GROUNDWORK FOR A BETTER VOCABULARY

THIRD EDITION

GROUNDWORK FOR A BETTER VOCABULARY

THIRD EDITION

BETH JOHNSON

CAROLE MOHR

JANET M. GOLDSTEIN

TOWNSEND PRESS

Books in the Townsend Press Vocabulary Series:

Vocabulary Basics
Groundwork for a Better Vocabulary
Building Vocabulary Skills
Building Vocabulary Skills, Short Version
Improving Vocabulary Skills
Improving Vocabulary Skills, Short Version
Advancing Vocabulary Skills
Advancing Vocabulary Skills, Short Version
Advanced Word Power

Books in the Townsend Press Reading Series:

Groundwork for College Reading
Groundwork for College Reading with Phonics
Ten Steps to Building College Reading Skills
Ten Steps to Improving College Reading Skills
Ten Steps to Advancing College Reading Skills
Ten Steps to Advanced Reading

Other Reading and Writing Books:

Everyday Heroes
The Townsend Thematic Reader
Voices and Values: A Reader for Writers
English at Hand
English Essentials

Supplements Available for Most Books:

Instructor's Edition
Instructor's Manual and Test Bank
Online Exercises

Copyright © 2004 by Townsend Press, Inc.
Printed in the United States of America
ISBN 1-59194-014-1
9 8 7 6 5

Send book orders and requests for desk copies or supplements to:
Townsend Press Book Center
439 Kelley Drive
West Berlin, New Jersey 08091

For even faster service, contact us in any of the following ways:
By telephone: 1-800-772-6410
By fax: 1-800-225-8894
By e-mail: cs@townsendpress.com
Through our website: www.townsendpress.com

Contents

Note: For ease of reference, the titles of the reading selections in each chapter are included.

Preface: To the Instructor

The problem is all too familiar: *students just don't know enough words.* Reading, writing, and content teachers agree that many students' vocabularies are inadequate for the demands of courses. Weak vocabularies limit students' understanding of what they read and the clarity and depth of what they write.

The purpose of *Groundwork for a Better Vocabulary* and the other books in the Townsend Press vocabulary series is to provide a solid, workable answer to the vocabulary problem. In the course of 30 chapters, *Groundwork for a Better Vocabulary* teaches 300 important basic words. Here are the book's distinctive features:

1 **An intensive words-in-context approach.** Studies show that students learn words best by reading and using them repeatedly in different contexts, not through rote memorization. The book gives students an intensive in-context experience by presenting each word in eight different settings. Each chapter takes students through a productive sequence of steps:

- Students infer the meaning of each word by considering two sentences in which it appears and then choosing a brief definition from multiple choice options.

- On the basis of their inferences, students identify each word's meaning in a matching activity. They are then in a solid position to deepen their knowledge of a word.

- Finally, they strengthen their understanding of a word by applying it in five different words-in-context passages, including sentence-completion activities and high-interest fill-in-the-blank passages.

Each encounter with a word brings it closer to becoming part of the student's permanent word bank. *No comparable vocabulary book gives such sustained attention to the words-in-context approach.*

2 **Abundant practice.** In addition to the extensive practice in each chapter, a crossword puzzle and a set of unit tests appear at the end of every five-chapter unit. The puzzle and tests reinforce students' knowledge of the words in each chapter. In addition, most chapters reuse several words from earlier chapters (such repeated words are marked with small circles, like this°), allowing for more reinforcement. Last, there are supplementary tests in the *Test Bank* and the online exercises that accompany the book. All this practice means that students learn in the surest possible way: by working closely and repeatedly with each word.

3 **Controlled feedback.** The opening activity in each chapter gives students three multiple-choice options to help them decide on the meaning of a given word. The multiple-choice options also help students to complete the matching exercise that is the second activity of each chapter. A limited answer key at the back of the book then provides answers for the third activity in the chapter. All these features enable students to take an active role in their own learning.

4 **Focus on essential words.** A good deal of time and research went into selecting the 300 words featured in the book. Word frequency lists were consulted, along with lists in a wide range of vocabulary books. In addition, the authors and editors each prepared their own lists. A computer was used to help in the consolidation of the many word lists. A long process of group discussion then led to final decisions about the words that would be most helpful for students reading at a basic level.

5 **Appealing content.** Dull practice materials work against learning. On the other hand, meaningful, lively, and at times even funny sentences and selections can spark students' attention and thus enhance their grasp of the material. For this reason, a great deal of effort was put into creating sentences and selections with both widespread appeal and solid context support. We have tried throughout to make the practice materials truly enjoyable for teachers and students alike. Look, for example, at the selections on page 15 that serve as the Final Check in Chapter 1.

6 **Clear format.** The book has been designed so that its very format contributes to the learning process. Each chapter consists of three two-page spreads. In the first two-page spread (the first such spread is on pages 10–11), students can easily refer to all ten words in context while working on the matching activity, in which they must choose a clear meaning for each word. The other two-page spreads allow students to see the words in a variety of contexts as they work through the fill-in activities.

7 **Helpful supplements.**

a A convenient *Instructor's Edition* is available at no charge to instructors using the book. It is identical to the student book except that it contains answers to all of the activities and tests.

b A combined *Instructor's Manual and Test Bank* is also offered at no charge to instructors who have adopted the book and ordered at least 20 student copies. This manual contains a general vocabulary placement test as well as a pretest and a posttest both for the entire book and for each of the six units in the text. It also includes teaching guidelines, suggested syllabi, and an answer key, as well as a "Related Words" activity and an additional mastery test for each chapter.

c *Online exercises,* available at the Online Learning Center area of **www.townsendpress.com**, also accompany the book. These exercises consist of two additional tests for each vocabulary chapter in the book. The program includes a number of user- and instructor-friendly features: brief explanations of answers, a sound option, frequent mention of the user's first name, a running score at the bottom of the screen, a record-keeping file, and and an actual, audible pronunciation of each word.

Probably in no other area of reading instruction is the computer more useful than in reinforcing vocabulary. This vocabulary program takes full advantage of the computer's unique capabilities and motivational appeal. Here's how the program works:

• Students are tested on the ten words in a chapter, with each word in a sentence context different from any in the book itself.

• After students answer each question, they receive immediate feedback: The program states that the answer is right or wrong and why, frequently using the student's first name and providing a running score.

- When the test is over, the program supplies a test score and a chance to take a retest on the ten words. Students then receive a score for this retest. What is so valuable about this, of course, is that the program gives students immediate additional practice with the words they need to review.

- In addition, the online exercise program offers a second, more challenging test in which students must identify the meanings of the chapter words without the benefit of context. This test is a final check that students have really learned the words. And, again, there is the option of a retest, with its own score.

Once students complete these exercises, their knowledge of each word in the chapter will have been carefully reinforced. And this reinforcement will be the more effective for having occurred in an electronic medium that especially engages today's students.

To obtain a copy of either print supplement, instructors who have adopted the book may e-mail Customer Service at **cs@townsendpress.com**. Alternatively, instructors may call our toll-free number, 1-800-772-6410, fax us at 1-800-225-8894, or write to us at the address shown on the copyright page.

8 **Realistic pricing.** As with the previous editions, the goal has been to offer the highest possible quality at the best possible price. While *Groundwork for a Better Vocabulary* is comprehensive enough to serve as a primary text, its modest price also makes it an inexpensive supplement.

9 **One in a sequence of books.** The most fundamental book in the Townsend Press vocabulary series is *Vocabulary Basics*. It is followed by *Groundwork for a Better Vocabulary* (a slightly more advanced basic text) and then by the three main books in the series: *Building Vocabulary Skills* (also a basic text), *Improving Vocabulary Skills* (an intermediate text), and *Advancing Vocabulary Skills* (a more advanced text). The most advanced book in the Townsend Press vocabulary series is *Advanced Word Power*. There are also short versions of the *Building, Improving*, and *Advancing* books. Suggested reading levels for the books are included in the *Instructor's Manual*. Together, the books can help create a vocabulary foundation that will make any student a better reader, writer, and thinker.

NOTES ON THE THIRD EDITION

A number of changes have been made in the third edition of *Groundwork for a Better Vocabulary*:

- Thirteen words have been changed, and an entirely new Unit Six, teaching fifty additional words, has been added. *Groundwork for a Better Vocabulary* now contains 300 words, as do the higher-level TP vocabulary books.

- To make room for Unit Six, the "Related Words" activities in each chapter have been moved to a special section in the *Instructor's Manual and Test Bank*. Instructors who have adopted the book may photocopy these activities (or anything else in the IMTB) for classroom use.

- A new section, "Topics for Discussion and Writing," contains the "Questions for Discussion" and "Ideas for Writing" that formerly concluded the vocabulary chapters. Each of the seven high-interest items uses one or more of the vocabulary words in the chapter in a brief scenario suitable for class or small-group discussion, writing, or both.

- Finally, many practice items throughout the book have been revised or updated to ensure that each item works as clearly and effectively as possible with students.

ACKNOWLEDGMENTS

We are grateful for the enthusiastic comments provided by users of the Townsend Press vocabulary books over the life of the first two editions. Particular thanks go to the following reviewers for their many helpful suggestions: Barbara Brennan Culhane, Nassau Community College; Carol Dietrick, Miami-Dade Community College; Larry Falxa, Ventura College; Jacquelin Hanselman, Copper Mountain College; Shiela P. Kerr, Florida Community College at Jacksonville; John M. Kopec, Boston University; Belinda E. Smith, Wake Technical Community College; Daniel Snook, Montcalm Community College; and William Walcott, Montgomery College. For help with the third edition, we are especially grateful to George Jiang of Riverside Community College and Terri Amici of Baltimore, Maryland. We appreciate as well the writing, editing, and proofreading assistance of Lisa Barsky in helping us make *Groundwork for a Better Vocabulary* even more effective and user-friendly than before.

Beth Johnson   *Carole Mohr*   *Janet M. Goldstein*

Introduction

WHY VOCABULARY DEVELOPMENT COUNTS

You have probably often heard it said, "Building vocabulary is important." Maybe you've politely nodded in agreement and then forgotten the matter. But it would be fair for you to ask, "Why is a good vocabulary so important? Can you prove it?" Here are four convincing reasons.

1 Common sense tells you what many research studies have also shown: vocabulary is a basic part of understanding what you read. A word here and there may not stop you, but if there are too many words you don't know, comprehension will suffer. The content of textbooks is often difficult enough; you don't want to work as well on understanding the words which express that content.

2 Vocabulary is a major part of almost every standardized test, including reading achievement tests, college entrance exams, and armed forces and vocational placement tests. Test developers know that vocabulary is a key measure of both one's learning and one's ability to learn. It is for this reason that they include a separate vocabulary section as well as a reading comprehension section. The more words you know, then, the better you are likely to do on such important tests.

3 Studies have shown that students with strong vocabularies are more successful in school. And one widely known study found that a good vocabulary, more than anything else, was common to people enjoying successful careers. Words are, in fact, the tools not just of better reading, but of better writing, speaking, listening, and thinking, as well. The more words you have at your command, the more effect you can have on the people around you.

4 In today's world, a good vocabulary counts more than ever. Far fewer people work on farms or in factories. Far more are in jobs that provide services or process information. More than ever, the tools of our trade are words: the words we use in reading, writing, listening, and speaking. In addition, experts say that workers of tomorrow will be called on to change jobs and learn new skills at an ever-increasing pace. The keys to survival and success will be the abilities to read, write, speak, and learn in a quick and skillful way. A solid vocabulary is essential for all of these skills.

Clearly, there is powerful proof that building vocabulary is a major key to success. The question then becomes, "What is the best way of going about it?"

1

WORDS IN CONTEXT: THE KEY TO VOCABULARY DEVELOPMENT

Memorizing lists of words is a traditional method of vocabulary development. However, a person is likely to forget such memorized lists quickly. Studies show that to master a word, you must see and use it in various contexts—that is, in different real-life sentences and paragraphs. By working actively and repeatedly with a word, you greatly increase your chance of really learning it.

The following activity will make clear how this book is organized and how it uses a words-in-context approach. In the spaces provided, answer the questions or fill in the missing words.

Inside Front Cover and Contents

Turn to the inside front cover.

- The inside front cover provides a _____ that will help you pronounce all the vocabulary words in the book.

Now turn to the table of contents on pages v–vi.

- How many chapters are in the book? _____

- Four short sections follow the last chapter. The first of these sections is a limited answer key, the second gives helpful information on using _____, the third contains _____, and the fourth is an index of the 300 words in the book.

Vocabulary Chapters

Turn to Chapter 1 on pages 10–15. This chapter, like all the others, consists of seven parts:

- The **first part** of the chapter, on pages 10–11, is titled _____.

    The left-hand column lists the ten words in the chapter. Under each **boldfaced** word is its _____ (in parentheses). For example, the pronunciation of *challenge* is _____. For a guide to pronunciation, see the inside front cover as well as "Dictionary Use" on pages 243–244.

    Below the pronunciation guide for each word is its part of speech. The part of speech shown for *challenge* is _____. The vocabulary words in this book are mostly nouns, adjectives, and verbs. **Nouns** are words used to name something—a person, place, thing, or idea. Familiar nouns include *boyfriend, city, hat*, and *truth*. **Adjectives** are words that describe nouns, as in the following word pairs: *former* boyfriend, *large* city, *red* hat, *whole* truth. All of the **verbs** in this book express an action of some sort. They tell what someone or something is doing. Common verbs include *read, drive, discover*, and *imagine*.

    To the right of each word are two sentences that will help you understand its meaning. In each sentence, the **context**—the other words in the sentence—provides clues you can use to figure out the definition. There are four common types of context clues—examples, synonyms, antonyms, and the general sense of the sentence. Each is briefly described on the pages that follow.

Common Context Clues

1 Examples

A sentence may include examples that show what an unfamiliar word means. For instance, take a look at the following item from Chapter 2 for the word *category*:

> When Jasmine was in high school, she didn't seem to fit into any **category**. She wasn't an athlete, a scholar, or a rebel.

The second sentence gives three examples of *category*—being "an athlete, a scholar, or a rebel." To figure out what *category* means, think about those examples. What is the speaker saying that Jasmine doesn't fit into? Look at the answer choices below, and in the space provided, write the letter of the answer you feel is correct.

> ____ *Category* means   A. goal.   B. feeling.   C. group.

Since the speaker is talking about the types of groups in high school, you may have correctly guessed that answer *C* is the right choice.

2 Synonyms

Synonyms are words that mean the same or almost the same as another word. The words *joyful, happy,* and *pleased* are synonyms; they all mean about the same thing. A synonym serves as a context clue by telling the meaning of an unknown word that is nearby. For instance, the sentence below from Chapter 1 includes a synonym clue for the vocabulary word *peculiar.*

> My brother thinks my chip-and-dip sandwiches are **peculiar**, but I don't think they're as strange as the peanut-butter-and-tuna sandwiches he eats.

Rather than repeat *peculiar* in the second part of the sentence, the author used a synonym. Find that synonym, and then from the choices below, write in the letter of the meaning of *peculiar.*

> ____ *Peculiar* means   A. attractive.   B. unusual.   C. innocent.

In the sentence from Chapter 1, *strange* is used as a synonym for *peculiar.* Since another word for *strange* is *unusual,* the answer is *B.*

3 Antonyms

Antonyms are words with opposite meanings. For example, *help* and *harm* are antonyms, as are *work* and *rest.* An antonym serves as a context clue by telling the opposite meaning of a nearby unknown word. The sentence below from Chapter 2 provides an antonym clue for the word *deliberate.*

> Manny's pushing me was quite **deliberate**; it wasn't accidental at all.

To emphasize the point, the author used an antonym of *deliberate.* Find the antonym, and use it to help you figure out what *deliberate* means. Then write in the letter of the meaning you choose.

> ____ *Deliberate* means   A. easy.   B. fair.   C. planned.

(Continues on next page)

The sentence suggests that *deliberate* pushing and *accidental* pushing are very different things. So we can guess that *deliberate* means the opposite of *accidental*. Another word that is the opposite of *accidental* is *planned*, so *C* is the correct answer—*deliberate* means "planned."

4 General Sense of the Sentence

Even when there are no example, synonym, or antonym clues in a sentence, you can still figure out the meaning of an unfamiliar word. For example, look at the sentence below from Chapter 1 for the word *surplus*.

> More and more restaurants are donating their **surplus** food to homeless people.

After thinking carefully about the context, you should be able to figure out what kind of food restaurants would be giving to homeless people. Write the letter of your choice.

___ *Surplus* means   A. strange.   B. extra.   C. main.

From the general sense of the sentence from Chapter 1 plus your own common sense, you probably guessed that the restaurants are donating "extra" food. Answer *B* is correct.

By looking closely at the pair of sentences provided for each word, as well as the answer choices, you should be able to decide on the meaning of a word. As you figure out each meaning, you are working actively with the word. You are creating the groundwork you need to understand and to remember the word. Getting involved with the word and developing a feel for it, based upon its use in context, is the key to word mastery.

It is with good reason, then, that the directions at the top of page 10 tell you to use the context to figure out each word's _____. Doing so deepens your sense of the word and prepares you for the next activity.

- The **second part** of the chapter, on page 11, is titled _____.

According to research, it is not enough to see a word in context. At a certain point, it is important to look at the actual meaning of a word. The matching exercise provides that meaning, but it also makes you look for and think about that meaning. In other words, it continues the active learning that is your surest route to learning and remembering a word.

Note the caution that follows this exercise: Do not go any further until you are sure that you know the correct meaning of each word as used in context.

Keep in mind that a word may have more than one meaning. In fact, some words have quite a few meanings. (If you doubt it, try looking up in a dictionary the word *make* or *draw*.) In this book, you will focus on one common meaning for each vocabulary word. However, many of the words have additional meanings. For example, in Chapter 1, you will learn that *challenge* means "a test of one's abilities," as in the sentence "My new job is a real challenge." If you then look up *challenge* in the dictionary, you will discover that it has other meanings. For example, it can also mean "a call to take part in a contest or fight," as in "Ted never turns down a challenge to play any kind of game." After you learn one common meaning of a word, you will find yourself gradually learning its other meanings in the course of your school and personal reading.

- The **third and fourth parts** of the chapter, on page 12, are titled _____ and _____.

   The first check consists of ten sentences that give you an opportunity to test your understanding of the ten words. After filling in the words, check your answers in the limited key at the back of the book. (But be sure to use the answer key as a learning tool only. Doing so will help you to master the words and to prepare for the remaining activities and the unit tests, for which answers are not provided.) The second check on page 12 then gives you another chance to deepen your understanding of the words.

- The **fifth part** of the chapter, on page 13, is titled _____. The practices on this page will make the meanings of the words come more alive through the use of vivid examples. Chances are you may find this activity to be one of the most enjoyable in the book.

- The **sixth part** of the chapter, on page 14, offers practice in one of three areas: word parts, synonyms and antonyms, or analogies. Each is explained below.

Word Parts, Synonyms-Antonyms, and Analogies

Word Parts

   The first and third chapters in each unit contain practice with word parts.

   Word parts are building blocks used in many English words. Learning word parts can help you to spell and pronounce words, unlock the meanings of unfamiliar words, and remember new words.

   This book covers twenty-four word parts. You will learn two types: prefixes and suffixes. A **prefix** is a word part that is found at the *beginning* of a word. When written separately, a prefix is followed by a hyphen to show that something follows it. For example, the prefix *sur* is written like this: *sur-*. *Sur-* can mean "beyond" or "additional," as in *surpass* (to go beyond) and *surcharge* (an additional charge).

   A **suffix** is a word part that is found at the *end* of a word. To show that something always comes before a suffix, a hyphen is placed at the beginning. For instance, the suffix *ly* is written like this: *-ly*. One common meaning of *-ly* is "in a certain way," as in the words *gratefully* (in a grateful way) and *angrily* (in an angry way).

   Each word-part practice begins with the meaning of a word part and examples. Fill-in items then help you remember and recognize the word parts. To see what these items are like, try the one below from Chapter 1 for the word part *sur*. On the answer line, write the word that best completes the sentence.

surcharge   surface   surpass   surplus   surtax

_____ In addition to the usual taxes, people who earn more than a certain amount will have to pay a ___.

(Continues on next page)

The sentence suggests that people who earn more than a certain amount will have to pay an additional tax. Since you now know that *sur-* can mean "additional," you probably wrote the correct word on the line: *surtax* (an additional tax).

(There is a third type of word part—a root. You will not be working with roots in this book. **Roots** are word parts that carry the basic meanings of words. For example, one common root is *vis*, which means "to see," as in the words *visit* and *vision*.)

Synonyms and Antonyms

The second and fourth chapters in each unit contain synonym-antonym practices. You have already learned in this introduction that a **synonym** is a word that means the same or almost the same as another word, and that an **antonym** is a word that means the opposite of another word. These practices will deepen your understanding of words by getting you to think about other words with the same or opposite meanings.

To see what the synonym questions are like, do the example below. Write the letter of the word that most nearly means the same as the first word, *hard*.

___ **hard**

A. new	B. difficult
C. far	D. bad

Since *difficult* is another way of saying *hard*, the correct answer is *B*. Now, to see what the antonym questions are like, do the sample item below. Write in the letter of the word that most nearly means the opposite of *kind*.

___ **kind**

A. silly	B. busy
C. young	D. cruel

The opposite of *kind* is *cruel*, so *D* is the correct answer.

Analogies

The last chapter in each unit contains an analogy practice, which is yet another way to deepen your understanding of words. An **analogy** is a similarity between two things that are otherwise different. Doing an analogy question is a two-step process. First you have to figure out the relationship in a pair of words. Those words are written like this:

LEAF : TREE

What is the relationship between the two words above? The answer can be stated like this: A leaf is a part of a tree.

Next, you must look for a similar relationship in a second pair of words. Here is how a complete analogy question looks:

LEAF : TREE ::

A. pond : river	B. foot : shoe
C. page : book	D. beach : sky

(Continues on next page)

And here is how the question can be read:

____ LEAF is to TREE as

    A. *pond* is to *river.*   B. *foot* is to *shoe.*

    C. *page* is to *book.*   D. *beach* is to *sky.*

To answer the question, you have to decide which of the four choices has a relationship similar to the first one. Check your answer by seeing if it fits in the same wording that you used to show the relationship between *leaf* and *tree:* A ____ is a part of a ____. Which answer would you choose?

The correct answer is *C.* Just as a *leaf* is a part of a *tree,* a *page* is a part of a *book.* On the other hand, a *pond* is not a part of a *river,* nor is a *foot* a part of a *shoe,* nor is a *beach* a part of the *sky.*

We can also state the complete analogy this way: *Leaf* is to *tree* as *page* is to *book.*

Here's another analogy question to try. Begin by figuring out the relationship between the first two words.

____ COACH : PLAYER ::

    A. soldier : military   B. infant : baby

    C. actor : famous   D. boss : worker

Coach and *player* have different responsibilities in an organization: a coach gives orders to a player. So you need to look at the other four pairs to see which has a similar relationship. When you think you have found the answer, check to see that the two words you chose can be compared in the same way as *coach* and *player:* a ____ gives orders to a ____.

In this case, the correct answer is *D*; a *boss* gives orders to a *worker.* (In other words, *coach* is to *player* as *boss* is to *worker.*)

By now you can see that there are basically two steps to doing analogy items:

1) Find out the relationship between the first two words.
2) Find the answer that expresses the same type of relationship that the first two words have.

Now try one more analogy question on your own. Write the letter of the answer you choose in the space provided.

____ SWING : BAT ::

    A. drive : car   B. run : broom

    C. catch : bat   D. fly : butterfly

If you chose answer *A,* you were right. *Swing* is what we do with a *bat,* and *drive* is what we do with a *car.*

- The **seventh part** of the chapter, on page 15, is titled _____.
Here you are given two interesting passages where you can practice applying the words in context. The first two such passages, on page 15, are titled _____

and _____.

FINAL NOTES

1 You now know how to proceed with the words in each chapter. Make sure that you do each page very carefully. Remember that as you work through the activities, you are learning the words.

How many times will you use each word? If you look, you'll see that each chapter gives you the opportunity to work with each word at least seven times. Each time that you work with a word adds to the likelihood that the word will become part of your active vocabulary. You will have further opportunities to use the word in the crossword puzzle and tests that end each unit. The computer software that is available with the book gives you even more practice.

In addition, many of the words are used again in later chapters of the book. Such repeated words are marked with small circles, like this°. For example, which words from Chapter 1 are repeated in the second Final Check passage on page 21 of Chapter 2? _____

and _____

Sometimes words related to the vocabulary words are used in the word-parts exercises. Those words are also marked with the small circle (°). For example, in Chapter 2, *deliberate* is defined as "Done on purpose; carefully planned." In the Word Parts section of Chapter 3, you will see that *deliberately* means "in a deliberate way" (or, in other words, "in a purposeful way").

2 At the bottom of the last page of each chapter is a "Check Your Performance" box, where you can enter your score for four of the practices. Note that these scores should also be entered into the vocabulary performance chart located on the inside of the _____ cover.

To get your score, count the number of items that you answered correctly in each section. Then add a zero. For example, if you got seven questions right in Check 2, you would write "70%" in the blank.

3 The facts are in. A strong vocabulary is a source of power. Words can make you a better reader, writer, speaker, thinker, and learner. They can dramatically increase your chances of success in school and in your job.

But a strong vocabulary will not be yours without effort. Words must be learned in a program of regular study. If you commit yourself to learning words, and you work actively and honestly with the chapters in this book, you will not only enrich your vocabulary—you will enrich your life, as well.

Unit One

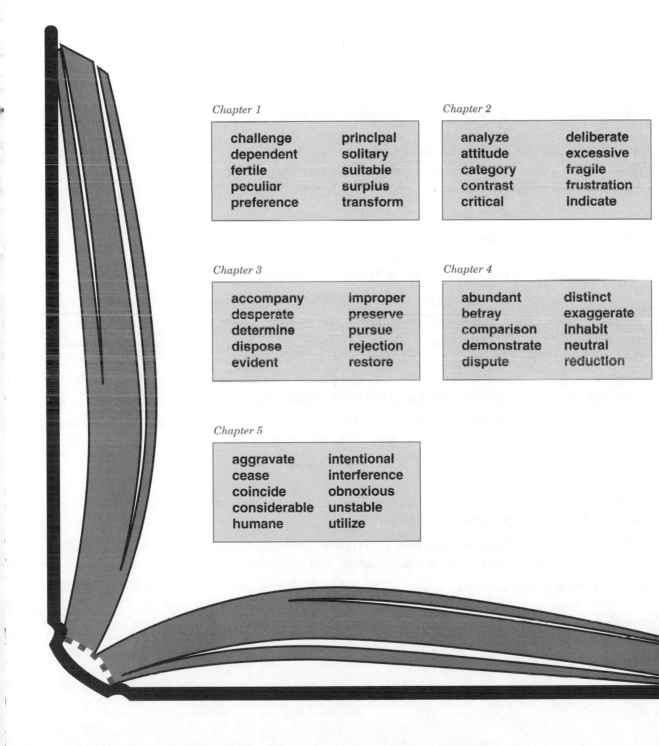

Chapter 1

challenge	principal
dependent	solitary
fertile	suitable
peculiar	surplus
preference	transform

Chapter 2

analyze	deliberate
attitude	excessive
category	fragile
contrast	frustration
critical	indicate

Chapter 3

accompany	improper
desperate	preserve
determine	pursue
dispose	rejection
evident	restore

Chapter 4

abundant	distinct
betray	exaggerate
comparison	inhabit
demonstrate	neutral
dispute	reduction

Chapter 5

aggravate	intentional
cease	interference
coincide	obnoxious
considerable	unstable
humane	utilize

challenge	principal
dependent	solitary
fertile	suitable
peculiar	surplus
preference	transform

Ten Words in Context

In the space provided, write the letter of the meaning closest to that of each **boldfaced** word. Use the context of the sentences to help you figure out each word's meaning.

1 challenge
(chăl'ĭnj)
– *noun*

• Ginny enjoys rock climbing. It's a difficult **challenge**, but she feels very proud after making a climb.

• When the babysitter arrived, he stared at the four active little boys he was expected to watch. "This will be quite a **challenge**," he sighed.

____ *Challenge* means   A. reason.   B. something boring.   C. something requiring effort.

2 dependent
(dĭ-pĕn'dənt)
– *adjective*

• Some animals can take care of themselves as soon as they are born, but human babies are **dependent** upon their parents for years.

• Tyrone's father said to him, "You are still much too **dependent** on me. It's about time you got a job and supported yourself."

____ *Dependent* means   A. relying.   B. leading.   C. puzzling.

3 fertile
(fûr'tl)
– *adjective*

• Because its soil is so **fertile**, Iowa has many farms.

• Our pet hamsters were so **fertile** that we ended up selling many baby hamsters back to the pet store.

____ *Fertile* means   A. common.   B. large.   C. able to produce.

4 peculiar
(pĭ-kyōōl'yər)
– *adjective*

• Jack didn't know why people were giving him **peculiar** looks until he realized there was a food stain on his shirt.

• My brother thinks my chip-and-dip sandwiches are **peculiar**, but I don't think they're as strange as the peanut-butter-and-tuna sandwiches he eats.

____ *Peculiar* means   A. attractive.   B. unusual.   C. innocent.

5 preference
(prĕf'ər-əns)
– *noun*

• There are Chinese, Italian, and Indian restaurants nearby. What's your **preference** for dinner tonight?

• What is your color **preference** for the living room? Do you like cool blues and greens, or warm oranges and yellows?

____ *Preference* means   A. choice.   B. skill.   C. effect.

6 principal
(prĭn'sə-pəl)
– *adjective*

• The **principal** cause of most success is hard work, not luck or talent.

• The queen of England has no real power. The **principal** leader of England is the prime minister.

____ *Principal* means   A. most recent.   B. false.   C. chief.

7 **solitary**
(sŏl'ĭ-tĕr'ē)
– *adjective*

- After taking a **solitary** vacation in a cabin for two weeks, Ned was ready to return to the company of other humans.
- In the mood to be by herself, Melba looked forward to spending the evening in such **solitary** activities as reading and taking a long bubble bath.

___ *Solitary* means   A. friendly.   B. proper.   C. done alone.

8 **suitable**
(sōō'tə-bəl)
– *adjective*

- Sharon asked her mother if her blue dress was **suitable** for a funeral, or if she had to wear black.
- Because the prices and food are so good, the team decided that the Red Lion Inn would be **suitable** for its annual banquet.

___ *Suitable* means   A. right.   B. too expensive.   C. important.

9 **surplus**
(sûr'plŭs)
– *adjective*

- More and more restaurants are donating their **surplus** food to homeless people.
- The Barkleys had more kitchen supplies than they needed, so they gave their **surplus** pots and pans to their son, who had just gotten his own apartment.

___ *Surplus* means   A. strange.   B. extra.   C. main.

10 **transform**
(trăns-fôrm')
– *verb*

- My sister plans to **transform** this messy attic into an attractive office.
- The magician seemed to **transform** a chicken's egg into an egg the size of a basketball.

___ *Transform* means   A. to accept.   B. to repeat.   C. to change.

Matching Words with Definitions

Following are definitions of the ten words. **Print** each word next to its definition. If you look closely at each word in context, you will be able to figure out its meaning.

1. _____   Producing or able to produce much fruit, large crops, or many children

2. _____   Most important; main; leading

3. _____   Relying on others for aid or support

4. _____   Extra; more than what is used or needed

5. _____   Odd; strange

6. _____   A test of one's abilities; anything that calls for a special effort

7. _____   Happening or done alone

8. _____   To change in form or appearance

9. _____   Right for a certain purpose; proper; fitting

10. _____   A choice; first choice; something preferred

CAUTION: Do not go any further until you are sure the above answers are correct. Then you can use the definitions to help you in the following practices. Your goal is eventually to know the words well enough so that you don't need to check the definitions at all.

➣ *Check 1*

Using the answer line, complete each item below with the correct word from the box.

A. challenge	B. dependent	C. fertile	D. peculiar	E. preference
F. principal	G. solitary	H. suitable	I. surplus	J. transform

_____ 1. Just one can of spinach ___s Popeye from a weakling into a hero.

_____ 2. If land is always planted with the same crop, it will become less ___. Changing crops from one year to the next keeps the soil rich.

_____ 3. Although Al's ___ is for a daytime job, he will work at night if necessary.

_____ 4. Max and Helen had more clothes than they needed, so they donated their ___ clothes to a thrift store.

_____ 5. I can't imagine what that ___ odor is from. It's like a mixture of burning tires and freshly cut grass.

_____ 6. A man lived by himself in a cave most of his life. His was a ___ life.

_____ 7. I know you have reasons for quitting your job. What's the ___ reason?

_____ 8. Baby-sitting with a lot of children isn't easy—it's a ___.

_____ 9. My neighbors are looking for ___ homes for the eight puppies their collie gave birth to. They want homes where the pups will be well cared for.

_____ 10. Sometimes Estela felt like giving up, but she knew she couldn't because she had three young children and an elderly mother who were ___ on her.

NOTE: Now check your answers to these questions by turning to page 239. Going over the answers carefully will help you prepare for the remaining practices, for which answers are not given.

➣ *Check 2*

Using the answer lines, complete each item below with **two** words from the box.

_____
_____ 1–2. When I'm not feeling well, my ___ is to have lots of company, but when my husband is sick, he would rather be ___.

_____
_____ 3–4. In the last year, our neighbors have ___ed their unattractive yard into something beautiful. The ___ change they made was to put in some lovely flowering plants; all of the other changes were small ones.

_____
_____ 5–6. Ben is happy to live at home, pay no rent, and use his mother's car, but I don't think it's ___ for a grown man to be so ___ on his parents.

_____
_____ 7–8. Our tomato plants are almost too ___. It is a ___ to use or give away all the tomatoes before they spoil.

_____
_____ 9–10. We had so many tomatoes that we ended up inventing some ___ recipes to use up the ___ fruit; perhaps the strangest was "Peanut Butter Tomato Pie."

➤ *Word Work*

A. In the space provided, write the letter of the choice that best completes each item.

_____ 1. A boy who is too **dependent** on his friends
    A. pays little attention to them.
    B. is too bossy with them.
    C. won't make any decisions without them.

_____ 2. Someone who enjoys **solitary** work would probably like a job
    A. selling a product that he or she believed in.
    B. working in a one-person office, rarely seeing other people.
    C. meeting people and answering their questions.

_____ 3. We knew for sure that our dog was **fertile** when she
    A. bit the mailman.
    B. did very well in training class.
    C. had puppies.

_____ 4. Most people would think it was **peculiar** if a teacher
    A. came into class dressed as Bozo the Clown.
    B. punished a student for cheating.
    C. dropped a piece of chalk on the floor.

_____ 5. If a friend came to you and sadly said, "My grandfather just died," what would be the most **suitable** response for you to make?
    A. "That's awful. I'm really sorry."
    B. "That's nothing; wait until you hear about my day."
    C. "Can you lend me some money?"

B. In the space provided, write the letter of the word that most closely relates to the situation in each item.

_____ 6. I like Pepsi more than I like Coca-Cola.

    A. preference   B. fertile   C. transform

_____ 7. The weightlifter is going to try to beat her own best record.

    A. dependent   B. challenge   C. surplus

_____ 8. Cream is the main ingredient in butter.

    A. challenge   B. dependent   C. principal

_____ 9. These pieces of cloth were left over after I made myself a shirt.

    A. surplus   B. fertile   C. preference

_____10. Cinderella's fairy godmother will change her rags into a beautiful gown, a pumpkin into a carriage, and mice into horses.

    A. solitary   B. principal   C. transform

➤ *Word Parts*

A. The prefix *trans-* can mean "across" or "change to."

    Examples: *transport* — to take from one place across to another

                   translate — to change from one language to another

On each answer line, write the word from the box that best completes the item.

A. **transatlantic**	B. **transform**	C. **translate**
D. **transplant**	E. **transportation**	

_____ 1. Trina's job is to ___ business letters from Spanish into English.

_____ 2. You can ___ a room simply by painting it a different color.

_____ 3. The doctor ___ed one of Mark's kidneys into his sister.

_____ 4. Since my grandmother doesn't drive and there is no public ___ in her area, she depends on Dad to take her shopping.

_____ 5. The ship will cross the Atlantic Ocean next week. The ship's ___ trip begins in New York City and ends in England.

B. The prefix *sur-* means "over," "upon," "beyond," or "additional."

    Examples: *surpass* — to go beyond

                   surtax — an additional tax

On each answer line, write the word from the box that best completes the item.

F. **surcharge**	G. **surface**	H. **surpass**
I. **surplus**	J. **surtax**	

_____ 6. I like to protect and shine the ___s of my wooden tables with wax.

_____ 7. Our garden produced so much zucchini that we gave big bagfuls of ___ squash to all our neighbors.

_____ 8. In addition to the usual taxes, people who earn more than a certain amount will have to pay a ___.

_____ 9. The drive to raise money for the children's hospital was so successful that the money raised ___ed the goal that was set.

_____ 10. Because we brought so much luggage on our trip, we had to pay the airline a ___.

➤ *Final Check*

Read the passages carefully. Then fill in each blank with the word that best fits the context.

A. Johnny Appleseed

A. **fertile**	B. **peculiar**	C. **solitary**	D. **surplus**	E. **transform**

John Chapman, who is known to the world as Johnny Appleseed, must have been a strange sight. His (1)_____ clothing included cloth sacks for shirts and a tin pot for a hat.

In western Pennsylvania, where Johnny lived, many people grew apples. But there weren't any apples in the lands further west, which were just then being cleared and settled. So Johnny wandered among his neighbors, asking them for their (2)_____ apple seeds. During his lifetime, Johnny walked thousands of miles, making many long trips from his home to the valleys of Ohio and Indiana. Everywhere he went, he scattered seeds. Many of those seeds fell on (3)_____ ground and grew into strong trees.

Johnny often wandered through areas where Native Americans fought with the white settlers. Since Johnny was a loner, his travels were always (4)_____. He carried no weapon, yet he was never harmed. The Indians believed that the Great Spirit especially loved people like Johnny, who was not like other people. In his own quiet way he (5)_____ed the American wilderness, filling it with thousands of flowering, fruit-filled trees.

B. The Lovable Leech?

F. **challenge**	G. **dependent**	H. **preference**	I. **principal**	J. **suitable**

As highly developed as we human beings like to think we are, the fact is that we are still (6)_____ upon many lower forms of life. The (7)_____ way that this is true, of course, is that we use meat for food and skins for clothing. But there are other ways, sometimes strange ways, that we rely on other creatures. Take, for example, the leech. It would be a (8)_____ for anyone to really like a leech. It is a disgusting-looking worm that lives in freshwater ponds and streams. As many people have discovered when they've gone swimming, a leech's (9)_____ for dinner is human blood. It loves to attach itself to a swimmer's foot and sink in its teeth—as many as three hundred of them. The bite does not cause any pain. But the leech can suck out eight times its own weight in blood. "How disgusting," you are probably thinking. But listen to this. In recent years, doctors have found that leeches are the most (10)_____ way to remove extra blood from a person after an injury, especially around the eyes. Yes, leeches are honored guests in many modern hospitals.

Enter your scores above and in the vocabulary performance chart on the inside back cover of the book.

analyze	deliberate
attitude	excessive
category	fragile
contrast	frustration
critical	indicate

Ten Words in Context

In the space provided, write the letter of the meaning closest to that of each **boldfaced** word. Use the context of the sentences to help you figure out each word's meaning.

1 analyze
(ăn'ə-līz)
– *verb*

- Someone in the laboratory will **analyze** the blood sample to see if the patient has an illness.
- Before we can suggest solutions, we must carefully **analyze** the city's money problems.

___*Analyze* means   A. to plan.   B. to study.   C. to create.

2 attitude
(ăt'ĭ-tood')
– *noun*

- Athletes need to have a positive **attitude**. Even if they have lost the previous game, they need to come into the next one ready to win.
- Rudy came to the party with a poor **attitude**; he was sure that he'd be bored and wouldn't have any fun.

___*Attitude* means   A. set of rules.   B. background.   C. way of thinking.

3 category
(kăt'ə-gôr'ē)
– *noun*

- When Jasmine was in high school, she didn't seem to fit into any **category**. She wasn't an athlete, a scholar, or a rebel.
- The small store had many jazz and rock recordings, but not much in the **category** of country music.

___*Category* means   A. goal.   B. feeling.   C. group.

4 contrast
(kŏn'trăst')
– *noun*

- Everyone is surprised to see that there's a **contrast** between Peggy's eyes. One eye is brown, and the other is green.
- I was struck by the **contrast** between the fancy houses west of Main Street and the poor neighborhoods to the east.

___*Contrast* means   A. disappointment.   B. place.   C. difference.

5 critical
(krĭt'ĭ-kəl)
– *adjective*

- My boss can be very **critical** of me when I don't do my best work, but she's also quick to praise me when I do well.
- My aunt is **critical** of her neighbors. She calls them lazy because their house needs painting and their yard is overgrown with weeds.

___*Critical* means   A. faultfinding.   B. jealous.   C. proud.

6 deliberate
(dĭ-lĭb'ər-ĭt)
– *adjective*

- Manny's pushing me was quite **deliberate**; it wasn't accidental at all.
- I'm sure our neighbor knew that the tall tree he was planting would keep the sun from our flowers. It was a **deliberate** dirty trick.

___*Deliberate* means   A. easy.   B. fair.   C. planned.

7 excessive
(ĭk-sĕs′ĭv)
– *adjective*

- **Excessive** speed caused the accident; the truck driver was going nearly eighty miles an hour.
- Mrs. Hill's concern about her little boy's health is **excessive**. She rushes him to the doctor every time he gets the sniffles or scrapes his knee.

___ *Excessive* means   A. overly great.   B. off and on.   C. normal.

8 fragile
(frăj′əl)
– *adjective*

- The lamp is **fragile**, so when you pack it, please put it in a deep box with plenty of newspaper around it.
- When my little sister was a toddler, we kept **fragile** dishes and glasses out of her reach. We knew she would break them.

___ *Fragile* means   A. broken.   B. strong.   C. breakable.

9 frustration
(frŭs-trā′shən)
– *noun*

- Trying to learn to roller-skate, I fell down twenty times and then crashed into a wall. Feeling more **frustration** than pain, I finally gave up.
- Elaine felt great **frustration** when she failed her driving test for the third time.

___ *Frustration* means   A. relief.   B. discouragement.   C. pleasure.

10 indicate
(ĭn′də-kāt′)
– *verb*

- Jeff's frown seemed to **indicate** that he was unhappy with our plan.
- The parking-lot attendant pointed to **indicate** that Lonnie should drive the car all the way up to the fence.

___ *Indicate* means   A. to hide.   B. to show.   C. to plan.

Matching Words with Definitions

Following are definitions of the ten words. **Print** each word next to its definition. If you look closely at each word in context, you will be able to figure out its meaning.

1. _____   A feeling of anger and helplessness that comes from bad luck, defeat, or failure; disappointment

2. _____   A point of view; state of mind; way of thinking or feeling

3. _____   A group of people or things having something in common; type

4. _____   Too much; more than is reasonable

5. _____   Done on purpose; carefully planned

6. _____   An obvious difference

7. _____   Disapproving; tending to find fault

8. _____   Easily broken or damaged

9. _____   To examine carefully; study closely

10. _____   To show; serve as a sign or signal

CAUTION: Do not go any further until you are sure the above answers are correct. Then you can use the definitions to help you in the following practices. Your goal is eventually to know the words well enough so that you don't need to check the definitions at all.

➢ *Check 1*

Using the answer line, complete each item below with the correct word from the box.

A. **analyze**	B. **attitude**	C. **category**	D. **contrast**	E. **critical**
F. **deliberate**	G. **excessive**	H. **fragile**	I. **frustration**	J. **indicate**

_____   1. To avoid the ___ of failing the driving test again, Elaine has decided to take driving lessons.

_____   2. A planned action is ___.

_____   3. ___ eating during the holidays led to my gaining three pounds.

_____   4. A road sign with a picture of a leaping deer ___s that deer often cross the road at that spot.

_____   5. After losing every game last season, the soccer players began training this year with a poor ___. If they don't transform° their outlook, they will have another losing season.

_____   6. Something that is ___ can be easily damaged.

_____   7. Which ___ of movie do you prefer, comedy or action-adventure?

_____   8. When Maggie ___d her reasons for wanting to marry Joe, she realized that they were not good ones.

_____   9. Many teenagers feel their parents are too ___ of their clothing, music, and friends.

_____   10. I was surprised by the ___ between kind, gentle Bill and his impatient, bad-tempered brother.

NOTE: Now check your answers to these questions by turning to page 239. Going over the answers carefully will help you prepare for the remaining practices, for which answers are not given.

➢ *Check 2*

Using the answer lines, complete each item below with **two** words from the box.

_____
_____   1–2. There is a large ___ between things that fit in the ___ of junk food and those foods needed for basic nutrition.

_____
_____   3–4. When a child is learning to play a musical instrument, parents should have an encouraging ___. Rather than being ___ of the child, parents should find things to praise.

_____
_____   5–6. When we broke three glasses while washing the dishes, it wasn't ___. They were just too ___.

_____
_____   7–8. Most people can deal with some ___, but if discouragement becomes ___, it can actually cause illness.

_____
_____   9–10. When we ___ the citywide election returns, they will ___ how each neighborhood voted.

➤ *Word Work*

A. In the space provided, write the letter of the choice that best completes each item.

_____ 1. A piano teacher who was very **critical** of a child's playing would

    A. not pay attention.   B. praise the child.   C. point out every mistake.

_____ 2. When the boss advised Jim to improve his **attitude**, he meant that Jim should

    A. have a better   B. be neater.   C. speed up his typing.
       outlook about work.

_____ 3. If a rash **indicates** an allergy, the rash

    A. has nothing to do   B. causes the allergy.   C. is a sign of the allergy.
       with the allergy.

_____ 4. My grandmother's lace wedding veil is too **fragile** for me to wear at my own wedding. The veil

    A. might get torn.   B. is too old-fashioned.   C. is stained.

_____ 5. There is a big **contrast** in the twins' personalities. Their personalities

    A. are very much alike.   B. are very different.   C. aren't very pleasant.

B. In the space provided, write the letter of the word that most closely relates to the situation in each item.

_____ 6. The fire that destroyed the store was no accident. Someone set it on purpose.

    A. category   B. deliberate   C. uncritical

_____ 7. Did the murdered man's coffee contain poison? The police laboratory will examine a sample of the coffee to find out.

    A. analyze   B. contrast   C. attitude

_____ 8. When the swimming class was divided into sections, I was put with the "beginners."

    A. excessive   B. category   C. fragile

_____ 9. The little girl can't get her snow boots off. She pulls and tugs, pulls and tugs, and finally bursts into tears.

    A. deliberate   B. contrast   C. frustration

_____ 10. The servings at the restaurant are much too large. Plates are heaped with more food than anyone could eat.

    A. indicate   B. excessive   C. fragile

➤ *Synonyms and Antonyms*

A. Synonyms. Write the letter of the word or phrase that most nearly means the **same** as each boldfaced word.

_____ 1. **analyze**

    A. remember   B. examine

    C. find fault with   D. use

_____ 2. **attitude**

    A. height   B. outlook

    C. knowledge   D. skill

_____ 3. **category**

    A. group   B. purpose

    C. reaction   D. problem

_____ 4. **critical**

    A. absent   B. frightened

    C. nervous   D. disapproving

_____ 5. **indicate**

    A. plan   B. conceal

    C. show   D. disappoint

B. Antonyms. Write the letter of the word or phrase that most nearly means the **opposite** of each boldfaced word.

_____ 6. **contrast**

    A. difference   B. environment

    C. enjoyment   D. sameness

_____ 7. **deliberate**

    A. accidental   B. harmful

    C. helpful   D. fortunate

_____ 8. **excessive**

    A. not real   B. not enough

    C. unexpected   D. required

_____ 9. **fragile**

    A. damaged   B. unbreakable

    C. unnecessary   D. beautiful

_____ 10. **frustration**

    A. showing ignorance   B. feeling hatred

    C. being satisfied   D. expressing surprise

➤ *Final Check*

Read the passages carefully. Then fill in each blank with the word that best fits the context.

A. Finding Fault—And What to Do About It

A. **attitude**	B. **category**	C. **critical**	D. **excessive**	E. **frustration**

Are you one of those people who are constantly finding fault? Are you very (1)_____ of everyone else's mistakes? If the washing machine or the stereo breaks down, is your reaction (2)_____ anger and (3)_____? If so, beware! Too much bad temper and discouragement could be harming your health. Scientists say that faultfinders and those who are often angry actually seem to have more heart attacks. So if you fall into this (4)_____ of people, it's a smart idea to try to change your outlook. Learn to take things more calmly; learn to be more patient when someone or something disappoints you. If your (5)_____ improves, your health may improve, too.

B. What Do Your Hobbies Reveal About You?

F. **analyze**	G. **contrast**	H. **deliberate**	I. **fragile**	J. **indicate**

Mira, Pat, and Celia are sisters, close in age and similar in looks—but what a (6)_____ there is in their leisure activities! Mira loves an exciting challenge° and often takes (7)_____ risks. She has mastered the skateboard, she drives in stock-car races, and she's even tried boxing. In fact, she says she'd go skydiving if only she could afford it. Pat is a collector. She spends her spare time searching for old crystal and china—and taking care of it. She never minds the hours it takes her to wash and dust her precious, (8)_____ treasures. Then there's Celia, whose preference° is to spend every possible minute reading—that's all she wants to do! You've never met Mira, Pat, and Celia, but doesn't this tell you a lot about them? If we (9)_____ how people spend leisure time, their interests and hobbies can reveal a great deal about their personalities. What do you think your hobbies and other activities would (10)_____ about you?

Scores Check 2 _____%	Word Work _____%	Synonyms and Antonyms _____%	Final Check _____%

Enter your scores above and in the vocabulary performance chart on the inside back cover of the book.

CHAPTER

3

accompany	improper
desperate	preserve
determine	pursue
dispose	rejection
evident	restore

Ten Words in Context

In the space provided, write the letter of the meaning closest to that of each **boldfaced** word. Use the context of the sentences to help you figure out each word's meaning.

1 **accompany**
(ə-kŭm′pə-nē)
– *verb*

- The Myers asked my sister to **accompany** them to the seashore to help take care of their young children.
- In popular music, words usually **accompany** the tune. In much classical music, there are no words to go with the notes.

___*Accompany* means   A. to go before.   B. to go after.   C. to go with.

2 **desperate**
(dĕs′pər-ĭt)
– *adjective*

- Extremely ill people may be so **desperate** for a cure that they will try anything.
- The earthquake victims are **desperate** for food and clothing.

___*Desperate for* means   A. harmed by.   B. in great need of.   C. surprised by.

3 **determine**
(dĭ-tûr′mĭn)
– *verb*

- The doctor in the emergency room **determined** from an x-ray that Chen's ankle was sprained, not broken.
- Using a calculator, I **determined** that the "super-giant" box of laundry soap was a better buy than the "family economy" box.

___*Determine* means   A. to regret.   B. to remember.   C. to discover.

4 **dispose**
(dĭ-spōz′)
– *verb*

- The sign said, "Lungs at work. Please **dispose** of all cigarettes, cigars, and pipes before entering."
- After losing forty pounds, Herb decided to **dispose** of all the clothes that reminded him of his old size. He never wanted to see them again.

___*Dispose of* means   A. to get rid of.   B. to pay for.   C. to use up.

5 **evident**
(ĕv′ĭ-dənt)
– *adjective*

- The fact that my aunt dyes her hair is **evident**—her gray roots show.
- To make it **evident** that she didn't want to go out with James again, Crystal sent him back all his letters and gifts.

___*Evident* means   A. useful.   B. easy to see.   C. unlikely.

6 **improper**
(ĭm-prŏp′ər)
– *adjective*

- A bathing suit is fine for the beach, but it's **improper** for church.
- Movies are rated PG-13 if they contain material that is **improper** for young children.

___*Improper* means   A. common.   B. useful.   C. wrong.

7 preserve
(pri-zûrv′)
– *verb*

- Steps are being taken to **preserve** the remaining giant redwood trees of California and Oregon for future generations.
- To **preserve** its valuable old fabrics, the museum keeps them away from bright lights and extreme temperatures.

____*Preserve* means   A. to keep safe.   B. to sell off.   C. to seek.

8 pursue
(pər-soō′)
– *verb*

- At the age of 49, the woman decided to **pursue** a degree in social work and become a social worker.
- Victor plans to **pursue** an acting career in New York City. His goal is to become a great actor, not a great star.

____*Pursue* means   A. to avoid.   B. to work toward.   C. to replace.

9 rejection
(ri-jĕk′shən)
– *noun*

- My brother was upset when he received a letter of **rejection** from a college he wanted to attend.
- Nita wasn't too disturbed when she didn't get the job she had interviewed for. "If you can't handle **rejection**, you have some growing up to do," she said.

____*Rejection* means   A. respect.   B. not being accepted.   C. bad taste.

10 restore
(ri-stôr′)
– *verb*

- During the 1980s, the Statue of Liberty was **restored**. The damaged torch and the 1,600 iron bands that hold the copper skin to the frame were replaced.
- Surprisingly, there have been cases where a bump on the head has **restored** the sight of a blind person.

____*Restore* means   A. to fix.   B. to harm.   C. to give away.

Matching Words with Definitions

Following are definitions of the ten words. **Print** each word next to its definition. If you look closely at each word in context, you will be able to figure out its meaning.

1. _____   Obvious; clear

2. _____   To find out exactly; figure out

3. _____   To throw or give away; get rid of

4. _____   Having a great need or desire

5. _____   Not in good taste; not right for a situation; not suitable°

6. _____   To bring back to a normal or former condition; repair

7. _____   To protect; keep in good condition

8. _____   A saying "no" (to a request or desire); refusal

9. _____   To try to get or succeed in; seek

10. _____   To go along with; be together with

CAUTION: Do not go any further until you are sure the above answers are correct. Then you can use the definitions to help you in the following practices. Your goal is eventually to know the words well enough so that you don't need to check the definitions at all.

➤ *Check 1*

Using the answer line, complete each item below with the correct word from the box.

A. **accompany**	B. **desperate**	C. **determine**	D. **dispose of**	E. **evident**
F. **improper**	G. **preserve**	H. **pursue**	I. **rejection**	J. **restore**

_____ 1. If you are ___ for food, that means you are in great need of it.

_____ 2. When we say that something is ___, we mean that it can be clearly seen or clearly understood.

_____ 3. Do you like ketchup to ___ your French fries, or do you prefer them plain?

_____ 4. At some fancy restaurants, it's considered ___ for a man to show up without a jacket and a tie.

_____ 5. There are several ways to ___ things you no longer want: put them in the garbage, recycle them, or give or sell them to someone who can use them.

_____ 6. The opposite of "acceptance" is "___."

_____ 7. To ___ a piece of furniture, protect it from too much heat, sun, and moisture.

_____ 8. You can always ___ which twin is which because Beth wears glasses, but her sister Lisa doesn't.

_____ 9. Many athletes ___ an Olympic medal by practicing hours a day for years, but only a few athletes can actually win one.

_____ 10. To ___ an old table, you must first remove all the old varnish and paint.

NOTE: Now check your answers to these questions by turning to page 239. Going over the answers carefully will help you prepare for the remaining practices, for which answers are not given.

➤ *Check 2*

Using the answer lines, complete each item below with **two** words from the box.

_____
_____ 1–2. It is ___ that this old movie theater has been very well taken care of. The original seats and wallpaper have been ___d since 1924.

_____
_____ 3–4. Jill can't ___ the scholarship offered by that company. Her father is on the committee that decides who wins the award, so it would be ___ for her to apply.

_____
_____ 5–6. The woman was ___ for money, so she decided to sell her grandmother's diamond ring. She was disappointed when the jeweler ___d that the diamond was a cheap imitation.

_____
_____ 7–8. The owners of the old car are trying to decide if they will ___ it with new parts and a lot of body work, or ___ it by giving it away.

_____
_____ 9–10. I offered to ___ my friend to the tryout for the play, thinking that if she did not get the part, she might need help in dealing with the ___.

➤ *Word Work*

A. In the space provided, write the letter of the choice that best completes each item.

_____ 1. **Dispose** of clothes that

   A. are old and no longer fit.   B. you just bought.   C. you will wear next summer.

_____ 2. Ernie experienced **rejection** when he

   A. was invited   B. moved into   C. was turned down
      to a party.   a new house.   for a date.

_____ 3. Yelling, screaming, and jumping up and down would be **improper** behavior at

   A. a baseball game.   B. a movie.   C. an amusement park.

_____ 4. You could **restore** an old piano with

   A. a large truck.   B. beautiful music.   C. new keys, strings,
                                                   and woodwork.

_____ 5. You might feel **desperate** if you were

   A. stuck on a   B. wearing attractive   C. standing in a long line
      desert island.   new clothes.   at the supermarket.

B. In the space provided, write the letter of the word that most closely relates to the situation in each item.

_____ 6. Keep your wedding gown carefully wrapped in plastic and stored in a box.

   A. restore   B. determine   C. preserve

_____ 7. In my opinion, waffles go best with butter and maple syrup.

   A. accompany   B. restore   C. dispose

_____ 8. It was clear where the missing brownie went—the little boy's face was full of chocolate.

   A. desperate   B. evident   C. preserve

_____ 9. To find out what was wrong with his patient, the doctor had to do several tests.

   A. dispose of   B. accompany   C. determine

_____10. Annamarie worked hard to reach her goal of owning her own restaurant.

   A. preserve   B. pursue   C. evident

➤ *Word Parts*

A. One meaning of the suffix *-ly* is "in a certain way."

Examples: *desperate* — in great need   *grateful* — thankful
              desperately — in a way that shows great need   *gratefully* — in a thankful way

On each answer line, write the word from the box that means the same as the *italicized* words.

A. **angrily**	B. **deliberately°**	C. **desperately**
D. **excessively°**	E. **skillfully**	

_____ 1. Eva *in a deliberate° way* stuck her foot out as her little brother came
    by. As he fell, he yelled, "Hey, you did that on purpose!"

_____ 2. If the wound is sewed up *in a skillful way,* it won't even leave a scar.

_____ 3. I guess I have been watching TV *in an excessive way* recently. I know
    the characters on my favorite programs better than I know my family
    members.

_____ 4. Many neighbors stayed up all night, searching *in a desperate way* for
    the missing child.

_____ 5. The principal said to the class *in an angry way,* "There's no good
    reason for such rude behavior toward a substitute teacher."

B. One meaning of the prefix *re-* is "back."

Examples: *reflect*—to bend light back
              recall—to call back to mind; remember

On each answer line, write the word from the box that best completes the item.

F. **recall**	G. **reflect**	H. **remove**
I. **repay**	J. **restore**	

_____ 6. To ___ this old lamp, you'll need to put in new electrical wiring.

_____ 7. My brother is constantly asking me for loans, promising he will ___ me
    when he gets his allowance.

_____ 8. I remember the man's face, but I cannot ___ his name.

_____ 9. According to legend, when a vampire looks in the mirror, he sees
    nothing. The mirror doesn't ___ his image.

_____ 10. "Please ___ your hand from my car," said the young man.

➤ *Final Check*

Read the passages carefully. Then fill in each blank with the word that best fits the context.

A. Fixing Up Furniture

A. **determine**	B. **dispose**	C. **evident**	D. **preserve**	E. **restore**

    I feel proud when I can fix up furniture that other people have (1)_____d of. Instead of spending a lot of money on new furniture, I'll recycle an old chair thrown out by a relative or an ugly bureau I've found in a neighbor's trash pile. I like the challenge° of trying to (2)_____ them to their original condition. I often find a beautiful piece of furniture hidden under many coats of paint or varnish. At first it is hard to (3)_____ how good or bad the piece underneath really is. I must carefully remove the old paint or varnish. If it becomes (4)_____ that the quality of the piece of furniture is good, I sand it until it is smooth. Then I stain it to bring out the wood's natural lines and colors. Finally, I apply new varnish to (5)_____ the wood from damage by water or heat. Fixing other people's "junk" has been an inexpensive way for me to get some beautiful furniture.

B. Barbara's Date with Her Cousin

F. **accompany**	G. **desperate**	H. **improper**	I. **pursue**	J. **rejection**

    Barbara can finally laugh about the time twenty years ago when she was so (6)_____ for a date that she paid her cousin twenty-five dollars to go with her to the senior prom. She admits that she had very few dates in high school. However, when the prom tickets first went on sale, Barbara hoped that some handsome fellow would fall for her charms and ask her to the prom, and maybe even ask her to go steady. It didn't happen.

    Back then, people didn't think it was very "ladylike" behavior to actively (7)_____ a date with a boy. But Barbara wanted to go to the prom so badly that she didn't care if her actions seemed (8)_____. Despite her fear of (9)_____, she got up her nerve to ask Gary. He already had a date. So she asked Emilio and then Chuck. They also said no.

    One week before the prom, she called her cousin. He said, "Okay, but it will cost you." He wanted ten dollars to (10)_____ her to the dance and another fifteen dollars not to tell anyone at the prom that they were related.

Scores	Check 2 _____%	Word Work _____%	Word Parts _____%	Final Check _____%

Enter your scores above and in the vocabulary performance chart on the inside back cover of the book.

abundant	**distinct**
betray	**exaggerate**
comparison	**inhabit**
demonstrate	**neutral**
dispute	**reduction**

Ten Words in Context

In the space provided, write the letter of the meaning closest to that of each **boldfaced** word. Use the context of the sentences to help you figure out each word's meaning.

1 abundant
(ə-bŭn′dənt)
– *adjective*

- Our apple tree bore such an **abundant** crop this year that we'll have plenty of applesauce all winter.
- Mom's energy is so **abundant** that the rest of us can't keep up with her. After a day's work, she'll bike ten miles and then say, "Let's shoot a few baskets before dinner!"

___*Abundant* means   A. different.   B. great.   C. reasonable.

2 betray
(bĭ-trā′)
– *verb*

- The prisoners refused to **betray** their country by telling its secrets.
- I didn't mean to **betray** my brother by telling our parents he was using drugs. I wanted to help him.

___*Betray* means   A. to turn against.   B. to give aid to.   C. to argue with.

3 comparison
(kəm-păr′ĭ-sən)
– *noun*

- LaTanya decided which car to buy after making a **comparison** of all the cars in her price range.
- A **comparison** between Tim's and Eric's rooms makes it clear that Tim is the neater of the two boys.

___*Comparison* means   A. check of what is alike and different.   B. argument.   C. explanation.

4 demonstrate
(dĕm′ən-strāt′)
– *verb*

- I asked the salesman to **demonstrate** how to use the camera, but it was clear he didn't know how.
- When the new copying machine arrives in our office, someone who knows how to use it will **demonstrate** how all its features work.

___*Demonstrate* means   A. to remember.   B. to imagine.   C. to show.

5 dispute
(dĭ-spyo͞ot′)
– *noun*

- My **dispute** with my brother about who would get the last piece of pie was settled when our father ate it.
- Business at the store was so slow that the salespeople had a **dispute** over who would get the next customer.

___*Dispute* means   A. answer.   B. disagreement.   C. explanation.

6 distinct
(dĭ-stĭngkt′)
– *adjective*

- The faces of the people in the faded old photo were not **distinct**. We couldn't identify anyone.
- Although the two bowls of onion dip looked the same, there was a **distinct** difference in their taste.

___*Distinct* means   A. definite.   B. healthy.   C. hard to notice.

7 exaggerate
(ĭg-zăj′ə-rāt′)
– *verb*

- Dad, reminding us not to stretch the truth, always jokes, "I've told you a million times never to **exaggerate**!"
- I didn't **exaggerate** when I called Randall a musical genius. He really does play the guitar amazingly well.

___*Exaggerate* means   A. to ask questions.   B. to overstate.   C. to explain.

8 inhabit
(ĭn-hăb′ĭt)
– *verb*

- Six billion people **inhabit** the Earth.
- Bats often **inhabit** the attics of houses, barns, and other buildings.

___*Inhabit* means   A. to show.   B. to live in.   C. to check.

9 neutral
(no͞o′trəl)
– *adjective*

- If you ever go to a marriage counselor, don't expect him or her to agree with just you or just your spouse. A counselor must remain **neutral**.
- Switzerland has been a **neutral** country since 1648. It doesn't participate in wars or support one country against another.

___*Neutral* means   A. clear.   B. not taking sides.   C. not loyal.

10 reduction
(rĭ-dŭk′shən)
– *noun*

- When the company offered to pay workers for sick time they didn't use, there was a sudden **reduction** in the number of sick days taken.
- It seems everyone who runs for public office promises a **reduction** in taxes.

___*Reduction* means   A. order.   B. quarrel.   C. cut.

Matching Words with Definitions

Following are definitions of the ten words. **Print** each word next to its definition. If you look closely at each word in context, you will be able to figure out its meaning.

1. _____   To live in

2. _____   Very plentiful; more than enough

3. _____   The act of checking or judging how two or more things are alike or different

4. _____   To say that something is larger or greater than it really is; overstate

5. _____   Clear; obvious; easy to see or notice

6. _____   Not taking sides in a quarrel

7. _____   An argument; a quarrel

8. _____   To be disloyal to; turn against

9. _____   A decrease; cutback

10. _____   To explain or teach by showing

CAUTION: Do not go any further until you are sure the above answers are correct. Then you can use the definitions to help you in the following practices. Your goal is eventually to know the words well enough so that you don't need to check the definitions at all.

➤ *Check 1*

Using the answer line, complete each item below with the correct word from the box.

A. **abundant**	B. **betray**	C. **comparison**	D. **demonstrate**	E. **dispute**
F. **distinct**	G. **exaggerate**	H. **inhabit**	I. **neutral**	J. **reduction**

_____ 1. If someone's new job pays less than the old job, he or she has taken a ___ in pay.

_____ 2. Benedict Arnold was an American officer who secretly helped the British enemy during the American Revolution; he is remembered as a man who ___ed his country.

_____ 3. You ___ a point when you overstate it, as in saying, "I'm dying of hunger."

_____ 4. We had such an ___ crop of tomatoes this year that we had enough to give some to our neighbors.

_____ 5. If you want to remain friends with two people who are quarreling, it is best to stay ___ and keep out of the fight.

_____ 6. A ___ of our backgrounds and interests revealed we had a lot in common.

_____ 7. The uncooperative salesman refused to ___ how to use the VCR, saying, "Just read the manual and figure it out yourself."

_____ 8. Even though I was only three years old at the time, I have a ___ memory of the first time I saw the ocean.

_____ 9. The people who ___ Canada are called Canadians.

_____ 10. When we say that two people had a ___, we mean that their fight consisted of words, not punches.

NOTE: Now check your answers to these questions by turning to page 239. Going over the answers carefully will help you prepare for the remaining practices, for which answers are not given.

➤ *Check 2*

Using the answer lines, complete each item below with **two** words from the box.

_____
_____ 1–2. My family is having a ___ over whether to paint the kitchen yellow or tan. I'm remaining ___; I don't care what color it is.

_____
_____ 3–4. There has been a ___ in crime in our city this year. In ___ with last year, far fewer crimes were committed.

_____
_____ 5–6. I'll admit that ants were ___ at our picnic, but let's not ___. There really were not a trillion of them.

_____
_____ 7–8. Although I'd never sent e-mail on a computer before, Corey ___d how it works so clearly that I now have a ___ idea of how to do it myself.

_____
_____ 9–10. Homeless people secretly ___ed the abandoned building, but when someone ___ed them and told the police, they were thrown out.

➤ *Word Work*

A. In the space provided, write the letter of the choice that best completes each item.

_____ 1. Polar bears **inhabit**
   A. fish.
   B. the North Pole.
   C. white fur.

_____ 2. The neighbors had a **dispute**
   A. to celebrate a birthday.
   B. because they got along so well together.
   C. over where the property line between them was.

_____ 3. The king's most trusted advisers **betrayed** him by
   A. giving him a surprise party.
   B. checking to be sure his food was safe.
   C. planning to kill him.

_____ 4. Surprisingly, there was a **reduction** in the prices of houses in our area. The prices were
   A. lowered.
   B. raised.
   C. kept the same.

_____ 5. In a **comparison** at the supermarket, Annie learned that
   A. it takes her forty-five minutes to shop.
   B. Wheatsies cereal is a better buy than Oatsies.
   C. her friend Cara shops at the same store.

B. In the space provided, write the letter of the word that most closely relates to the situation in each item.

_____ 6. "My grandchildren are the smartest youngsters in the world, and as for their behavior—they're perfect, that's all. They're angels."

   A. neutral   B. betray   C. exaggerate

_____ 7. In the the woods and fields around my hometown, blueberries grow everywhere. You can pick them by the bucketful.

   A. neutral   B. abundant   C. betray

_____ 8. The view of the moon through the new telescope was extremely clear and sharp.

   A. abundant   B. reduction   C. distinct

_____ 9. "When my husband and I have an argument," Naomi said, "my mother-in-law never takes sides."

   A. neutral   B. demonstrate   C. abundant

_____10. To show the new soldiers how to take a rifle apart and put it together again, the instructors go through the whole process themselves.

   A. inhabit   B. demonstrate   C. neutral

➤ *Synonyms and Antonyms*

A. Synonyms. Write the letter of the word or phrase that most nearly means the **same** as each boldfaced word.

_____ 1. **betray**

   A. encourage   B. annoy
   C. escape   D. be disloyal

_____ 2. **comparison**

   A. thoughts and feelings   B. check of how things are alike or different
   C. questions and answers   D. time and effort

_____ 3. **demonstrate**

   A. show   B. confuse
   C. entertain   D. judge

_____ 4. **dispute**

   A. argument   B. agreement
   C. fact   D. condition

_____ 5. **inhabit**

   A. go away from   B. approach
   C. live in   D. explore

B. Antonyms. Write the letter of the word or phrase that most nearly means the **opposite** of each boldfaced word.

_____ 6. **abundant**

   A. not enough   B. effective
   C. lucky   D. great

_____ 7. **distinct**

   A. quiet   B. not constant
   C. large   D. not clear

_____ 8. **exaggerate**

   A. admire   B. destroy
   C. understate   D. defend

_____ 9. **neutral**

   A. unusual   B. favoring one side over another
   C. frightened   D. possible

_____10. **reduction**

   A. comment   B. increase
   C. agreement   D. answer

➤ *Final Check*

Read the passages carefully. Then fill in each blank with the word that best fits the context.

A. The Vacuum-Cleaner Salesman

A. **abundant**	B. **demonstrate**	C. **distinct**	D. **exaggerate**	E. **reduction**

I'll never forget the day a salesman (1)_____d his vacuum cleaner on my living room rug. I know some salespeople (2)_____ their product's good qualities, so I didn't believe everything he said. But I let him show me what his machine could do.

The first thing he did was deliberately° wipe his muddy feet on my rug. Next, he dumped an (3)_____ amount of ashes onto it. Then he vacuumed the mess up. In no time, there was a difference between the rest of the rug and the part he had dirtied and then cleaned. A clear light stripe now ran down the middle of my rug. The machine was great. He told me how lucky I was to have a chance to buy it then, because of a great (4)_____ in the price. Sadly, I had to tell him that even the lower price was too high for me. He then quickly thanked me and left.

Then I realized that he hadn't finished cleaning up all of the mess he had made. So I used my own vacuum cleaner, which did not do a very good job. As a result, I'm reminded of the frustration° of that day every time I walk through my living room. It still has a (5)_____ light stripe right down the middle.

B. Peace at Last

F. **betray**	G. **comparison**	H. **dispute**	I. **Inhabit**	J. **neutral**

My new apartment is so nice and quiet in (6)_____ with my last one. In my old building, the people who (7)_____ed the apartments on both sides of me were always having (8)_____s. For example, the woman in 401 and the man in 403 would argue all the time about politics. Once she yelled that she had trusted him to keep her secrets, but that he had (9)_____ed her by telling everyone in the building. He then loudly insisted that she was the one with the big mouth. In addition, his wife sometimes screamed at the woman for leaving her trash bags in the hall. Although they tried to get me to take sides, I remained completely (10)_____. I don't know who was right or wrong. I just know that the excessive° number of noisy arguments was too much for me to bear, and I'm glad to be out of there.

Scores	Check 2 _____%	Word Work _____%	Synonyms and Antonyms _____%	Final Check _____%

Enter your scores above and in the vocabulary performance chart on the inside back cover of the book.

aggravate	intentional
cease	interference
coincide	obnoxious
considerable	unstable
humane	utilize

Ten Words in Context

In the space provided, write the letter of the meaning closest to that of each **boldfaced** word. Use the context of the sentences to help you figure out each word's meaning.

1 **aggravate**
(ăg′rə-vāt)
– *verb*

- If you walk on your sprained ankle, you'll only **aggravate** the injury. The pain and swelling will get worse.
- If your next-door neighbors hate your dog, it's a difficult situation; so don't **aggravate** the problem by walking the dog on their lawn.

____*Aggravate* means A. to make use of. B. to make worse. C. to create.

2 **cease**
(sēs)
– *verb*

- After the police warned him twice, our landlord **ceased** burning trash in the backyard, an illegal activity in our town.
- When the snowfall finally **ceased**, we went out to shovel the driveway.

____*Cease* means A. to repeat. B. to start. C. to stop.

3 **coincide**
(kō′ĭn-sīd′)
– *verb*

- My best friend and I have moved to different states. We try to make our visits to our hometown **coincide** so that we can see each other.
- Our neighbor is getting married on the same day as my cousin. I wish the weddings were not going to **coincide** because I'd really like to go to both.

____*Coincide* means A. to happen at the same time. B. to be stopped. C. to be interesting.

4 **considerable**
(kən-sĭd′ər-ə-bəl)
– *adjective*

- After two hours and **considerable** effort, I finally found Vernon's apartment.
- Elena loves gardening, so she spends a **considerable** amount of time caring for flowers, vegetables, and herbs.

____*Considerable* means A. too little. B. gentle. C. quite a bit.

5 **humane**
(hyōō-mān′)
– *adjective*

- When our cat developed a fatal blood disease, we didn't want her to suffer. We felt it was more **humane** to have her painlessly "put to sleep."
- In the past, zoo animals were usually kept in bare concrete cages. In an attempt to be more **humane**, many zoos have built more natural, comfortable animal housing.

____*Humane* means A. wasteful. B. fast. C. caring.

6 **intentional**
(ĭn-tĕn′shə-nəl)
– *adjective*

- The police believe the fire was **intentional**, although they don't know why someone would purposely burn down the movie theater.
- I know I'm an hour late, but it wasn't **intentional**. A huge traffic accident held me up.

____*Intentional* means A. important. B. planned. C. late.

7 interference
(ĭn′tər-fēr′əns)
– *noun*

- Because the street workers outside our classroom window were such an **interference**, the class was moved to the library.
- My mom rarely gets involved in my arguments with my brother and sister. "You must learn to settle your problems without my **interference**," she says.

___*Interference* means   A. help.   B. getting in the way.   C. silence.

8 obnoxious
(əb-nŏk′shəs)
– *adjective*

- The children visiting the chicken farm held their noses because of the **obnoxious** smell.
- I won't go to the party if Lester is there. He always makes himself **obnoxious** by insulting and making fun of people.

___*Obnoxious* means   A. not interesting.   B. popular.   C. not pleasant.

9 unstable
(ŭn-stā′bəl)
– *adjective*

- The ladder felt so **unstable** that I was afraid to climb any higher than the third step.
- The young man's personality was **unstable**. One minute he seemed quiet and satisfied, and the next minute he was angry about something.

___*Unstable* means   A. not steady.   B. useful.   C. secure.

10 utilize
(yōōt′l-īz′)
– *verb*

- Don't throw bread away just because it's stale. Stale bread can be **utilized** to make bread crumbs and croutons.
- Last summer, Cindy **utilized** her swimming skills as a camp lifeguard.

___*Utilize* means   A. to sell.   B. to replace.   C. to use.

Matching Words with Definitions

Following are definitions of the ten words. **Print** each word next to its definition. If you look closely at each word in context, you will be able to figure out its meaning.

1. _____   Very unpleasant; distasteful; disgusting

2. _____   To stop; discontinue; quit

3. _____   Unsteady; wobbly; not reliable

4. _____   Done on purpose; planned

5. _____   To make worse

6. _____   Kind; sympathetic; merciful; gentle

7. _____   To happen at the same time

8. _____   Rather great; rather large

9. _____   The act of getting in the way of something; meddling in someone else's business; something that gets in the way

10. _____   To make use of; put to use, especially to good use

CAUTION: Do not go any further until you are sure the above answers are correct. Then you can use the definitions to help you in the following practices. Your goal is eventually to know the words well enough so that you don't need to check the definitions at all.

➤ *Check 1*

Using the answer line, complete each item below with the correct word from the box.

| A. **aggravate** | B. **cease** | C. **coincide** | D. **considerable** | E. **humane** |
| F. **intentional** | G. **interference** | H. **obnoxious** | I. **unstable** | J. **utilize** |

_____ 1. It's no wonder the vase fell over; the flowers were so top-heavy that the whole arrangement was ___.

_____ 2. My brother is glad he'll be able to ___ his skills as a mechanic in his new job at a garage.

_____ 3. Surprisingly, going to bed and taking it easy can actually ___ back pain. Gentle movement is often more helpful.

_____ 4. A ___ amount of time is the opposite of a rather small amount of time.

_____ 5. You may feel that slurping with straws is ___, but many kids don't find it disgusting at all.

_____ 6. The young man was charged with arson—the ___ setting of a harmful fire.

_____ 7. The two funerals will ___; that is, they will take place on the same day.

_____ 8. My nosy neighbor calls what she does just "taking a healthy interest in people's lives," but I call what she does "___."

_____ 9. It really isn't ___ to give small children chicks and baby ducks as presents. The poor little birds are almost sure to die soon.

_____ 10. The opposite of "begin" is ___.

NOTE: Now check your answers to these questions by turning to page 239. Going over the answers carefully will help you prepare for the remaining practices, for which answers are not given.

➤ *Check 2*

Using the answer lines, complete each item below with **two** words from the box.

_____
_____ 1–2. "No pain, no gain" is bad advice when it comes to sports injuries. You can easily ___ an injury by playing before the pain has ___d.

_____
_____ 3–4. If a couple's marriage seems ___, family members may try to get involved. But ___ from relatives sometimes does more harm than good.

_____
_____ 5–6. It may take ___ effort to get along with an ___ classmate or coworker, but learning how to deal with difficult people is a valuable skill.

_____
_____ 7–8. Animal-rights activists say it is not right to ___ cats, dogs, and monkeys in medical experiments. However, many researchers argue that their treatment of the animals is ___.

_____
_____ 9–10. The vocabulary skills class and the study skills class ___ this semester. Scheduling them for the same day and time probably wasn't ___, but students who wanted to take them both are annoyed.

➤ *Word Work*

A. In the space provided, write the letter of the choice that best completes each item.

_____ 1. According to the weather report, the rain should **cease** tonight. Tonight the rain should

    A. start, after a period   B. get much worse, with   C. stop, probably after raining
       of dry weather.   flooding in some areas.   most or all of the day.

_____ 2. Maria works at home, and sometimes there is a great deal of **interference** from her children. The children

    A. help her with her work.   B. bother her when she   C. leave for long
                             is trying to work.   periods of time.

_____ 3. The bus strike **coincided** with a blizzard, so many offices downtown were closed. The strike

    A. took place a week   B. was called off because   C. happened at the same time
       after the blizzard.   of the blizzard.   as the blizzard.

_____ 4. "If I hurt your feelings, you can be sure it was not **intentional**." I

    A. tried to hurt   B. have hurt you before.   C. did not mean to
       your feelings.   hurt your feelings.

_____ 5. The cost of getting wisdom teeth removed is **considerable**. It is

    A. quite expensive.   B. much cheaper   C. free.
                   than expected.

B. In the space provided, write the letter of the word that most closely relates to the situation in each item.

_____ 6. Mom doesn't like to dispose° of anything. She uses the comics as wrapping paper, cuts up worn-out rubber gloves to make rubber bands, and saves old stockings to use as dust cloths.

    A. interference   B. humane   C. utilize

_____ 7. My grandmother took in foster children and also gave much of her time to a program for pregnant teenagers.

    A. humane   B. aggravate   C. obnoxious

_____ 8. A man at the restaurant was loudly critical° of other customers and tried to start a fight.

    A. utilize   B. coincide   C. obnoxious

_____ 9. My cold got much worse when I went ice skating on the coldest day of the winter.

    A. intentional   B. aggravate   C. utilize

_____ 10. Our restaurant table was distinctly° rocking back and forth, so we put a matchbook under one leg to steady it.

    A. coincide   B. humane   C. unstable

➤ *Analogies*

Each item below starts with a pair of words in CAPITAL LETTERS. For each item, figure out the relationship between these two words. Then decide which of the choices (A, B, C, or D) expresses a similar relationship. Write the letter of your choice on the answer line. (All the repeated words in these items are from this unit.)

Note: To review analogies, see pages 6–7.

_____ 1. AGGRAVATE : WORSEN ::

    A. improve : make better   B. improve : make worse

    C. heal : injure   D. raise : lower

_____ 2. CEASE : BEGIN ::

    A. continue : go on   B. stop : quit

    C. stop : start   D. hurry : rush

_____ 3. PRESERVE° : FURNITURE ::

    A. restore° : repair   B. chair : furniture

    C. find : lose   D. analyze° : problem

_____ 4. OBNOXIOUS : PLEASANT ::

    A. harmful : unpleasant   B. annoying : irritating

    C. annoying : nice   D. pleasure : enjoyment

_____ 5. UTILIZE : TOOL ::

    A. catch : run   B. shaky : wobbly

    C. ship : car   D. swing : bat

_____ 6. UNSTABLE : STEADY ::

    A. large : big   B. evident° : unclear

    C. abundant° : plentiful   D. busy : happy

_____ 7. INTENTIONAL : ON PURPOSE ::

    A. untrue : false   B. accidental : on purpose

    C. planned : prevented   D. hoped for : feared

_____ 8. REJECTION° : ACCEPTANCE ::

    A. hour : time   B. child : children

    C. school : college   D. contrast° : similarity

_____ 9. INTERFERENCE : ASSISTANCE ::

    A. reduction°: decrease   B. garbage : bag

    C. teacher : subject   D. dispute° : agreement

_____ 10. VALUABLE : GOLD ::

    A. fragile° : glass   B. new : old

    C. diamond : ruby   D. excessive° : deliberate°

➤ *Final Check*

Read the passages carefully. Then fill in each blank with the word that best fits the context.

A. Study Skills to the Rescue!

| A. **aggravate** | B. **coincide** | C. **considerable** | D. **interference** | E. **utilize** |

Students say that one of their biggest headaches is what to do when several exams and assignments (1)_____; for example, when they have a test and a quiz the same week that a paper and a report are due. To deal with this situation, don't panic—that will only (2)_____ your problem. Instead, (3)_____ some study skills that will make you a better manager of your time. First, you can get (4)_____ help simply by planning well. Figure out what will take the most time; probably the test will need more study time than the quiz, and a long report might take more time than a short paper. Setting aside suitable° amounts of time will give you a sense of control. Second, be sure you get the most out of the time you've planned. Find a quiet place to work, and don't allow any (5)_____ from your friends or roommates, TV, radio, or CD player. And third? Well, try adding your own ideas to the list. The more you add, the more self-confident you'll feel.

B. Training a Puppy

| F. **cease** | G. **humane** | H. **intentional** | I. **obnoxious** | J. **unstable** |

Training a puppy is always a challenge. Although puppies are adorable creatures, their chewing and snapping can be (6)_____. Their naughtiness is not (7)_____, of course. They're just doing what comes naturally. However, in order for puppies to be good members of the household, these improper° behaviors have to (8)_____. It's up to the human owners to teach puppies good manners.

There are two important points to remember when it comes to training a puppy. The first is to treat the puppy in a (9)_____ manner, rather than a cruel one. For example, scold it by shaking a can of pennies at it instead of slapping it. Secondly, don't do things that confuse your dog. If you let it play tug-of-war with an old sneaker, don't be surprised when it chews up your brand-new Nikes. If your dog doesn't understand what you want of it, it is likely to develop an (10)_____ personality instead of a calm, pleasant one.

| *Scores*   Check 2 _____%   Word Work _____%   Analogies _____%   Final Check _____% |

Enter your scores above and in the vocabulary performance chart on the inside back cover of the book.

UNIT ONE: *Review*

The box at the right lists twenty-five words from Unit One. Using the clues at the bottom of the page, fill in these words to complete the puzzle that follows.

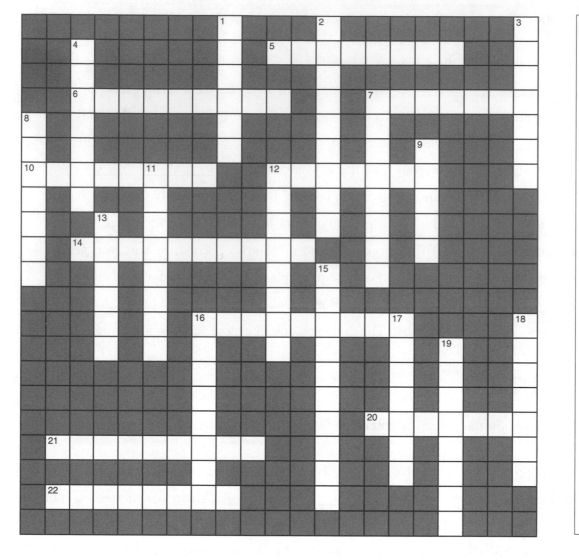

accompany
attitude
betray
cease
challenge
coincide
critical
deliberate
dispute
evident
fertile
fragile
humane
improper
indicate
inhabit
neutral
preference
preserve
reduction
rejection
solitary
surplus
unstable
utilize

ACROSS

5. To protect; keep in good condition
6. To go along with; be together with
7. To live in
10. Happening or done alone
12. To make use of; put to use, especially to good use
14. Done on purpose
16. A test of one's abilities
20. Not taking sides in a quarrel
21. A saying "no" (to a request or desire); refusal
22. Not in good taste; not right for a situation

DOWN

1. Kind; sympathetic; merciful; gentle
2. A decrease; cutback
3. Producing or able to produce much fruit, large crops, or many children
4. Easily broken or damaged
7. To show; serve as a sign or signal
8. An argument; a quarrel
9. To stop; discontinue
11. A point of view; state of mind; way of thinking or feeling
12. Unsteady; wobbly; not reliable
13. To be disloyal to; turn against
15. Choice; first choice; something desired
16. To happen at the same time
17. Obvious; clear
18. Extra; more than what is used or needed
19. Disapproving; tending to find fault

UNIT ONE: Test 1

PART A
Choose the word that best completes each item and write it in the space provided.

_____ 1. A bucket of paint can ___ a room's looks.

    A. transform   B. accompany   C. challenge   D. utilize

_____ 2. Jenna was afraid to touch the ___ house of cards—it looked ready to collapse.

    A. improper   B. distinct   C. neutral   D. unstable

_____ 3. Kwan thought my not inviting her to my party was a ___ insult. In reality, her invitation slipped under a book, so it never was mailed.

    A. deliberate   B. suitable   C. humane   D. improper

_____ 4. Don't scratch a mosquito bite! You'll only ___ the itching and end up feeling even worse.

    A. analyze   B. aggravate   C. indicate   D. utilize

_____ 5. Julio's ___ aim in going to college is to get a good job when he graduates, but he hopes to have a good time while he's there, as well.

    A. abundant   B. obnoxious   C. principal   D. desperate

_____ 6. It took a long time for doctors to ___ what Felicia was allergic to, but they finally figured out that it was her lipstick.

    A. utilize   B. preserve   C. determine   D. restore

_____ 7. After hours of ___ work at my desk, I am ready to spend some time with other people.

    A. abundant   B. solitary   C. humane   D. dependent

_____ 8. My grandmother's old china doll is much too ___ to play with; it would soon be broken.

    A. fragile   B. suitable   C. distinct   D. improper

_____ 9. "Your secret is safe with me," said the handsome prince to the fair maiden. "I swear I will never ___ you!"

    A. restore   B. demonstrate   C. preserve   D. betray

_____ 10. The students in history class noticed a ___ odor coming from the science lab across the hall. The odor smelled like a mixture of rotten eggs and gasoline.

    A. suitable   B. humane   C. fertile   D. peculiar

(Continues on next page)

_____ 11. It is ___ that Wayne is interested in Shawna; he can't stop looking at her.

        A. humane   B. evident   C. dependent   D. critical

_____ 12. Animals that ___ a desert region are able to live there because they can go a long time without water.

        A. analyze   B. indicate   C. dispose of   D. inhabit

_____ 13. A salesperson came to the office to ___ how the new copier worked, but he didn't explain very clearly how to use the machine.

        A. preserve   B. restore   C. demonstrate   D. utilize

PART B

Write **C** if the italicized word is used **correctly**. Write **I** if the word is used **incorrectly**.

_____ 14. Suddenly, the music *ceased*, and the room was very quiet.

_____ 15. That jigsaw puzzle is a *challenge* because it is too easy. It's meant for very young children and has only six pieces.

_____ 16. Because of *interference* by a fan who ran onto the playing field, the game was temporarily stopped by a referee.

_____ 17. Bullies are praised for the *humane* way they treat their victims.

_____ 18. Maya's elderly parents are too *dependent* on her. They constantly call her for help and advice.

_____ 19. The bare, dry, stony fields look very *fertile*.

_____ 20. Raspberries are so *abundant* in our city that it's hard to find them. When you do, they cost as much as five or six dollars for a tiny box.

_____ 21. My *preference* is to go to an Italian restaurant tonight because I dislike spaghetti and pizza.

_____ 22. The notice in the airplane said, "Seat cushions can be *utilized* for flotation." In other words, you can use the cushions to float on if the plane crashes in water.

_____ 23. The teenagers on the subway were especially *obnoxious*. They gave up their seats so some elderly people and a pregnant woman could sit down.

_____ 24. It was very *improper* of you to thank Mrs. Wilson for sending you a birthday card.

_____ 25. Teenage boys are sometimes nervous about asking a girl for a date because they fear *rejection*.

Score   (Number correct) _____ × 4 = _____ %

UNIT ONE: Test 2

PART A
On the answer line, write the word from the box that completes each item below. Use each word once.

A. **accompany**	B. **analyze**	C. **category**	D. **coincide**	E. **comparison**
F. **desperate**	G. **dispose of**	H. **intentional**	I. **neutral**	J. **reduction**
K. **restore**	L. **suitable**	M. **surplus**		

_____ 1. The man on the bus who stepped on my foot said, "Sorry! It wasn't ___. I didn't mean to do it!"

_____ 2. Darin's vegetable garden grew so well and produced so much that he didn't know what to do with the ___ tomatoes and zucchinis.

_____ 3. A ___ between the two jobs didn't make it much easier for Marnie to decide; one paid better, but the other was more interesting.

_____ 4. Why do Easter and Passover ___ in some years, while in other years they are weeks apart rather than at the same time?

_____ 5. That child hates to fight. When his brother and sister get into a quarrel, he always stays ___.

_____ 6. Americans think too much about weight ___. There is more to life than just losing weight!

_____ 7. The town will ___ traffic patterns to find out if more traffic lights are needed.

_____ 8. Some psychologists think there are two types of people: type A's, who are hard-working and uptight, and type B's, who are relaxed and easygoing. Which ___ do you belong in?

_____ 9. If a poor man is ___ for money to buy medicine for his sick wife, do you think he should steal?

_____ 10. Don't ___ the comic section of the Sunday paper. Save it and use it as wrapping paper; it's colorful and fun!

_____ 11. When Josie had a tooth pulled, she asked Mark to ___ her to the dentist and see that she got home all right afterward.

_____ 12. Cut-off jeans might be ___ to wear to a ball game, but they would be out of place at a funeral.

_____ 13. The town wants to ___ the old firehouse instead of tearing it down and building a new one.

(Continues on next page)

PART B
Write **C** if the italicized word is used **correctly**. Write **I** if the word is used **incorrectly**.

_____14. Ronda has an unusual *attitude* toward weekends, vacations, and holidays; she doesn't like them much and would just as soon go to work every day of the year.

_____15. Corey's fame as a football player is *considerable*. Nobody has ever heard of him.

_____16. Imagine my *frustration* when I learned I had earned straight A's for the semester!

_____17. Helen is far too *critical* of her husband. She adores him and never finds fault with him no matter how inconsiderately he treats her.

_____18. To *preserve* the seat covers in his car, Denny had slipcovers put on. Then he put plastic over the slipcovers. Then he spread old sheets over the plastic.

_____19. Denny's concern for his car's seat covers seems to be *excessive*. Who ever heard of using so many layers of covers at once?

_____20. The old photograph was so *distinct* that the faces of the people in it were just a blur.

_____21. "If you get robbed on the street," said the police officer, "never try to *pursue* the thief yourself. Call us and let us do the chasing!"

_____22. There is a real *contrast* between the twins. They look so much alike that sometimes even their mother can't tell them apart.

_____23. Don't *exaggerate* when you fill out a job application. If you were a store clerk, for instance, don't say you were the manager.

_____24. When President Calvin Coolidge wanted to *indicate* that he was not a candidate for reelection, he said, "I do not choose to run."

_____25. Lupe and Jorge agree about everything, so they have one *dispute* after another.

Score   (Number correct) _____ × 4 = _____%

UNIT ONE: Test 3

PART A: Synonyms
In the space provided, write the letter of the choice that is most nearly the **same** in meaning as the **boldfaced** word.

_____ 1. **accompany**   A) go   B) seek   C) figure out   D) go with

_____ 2. **analyze**   A) worry about   B) argue about   C) study   D) change

_____ 3. **attitude**   A) height   B) disappointment   C) point of view   D) skill

_____ 4. **category**   A) a type   B) a book   C) a difference
D) a check for similarities and differences

_____ 5. **challenge**   A) quarrel   B) something needing effort   C) change   D) use

_____ 6. **coincide**   A) change   B) live in   C) happen at the same time   D) show

_____ 7. **comparison**   A) a check for similarities and differences   B) an increase
C) a feeling of anger   D) a first choice

_____ 8. **considerable**   A) unpleasant   B) difficult   C) quite large   D) producing much

_____ 9. **critical**   A) kind   B) hard to get   C) disapproving   D) harmful

_____ 10. **demonstrate**   A) show   B) get rid of   C) turn against   D) overstate

_____ 11. **desperate**   A) relying on others   B) in great need   C) clear   D) alone

_____ 12. **determine**   A) prevent   B) explain   C) figure out   D) protect

_____ 13. **evident**   A) hard to get   B) fitting   C) clear   D) too much

_____ 14. **fertile**   A) careful   B) helpful   C) fearful   D) fruitful

_____ 15. **indicate**   A) disapprove of   B) show   C) turn against   D) protect

_____ 16. **inhabit**   A) make a habit of   B) seek   C) live in   D) leave

_____ 17. **interference**   A) getting in the way   B) difference   C) decrease   D) refusal

_____ 18. **preference**   A) first choice   B) disappointment   C) extra   D) test

_____ 19. **preserve**   A) teach   B) turn against   C) destroy   D) protect

_____ 20. **principal**   A) main   B) on purpose   C) plentiful   D) unusual

_____ 21. **pursue**   A) examine   B) chase   C) get rid of   D) stop

_____ 22. **restore**   A) remove   B) seek   C) give away   D) repair

_____ 23. **solitary**   A) rare   B) alike   C) done alone   D) not reliable

_____ 24. **transform**   A) bring back   B) send   C) change   D) end

_____ 25. **utilize**   A) protect   B) use   C) show   D) stop

(Continues on next page)

PART B: Antonyms

In the space provided, write the letter of the choice that is most nearly **opposite** in meaning to the **boldfaced** word.

_____26. **abundant**   A) healthy   B) unplanned   C) rare   D) unkind

_____27. **aggravate**   A) attack   B) learn   C) move   D) make better

_____28. **betray**   A) grow   B) be happy   C) keep   D) be loyal to

_____29. **cease**   A) give   B) learn   C) ruin   D) start

_____30. **contrast**   A) similarity   B) help   C) agreement   D) success

_____31. **deliberate**   A) unusual   B) unclear   C) unplanned   D) unnecessary

_____32. **dependent**   A) relying on oneself   B) working alone   C) knowing oneself
D) not obvious

_____33. **dispose of**   A) like   B) keep   C) leave   D) remember

_____34. **dispute**   A) test   B) agreement   C) group   D) choice

_____35. **distinct**   A) helpful   B) broken   C) unclear   D) well-known

_____36. **exaggerate**   A) understate   B) go away from   C) think about   D) support

_____37. **excessive**   A) not clear   B) not enough   C) strong   D) not able

_____38. **fragile**   A) not proper   B) unhappy   C) unpleasant   D) unbreakable

_____39. **frustration**   A) failure   B) kindness   C) too much   D) satisfaction

_____40. **humane**   A) cruel   B) forgotten   C) important   D) too little

_____41. **improper**   A) well-known   B) recent   C) too little   D) in good taste

_____42. **intentional**   A) proper   B) done poorly   C) plentiful   D) accidental

_____43. **neutral**   A) paying attention   B) taking sides   C) proper   D) pleasant

_____44. **obnoxious**   A) approving   B) common   C) pleasant   D) intelligent

_____45. **peculiar**   A) difficult   B) ordinary   C) weak   D) excellent

_____46. **reduction**   A) last choice   B) increase   C) start   D) answer

_____47. **rejection**   A) approval   B) addition   C) lack   D) loss

_____48. **suitable**   A) improved   B) unkind   C) improper   D) immediate

_____49. **surplus**   A) success   B) lack   C) luck   D) trouble

_____50. **unstable**   A) steady   B) easy   C) usual   D) quite small

Score   (Number correct) _____ × 2 = _____ %

Enter your score above and in the vocabulary performance chart on the inside back cover of the book.

Unit Two

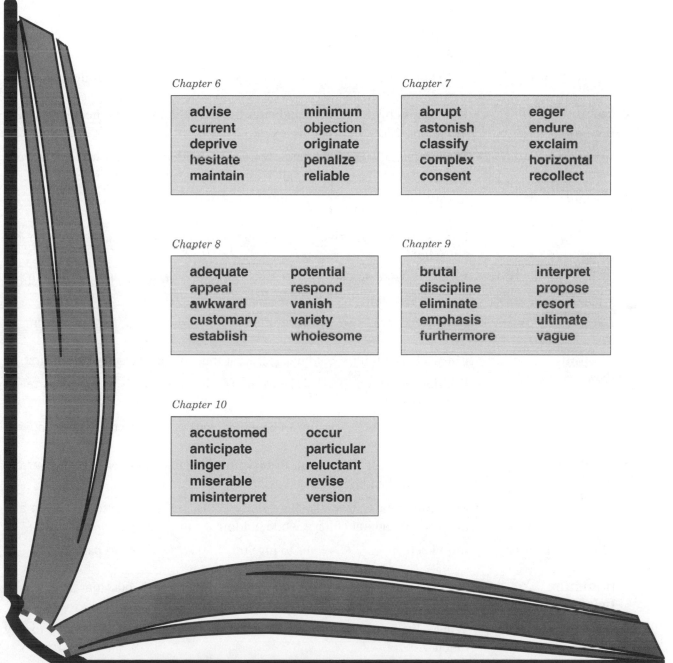

Chapter 6

advise	minimum
current	objection
deprive	originate
hesitate	penalize
maintain	reliable

Chapter 7

abrupt	eager
astonish	endure
classify	exclaim
complex	horizontal
consent	recollect

Chapter 8

adequate	potential
appeal	respond
awkward	vanish
customary	variety
establish	wholesome

Chapter 9

brutal	interpret
discipline	propose
eliminate	resort
emphasis	ultimate
furthermore	vague

Chapter 10

accustomed	occur
anticipate	particular
linger	reluctant
miserable	revise
misinterpret	version

advise	minimum
current	objection
deprive	originate
hesitate	penalize
maintain	reliable

Ten Words in Context

In the space provided, write the letter of the meaning closest to that of each **boldfaced** word. Use the context of the sentences to help you figure out each word's meaning.

1 advise
(ăd-vīz′)
– *verb*

- I'd like to **advise** Alan to break up with Elaine, but I know he'll get angry if I offer my opinion.
- The park ranger said, "I **advise** you to hang your food from a tree if you don't want the bears to get it."

_____*Advise* means   A. to punish.   B. to suggest to.   C. to follow.

2 current
(kûr′ənt)
– *adjective*

- Rita keeps up with fashion and buys the **current** styles, but her sister wears the same basic style, year after year.
- Doctors once suggested total bed rest after surgery. However, **current** practice is to have patients walk as soon as possible after an operation.

_____*Current* means   A. up-to-date.   B. little known.   C. older.

3 deprive
(dĭ-prīv′)
– *verb*

- Isaac's mother **deprives** him of his allowance when he doesn't do his household jobs.
- Dad complains that his low-fat, low-calorie diet **deprives** him of everything he enjoys eating.

_____*Deprive of* means   A. to keep from.   B. to offer to.   C. to protect from.

4 hesitate
(hĕz′ĭ-tāt′)
– *verb*

- I **hesitated** so long about buying the car that someone else bought it first.
- Rodrigo **hesitated** to ask Julie to marry him. He wasn't sure he was ready to get married.

_____*Hesitate* means   A. to act quickly.   B. to be undecided.   C. to be pleased.

5 maintain
(mān-tān′)
– *verb*

- When driving, it's important to **maintain** a safe distance between your car and the car ahead of you.
- My brother must have excellent study skills. He was able to **maintain** a B average throughout college while holding a full-time job.

_____*Maintain* means   A. to keep up.   B. to give up.   C. to pass up.

6 minimum
(mĭn′ə-məm)
– *adjective*

- The **minimum** number of people allowed for each bus tour is eight. If fewer people sign up, the trip will be canceled.
- What's the **minimum** price you'll take for your car? I can't afford to pay much.

_____*Minimum* means   A. oldest.   B. biggest.   C. lowest.

7 objection
(əb-jĕk′shən)
– *noun*

• Luz had a strong **objection** to the wallpaper her husband picked out for their living room. "It looks like a doctor's waiting room," she complained.

• Granddad had a strong **objection** to boys' wearing long hair. Once when my father refused to get a haircut, Granddad cut his hair while he was asleep.

___ *Objection* means   A. interest in.   B. memory of.   C. dislike of.

8 originate
(ə-rĭj′ə-nāt′)
– *verb*

• The ice-cream cone **originated** at the 1904 World's Fair in St. Louis. An ice-cream seller ran out of cups, so he wrapped a waffle around the ice cream and sold it that way.

• Many people believe that baseball **originated** in Cooperstown, New York, in 1839. However, it must have started earlier, since the sport was mentioned in English publications as early as 1744.

___ *Originate* means   A. to continue.   B. to begin.   C. to delay.

9 penalize
(pē′nə-līz′)
– *verb*

• Whenever my parents heard I had been kept after school, they would **penalize** me again at home.

• The judge decided to **penalize** the young thief with one hundred hours of volunteer work.

___ *Penalize* means   A. to depend upon.   B. to answer.   C. to punish.

10 reliable
(rĭ-lī′ə-bəl)
– *adjective*

• Joe Sherman is a **reliable** mechanic. You can count on him to tell you the truth and to fix whatever is wrong with your car.

• The ad said, "**Reliable** store clerk needed. Don't bother to apply unless you are willing to show up on time every day."

___ *Reliable* means   A. modern.   B. able to be trusted.   C. not expensive.

Matching Words with Definitions

Following are definitions of the ten words. **Print** each word next to its definition. If you look closely at each word in context, you will be able to figure out its meaning.

1. _____   A dislike; feeling of being against something; disapproval
2. _____   To stop because of not being able to decide; put off acting because of feeling unsure
3. _____   To take away from; keep from having or enjoying
4. _____   Smallest in size or amount that is allowed or possible; least
5. _____   To continue; carry on; keep in existence
6. _____   Modern; existing now; in general use or practice today
7. _____   To come into being; start
8. _____   To punish; cause to suffer for doing something wrong
9. _____   To give advice to; recommend
10. _____   Able to be depended upon; trustworthy

CAUTION: Do not go any further until you are sure the above answers are correct. Then you can use the definitions to help you in the following practices. Your goal is eventually to know the words well enough so that you don't need to check the definitions at all.

➤ *Check 1*

Using the answer line, complete each item below with the correct word from the box.

| A. **advise** | B. **current** | C. **deprive** | D. **hesitate** | E. **maintain** |
| F. **minimum** | G. **objection** | H. **originate** | I. **penalize** | J. **reliable** |

_____ 1. A worker who is honest and does his job carefully would be called a ___ worker.

_____ 2. My aunt is not a good patient. She rarely does what her doctor ___s her to do.

_____ 3. The opposite of the highest salary the company allows would be its ___ salary.

_____ 4. To ___ the team member who skipped practice, the coach made her do fifty pushups.

_____ 5. We can say that the place where a river starts is where it ___s.

_____ 6. We might refer to styles that are widely worn today as ___ fashions.

_____ 7. Prisons ___ people of much of their freedom.

_____ 8. Larry ___s to work more than ten hours a week after school. He has such difficult classes that he may need more time than usual for studying.

_____ 9. I have an ___ to that comedian. His jokes often hurt other people.

_____ 10. You must keep up a B average to keep your football uniform. In other words, if you don't ___ good grades, you're off the team.

NOTE: Now check your answers to these questions by turning to page 239. Going over the answers carefully will help you prepare for the remaining practices, for which answers are not given.

➤ *Check 2*

Using the answer lines, complete each item below with **two** words from the box.

_____
_____ 1–2. The best way to ___ Eric when he does something bad is to ___ him of his bicycle for a day.

_____
_____ 3–4. The girls accepted jobs that paid the ___ wage, hoping that they would get raises once they proved they were ___ workers.

_____
_____ 5–6. My doctor has an ___ to "crash diets." Although they cause a quick reduction° in weight, they do not help the dieter ___ that new, lower weight.

_____
_____ 7–8. Keisha likes her hair cut in the most ___ style. Her hairdresser ___s her about the newest fashionable looks.

_____
_____ 9–10. The fox terrier is a dog that ___d in England, where fox hunting was popular. It was valued there by hunters because it would not ___ to run into a fox's tunnel and drive the animal out.

➤ *Word Work*

A. Write each word next to the examples that best match it.

A. **advise**	B. **hesitate**	C. **originate**
D. **penalize**	E. **reliable**	

_____ 1. Send a murderer to prison.
Keep a teenager from a party because of poor behavior.
Tell a wild four-year-old to go to her room.

_____ 2. A car that always starts
A friend who is there when you need her
A bus that is never late

_____ 3. Tell a good friend to try harder in school.
Suggest to your sister that she should develop her musical talent.
Encourage an elderly person to get a pet.

_____ 4. Being unable to decide whether to ask Gil to the dance
Stopping because of being uncertain about which way to go
Delaying the purchase of a new car because of doubt about paying so much

_____ 5. Friday gets its name from "Freya," the name of a Norse goddess.
Ice-cream sundaes get their name because they were first sold only on Sundays.
Floating Ivory soap was invented accidentally when a soap-mixing machine was left on too long.

B. In the space provided, write the letter of the choice that best completes each item.

_____ 6. You are likely to have an **objection** to something

    A. helpful.   B. harmful.   C. recent.

_____ 7. To **maintain** good health, you should

    A. start smoking.   B. shop.   C. exercise.

_____ 8. **Current** movies are

    A. playing now.   B. old classics.   C. comedies.

_____ 9. "When your cousin visits, he'll be sharing your room," Tim's mother announced. Tim realized he would be **deprived** of his

    A. meals.   B. relatives.   C. privacy.

_____ 10. To buy clothing at the **minimum** cost, go to

    A. department stores.   B. garage sales.   C. France.

➤ *Word Parts*

A. The suffixes *-ance* and *-ence* often mean "the act, state, or quality of."

Examples: *maintain* — to keep in existence   *patient* — willing to put up with something
maintenance — the act of keeping   *patience* — the quality of being patient
in existence

On each answer line, write the word from the box that means the same as the *italicized* words.

A. **avoidance**	B. **excellence**	C. **dependence**
D. **interference°**	E. **maintenance**	

_____   1. "I know you mean well," the woman said to her mother. "But I'm 25 now, and your *act of interfering* in how I do my job is not helpful."

_____   2. My father's *state of depending* on caffeine is not healthy for him.

_____   3. Takeo aims for *the quality of being excellent* in everything he does.

_____   4. The *act of maintaining* of good grades requires a lot of willpower.

_____   5. Anna's *act of avoiding* milk is easily explained—she is allergic to it.

B. The prefix *in -* often means "not," which can change words to their opposites.

Examples: *direct* — in a straight line   *humane°* — kind
indirect — not in a straight line   *inhumane* — not kind

On each answer line, write the word from the box that best completes the item.

F. **incapable**	G. **inconvenient**	H. **indistinct°**
I. **inexpensive**	J. **inhumane**	

_____   6. The fog was so thick that the road signs were ___, and I could barely see them.

_____   7. I wish there were a grocery store nearby. It is ___ to have to drive all the way across town.

_____   8. "It's ___ to give me a ten o'clock curfew!" Claudia complained. Her father replied, "I'm sorry you think I'm unkind, but I think 10 p.m. is a perfectly reasonable time to be home."

_____   9. Most people are ___ of wiggling their ears, but not my dad! He can make them flap like wings.

_____   10. Since we are on a budget, we buy ___ furniture at flea markets. In comparison° with our friends' new furniture, the old pieces we buy are often of better quality.

➤ *Final Check*

Read the passages carefully. Then fill in each blank with the word that best fits the context.

A. Toasters

A. **current**	B. **maintain**	C. **minimum**	D. **originate**	E. **reliable**

Although the practice of eating toasted bread (1)_____d about 4,600 years ago, the pop-up electric toaster was not invented until 1919. These early pop-up toasters were not very (2)_____—they broke down often. Also, they weren't able to (3)_____ an even temperature, but grew hotter and hotter with each piece of bread toasted. Some poor-quality machines even popped the toast all the way across the room. Over the years, toasters have certainly improved. (4)_____ ones give us a (5)_____ number of problems with repairs and temperature control.

B. A Mean Man

F. **advise**	G. **deprive**	H. **hesitate**	I. **objection**	J. **penalize**

Mr. Barker says that he has no (6)_____ to kids—as long as they don't come into his yard, as long as they don't (7)_____ him of peace and quiet, and as long as they don't grow up to be teenagers.

Neighborhood kids say he's the meanest man they ever met. Who can blame them? If he sees them choosing up sides for a ball game in the street, for example, he doesn't (8)_____ a minute. He runs right to his window and yells, "You can't do that in front of MY house!" The kids are afraid of him, but they yell back that the street belongs to everybody. "Well, I (9)_____ you to watch your step!" he replies. "If you kids break my window or step on my flowers, you will be (10)_____d." Then he slams his window shut. Maybe a hard life has made Mr. Barker the way he is, but it's hard to have warm feelings for someone so obnoxious°.

Scores Check 2 _____%	Word Work _____%	Word Parts _____%	Final Check _____%

Enter your scores above and in the vocabulary performance chart on the inside back cover of the book.

abrupt	eager
astonish	endure
classify	exclaim
complex	horizontal
consent	recollect

Ten Words in Context

In the space provided, write the letter of the meaning closest to that of each **boldfaced** word. Use the context of the sentences to help you figure out each word's meaning.

1 abrupt
(ə-brŭpt´)
– *adjective*

- Seat belts in cars protect passengers from injuries caused by **abrupt** stops.
- An **abrupt** burst of laughter during the church service surprised everyone.

___*Abrupt* means   A. silent.   B. simple.   C. not expected.

2 astonish
(ə-stŏn´ĭsh)
– *verb*

- A magician **astonished** the audience by making seemingly impossible things happen.
- The announcement that the factory was closing forever **astonished** the employees, who had not known their jobs were in danger.

___*Astonish* means   A. to delay.   B. to encourage.   C. to surprise.

3 classify
(klăs´ə-fī´)
– *verb*

- The stamp collector **classified** her stamps by countries—she put all the stamps from France together, all the stamps from Spain together, and so on.
- I was surprised to learn that the sea horse is **classified** by scientists as a fish.

___*Classify* means   A. to lose.   B. to group.   C. to remember.

4 complex
(kəm-plĕks´)
– *adjective*

- Because income tax forms are so **complex**, many people hire professionals to prepare their tax returns.
- Our family is rather **complex**—it includes many second marriages and stepfamilies. At family reunions we spend a lot of time trying to figure out how we are all related.

___*Complex* means   A. hard to understand.   B. helpful.   C. small.

5 consent
(kən-sĕnt´)
– *verb*

- Only applicants who **consented** to a drug test were considered for the job.
- Enrique proposed to Anna by putting up a billboard saying, "Will you marry me?" She **consented** with her own sign that said, "Of course I will."

___*Consent* means   A. to say yes.   B. to listen.   C. to disagree.

6 eager
(ē´gər)
– *adjective*

- I am always **eager** to read the latest story by my favorite mystery writer.
- Our dog is **eager** to greet us when we come home. She jumps up on us and begins licking our hands before the door is even shut.

___*Eager* means   A. bored.   B. patient.   C. happily excited.

7 endure
(ĕn-dŏŏr′)
– *verb*

- We'll have to **endure** a few more weeks of cold, gray winter before spring arrives.
- Until someone finds a cure for the common cold, there's not much to do but **endure** the runny noses and sneezes.

____*Endure* means   A. to enjoy.   B. to organize.   C. to live with unwillingly.

8 exclaim
(ĭk-sklām′)
– *verb*

- "Wow!" "Ooooh!" "Aaah!" the crowd **exclaimed** as the colorful fireworks burst in the sky.
- When a cardinal landed on the bird feeder, the little girl **exclaimed**, "Look! A red blue jay!"

____*Exclaim* means   A. to remember.   B. to complain.   C. to call out.

9 horizontal
(hŏr′ĭ-zŏn′tl)
– *adjective*

- The surgery left a **horizontal** scar that runs from one side of my stomach to the other.
- The American flag contains **horizontal** red and white stripes.

____*Horizontal* means   A. dirty.   B. little.   C. running from side to side.

10 recollect
(rĕk′ə-lĕkt′)
– *verb*

- Can you **recollect** much about being in first grade?
- I couldn't **recollect** my aunt's phone number, so I had to call the phone company's information number.

____*Recollect* means   A. to agree with.   B. to remember.   C. to arrange.

Matching Words with Definitions

Following are definitions of the ten words. **Print** each word next to its definition. If you look closely at each word in context, you will be able to figure out its meaning.

1. _____   Lying flat; lying or extending from side to side (as opposed to going up and down)

2. _____   To put up with; bear patiently

3. _____   Looking forward to with great interest or desire

4. _____   Not simple; not easy to understand or figure out

5. _____   To agree to something

6. _____   To speak or cry out suddenly, as from strong feelings or surprise

7. _____   To arrange or organize into groups or types; place in a category°

8. _____   To remember; bring an image or idea back to mind

9. _____   To surprise greatly; amaze

10. _____   Sudden and unexpected

CAUTION: Do not go any further until you are sure the above answers are correct. Then you can use the definitions to help you in the following practices. Your goal is eventually to know the words well enough so that you don't need to check the definitions at all.

➤ *Check 1*

Using the answer line, complete each item below with the correct word from the box.

A. **abrupt**	B. **astonish**	C. **classify**	D. **complex**	E. **consent**
F. **eager**	G. **endure**	H. **exclaim**	I. **horizontal**	J. **recollect**

_____ 1. Sometimes I think I can't ___ one more day of winter, but I know I have to put up with it until spring.

_____ 2. Did you know that scientists ___ the whale as a mammal? Most people think of it as a fish.

_____ 3. Although I remember little about first grade, I ___ my year in third grade very clearly.

_____ 4. The great magician Houdini would ___ audiences by escaping from chains, locked trunks, and even sealed coffins.

_____ 5. The day after Jackie had her waist-length hair cut short, nearly everyone she met ___ed, "Oh! Your hair!"

_____ 6. A car would probably come to an ___ stop if a dog ran out in front of it.

_____ 7. Knowing that she had done well on every test, Phyllis was ___ to see her final grade for the course.

_____ 8. Why must tax forms be so ___? Why can't the government make them easier to understand?

_____ 9. It's true that ___ stripes on clothing make you look wider, and stripes that go up and down make you look taller.

_____ 10. If you won the lottery, would you ___ to having your name and picture printed in the newspaper?

NOTE: Now check your answers to these questions by turning to page 239. Going over the answers carefully will help you prepare for the remaining practices, for which answers are not given.

➤ *Check 2*

Using the answer lines, complete each item below with **two** words from the box.

_____
_____ 1–2. In early spring, ___ changes in the weather can ___ everyone. It may be mild and sunny in the morning, then snowing by bedtime.

_____
_____ 3–4. I didn't want to have dental surgery, but I decided to ___ to it rather than ___ my toothache any longer. I just want the pain to cease°.

_____
_____ 5–6. I am thinking of buying Felix a striped T-shirt for his birthday, but I can't ___ if he likes to wear ___ stripes or stripes that go up and down.

_____
_____ 7–8. Scientists ___ animals in a ___ system of groupings, using features such as being warm- or cold-blooded and having feathers or scales.

_____
_____ 9–10. My kids are not exactly ___ to go to school. When I wake them every morning, they ___, "Oh, no! Isn't it Saturday yet?"

➤ *Word Work*

A. In the space provided, write the letter of the choice that best completes each item.

_____ 1. Thelma **recollects** her neighbor's kindness. She

    A. is disappointed   B. remembers that her   C. doubts that her neighbor
        in her neighbor.   neighbor was kind.   can be kind.

_____ 2. You are likely to **exclaim**

    A. a grocery list.   B. a stamp collection.   C. an expression of surprise.

_____ 3. The rich heroine in the story announces that she wants to marry a poor woodcutter. Her father tells her, "I will never **consent** to such a marriage!" Her father feels that the woodcutter would be

    A. a good match for his daughter.   B. a poor match for his daughter.

_____ 4. When our neighbors told us they were divorcing, we were **astonished**. Obviously, we

    A. had expected the   B. had not expected   C. were not very interested.
        divorce for a long time.   it to happen.

_____ 5. It is difficult to **endure**

    A. a terrible headache.   B. a good dinner.   C. a sunny day.

B. In the space provided, write the letter of the word that most closely relates to the situation in each item.

_____ 6. At one point on the highway, there are eight lanes of traffic, three different levels, and about twenty signs with arrows pointing every which way.

    A. eager   B. complex   C. consent

_____ 7. Len's leaving his job was very sudden; one day he just marched in and said, "I quit."

    A. abrupt   B. horizontal   C. classify

_____ 8. The trees that had fallen during the storm lay flat on the ground.

    A. recollect   B. consent   C. horizontal

_____ 9. When the doors of the store opened on the day of the big sale, shoppers rushed in, excited about finding the best bargains.

    A. eager   B. horizontal   C. consent

_____ 10. The boys sort the coins they've saved into separate piles: pennies here, nickels there, dimes next, and then quarters.

    A. endure   B. exclaim   C. classify

➤ *Synonyms and Antonyms*

A. Synonyms. Write the letter of the word or phrase that most nearly means the **same** as each boldfaced word.

_____ 1. **abrupt**

      A. expected   B. delayed

      C. sudden   D. polite

_____ 2. **astonish**

      A. borrow   B. request

      C. allow   D. surprise

_____ 3. **classify**

      A. set aside for later   B. have no use for

      C. decide the value   D. organize into groups

_____ 4. **endure**

      A. bear up under   B. remember

      C. agree   D. deny

_____ 5. **exclaim**

      A. tell   B. call out

      C. notice   D. bear

B. Antonyms. Write the letter of the word or phrase that most nearly means the **opposite** of each boldfaced word.

_____ 6. **complex**

      A. simple   B. true

      C. interesting   D. wise

_____ 7. **consent**

      A. try   B. disagree

      C. begin   D. practice

_____ 8. **eager**

      A. unsteady   B. perfect

      C. expected   D. not interested

_____ 9. **horizontal**

      A. in a circle   B. lying at a slant

      C. straight up and down   D. outside

_____ 10. **recollect**

      A. forget   B. forgive

      C. plan   D. wonder

➤ *Final Check*

Read the passages carefully. Then fill in each blank with the word that best fits the context.

A. A Special Memory

A. **astonish**	B. **consent**	C. **eager**	D. **horizontal**	E. **recollect**

Tony and I often did things without asking our mom to (1)_____ to our activities—because she probably wouldn't. Besides, we loved secret projects. One summer we built a treehouse hidden among some tall trees on Mr. Leary's lot. The window was crooked, and the floor wasn't exactly (2)_____, although the tilt wasn't too bad. We took Mom's ladder to use as our stairs and decorated the place with an old rug and some pillows.

One day we heard Mom yelling up to us, "So that's where my ladder went!" Then she told us that Mr. Leary had called to say that the treehouse had to come down. "You could fall and get hurt," she explained, "and he doesn't want to get sued—and he's right. That treehouse is dangerous. I advise° you to come down from there right now."

But that night, (3)_____ to spend one last hour there, Tony and I sneaked out and headed for the treehouse. As we got near it, we were (4)_____ed to see a candle glowing in the crooked window. So we climbed up very quietly and peeked in. I can still (5)_____ the scene clearly. There was Mom, sitting on one of our pillows, smiling. Next to her were a pitcher of lemonade and three glasses. "It's about time you got here," she said. "What took you so long?"

B. Watch Your Manners!

F. **abrupt**	G. **classify**	H. **complex**	I. **endure**	J. **exclaim**

Most of us think we know how to be polite. But some things that Americans (6)_____ as good manners may seem rude in other parts of the world. Every culture has its own (7)_____ set of rules about what is and isn't acceptable.

For example, an American who went to a birthday party in Japan brought the fun to an (8)_____ end by giving a clock as a present. In Japan, giving anyone a clock is a way of saying "I hope your time is running out"—in other words, "I hope you die soon." Also, Americans in China are seen as bad-tempered when they (9)_____ something loudly, out of excitement or to make a point. In China, a loud voice is a sign of strong anger.

Of course, foreign visitors to the United States can also misunderstand our ways. For instance, an Arab who was a guest at a banquet in Washington later complained, "I didn't get a thing to eat." It turned out he had said, "No, thank you," each time he was offered food. In his country, it was good manners to refuse food several times before accepting it. His American hosts didn't know that, so they just let the poor fellow (10)_____ his hunger.

Scores   Check 2 _____%   Word Work _____%   Synonyms and Antonyms _____%   Final Check _____%

Enter your scores above and in the vocabulary performance chart on the inside back cover of the book.

adequate	potential
appeal	respond
awkward	vanish
customary	variety
establish	wholesome

Ten Words in Context

In the space provided, write the letter of the meaning closest to that of each **boldfaced** word. Use the context of the sentences to help you figure out each word's meaning.

1 adequate
(ăd′ĭ-kwĭt)
– *adjective*

- When I didn't have time to wash the windows, I hired a neighbor's child to do it. He did an **adequate** job—not perfect, but good enough.
- Open sandals are not **adequate** footwear for factory work. Workers should wear heavy shoes to protect their feet.

___*Adequate* means   A. OK.   B. poor.   C. popular.

2 appeal
(ə-pēl′)
– *verb*

- Every year, charities such as the American Cancer Society and the March of Dimes **appeal** to us for money to help cure disease.
- When police can't solve a crime, they sometimes **appeal** to the public for help.

___*Appeal to* means   A. to answer.   B. to run.   C. to make a request.

3 awkward
(ôk′wərd)
– *adjective*

- When I was 13, I was very **awkward**. My feet seemed too big, and I was always tripping over things.
- Rico is such an **awkward** dancer that he constantly steps on his partner's feet.

___*Awkward* means   A. not strong.   B. not graceful.   C. kind.

4 customary
(kŭs′tə-měr′ē)
– *adjective*

- In some towns, it's **customary** for the "Welcome Wagon" to visit newcomers and tell them about the town.
- Americans usually eat their big meal in the evening. In Ireland, however, it is **customary** to eat a big dinner in the afternoon and a light meal at night.

___*Customary* means   A. not polite.   B. normal.   C. rare.

5 establish
(ĭ-stăb′lĭsh)
– *verb*

- The first lending library was **established** in Scotland in 1725.
- The first movie theater in the United States was **established** in New Orleans in 1896.

___*Establish* means   A. to leave.   B. to stop.   C. to start.

6 potential
(pə-tĕn′shəl)
– *noun*

- My grandmother had the **potential** to be a great teacher, but she couldn't afford to go to college.
- Everyone agrees that Carlos has the **potential** to be a major-league baseball player. To become that good, he must continue to work hard.

___*Potential* means   A. request.   B. memory.   C. ability.

7 respond
(rĭ'spŏnd')
– verb

- You asked me a question, so why don't you stop talking for a minute so that I can **respond**?
- When very little children talk on the telephone, they sometimes don't realize they have to say "yes" or "no" out loud. They think they can **respond** to a question by nodding or shaking their heads.

___ *Respond* means   A. to reply.   B. to repeat.   C. to leave.

8 vanish
(văn'ĭsh)
– verb

- The magician made the rabbit **vanish** by slipping it under a secret door.
- You gave a stranger $500 in cash to paint your house? How do you know he won't **vanish** with the money?

___ *Vanish* means   A. to answer.   B. to begin.   C. to go out of sight.

9 variety
(və-rī'ə-tē)
– noun

- In the spring, the woods contain a **variety** of wildflowers, including bluebells, daffodils, and violets.
- Instead of being a **variety** of colors, all of Gale's clothes were lavender or purple.

___ *Variety* means   A. mixture.   B. absence.   C. shade.

10 wholesome
(hōl'səm)
– adjective

- The city residents are planning a community garden where they can grow their own fresh, **wholesome** fruits and vegetables.
- We now know smoking is not **wholesome**, but early cigarette ads claimed physical and mental benefits for smokers.

___ *Wholesome* means   A. obvious.   B. expensive.   C. healthy.

Matching Words with Definitions

Following are definitions of the ten words. **Print** each word next to its definition. If you look closely at each word in context, you will be able to figure out its meaning.

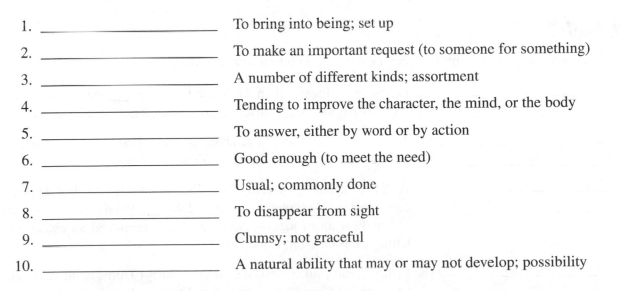

1. _____ To bring into being; set up

2. _____ To make an important request (to someone for something)

3. _____ A number of different kinds; assortment

4. _____ Tending to improve the character, the mind, or the body

5. _____ To answer, either by word or by action

6. _____ Good enough (to meet the need)

7. _____ Usual; commonly done

8. _____ To disappear from sight

9. _____ Clumsy; not graceful

10. _____ A natural ability that may or may not develop; possibility

CAUTION: Do not go any further until you are sure the above answers are correct. Then you can use the definitions to help you in the following practices. Your goal is eventually to know the words well enough so that you don't need to check the definitions at all.

➤ *Check 1*

Using the answer line, complete each item below with the correct word from the box.

A. **adequate**	B. **appeal**	C. **awkward**	D. **customary**	E. **establish**
F. **potential**	G. **respond**	H. **vanish**	I. **variety**	J. **wholesome**

_____ 1. An acorn has the ___ to be an oak tree.

_____ 2. I looked everywhere for my car keys, but they seem to have ___ed into thin air.

_____ 3. Rodney has worked in a ___ of positions, including trucker, carpenter, and rancher.

_____ 4. The signs the children put up on telephone poles ___ed to people to help find their lost cat.

_____ 5. Starting a day with exercise is more ___ than starting the day with a cigarette. Unlike cigarettes, exercise is good for us.

_____ 6. I'd love a huge apartment, but this small one is ___; it serves my needs.

_____ 7. The American Girl Scouts were ___ed in 1912.

_____ 8. People's habits can be referred to as their ___ behavior.

_____ 9. When asked a question, we usually ___, even if it's only to say, "I don't know."

_____ 10. On land, crocodiles seem slow and ___. However, once they are in the water, they are fast and graceful swimmers.

NOTE: Now check your answers to these questions by turning to page 239. Going over the answers carefully will help you prepare for the remaining practices, for which answers are not given.

➤ *Check 2*

Using the answer lines, complete each item below with **two** words from the box.

_____
_____ 1–2. Parents were happy when the Youth Club was ___ed in town because it gave their kids a ___ place to go, meet friends, and have fun.

_____
_____ 3–4. The ___ of fruits and vegetables at Fresh Foods is ___, but not as good as the selection at Grocery Giant.

_____
_____ 5–6. A talent agent ___ed to Christi's parents to let her appear in commercials. He thought Christi had the ___ to be a very good model and make a lot of money. However, her parents had an objection° to letting a ten-year-old work.

_____
_____ 7–8. In my dream, an old woman says, "Hurry! Come with me!" But I never go with her. She ___es before I have a chance to ___.

_____
_____ 9–10. It is ___ for people to bow to one another in Japan. When Fred visited that country, he bowed, too, even though he felt ___ doing it.

➤ *Word Work*

A. Write each word next to the examples that best match it.

A. **appeal**	B. **awkward**	C. **customary**
D. **variety**	E. **wholesome**	

_____ 1. Ice cream and cake at a birthday party
Saying "Bless you" when someone sneezes
Saying "Hello" when answering the phone

_____ 2. Ask people to become blood donors for the Red Cross.
Seek new volunteers for the public library.
Call upon the public to provide tips to help the police solve a crime.

_____ 3. A teen dance that is alcohol- and smoke-free
A bowl of shredded-wheat cereal, topped with sliced banana and skim milk
A G-rated movie

_____ 4. Bumping into someone in the doorway
Tripping over your shoelace
Spilling your coffee

_____ 5. Dogs: German shepherds, cocker spaniels, Italian bulldogs
Ice cream: strawberry, peach, butter pecan
Art supplies: crayons, markers, oil paints, watercolors

B. In the space provided, write the letter of the word that most closely relates to the situation in each item.

_____ 6. The Spanish-speaking students are going to set up their own Latino Club.

A. establish   B. vanish   C. variety

_____ 7. The wading pool is big enough for the children to splash around and cool off, even if they can't really swim in it.

A. vanish   B. adequate   C. respond

_____ 8. After watching Pablo play basketball with his friends, the coach said, "You ought to try out for the team. I think you could become a terrific player."

A. variety   B. awkward   C. potential

_____ 9. Jen taught her dog to obey whenever he hears her say, "Sit!"

A. respond   B. various   C. vanish

_____ 10. The famous pilot Amelia Earhart took off on an around-the-world flight in the summer of 1937 and was never seen again.

A. appealed   B. vanished   C. established

➤ *Word Parts*

A. The prefix *re-* often means "again."

> *Examples:* *utilize°* — to make use of
> *reutilize* — to make use of again

On each answer line, write the word from the box that best completes the item.

A. **reanalyze°**	B. **reheat**	C. **relearn**
D. **relocate**	E. **reutilize°**	

_____ 1. When I get home late from work, I usually find some leftovers that I can ___ for dinner.

_____ 2. It is easier to ___ something that you once knew and forgot, than to learn something for the first time.

_____ 3. Mr. Amin did not give up when a highway was built where his store had once been. He decided to ___ his business in another part of town.

_____ 4. After finishing a difficult math problem, I often ___ it, just to be sure I have the correct answer.

_____ 5. After I empty plastic bags from the supermarket, I ___ them. I may use them as storage bags or even bring them back to the supermarket to use there again.

B. The prefix *un-* often means "not." It can change words to their opposites.

> *Examples:* *intentional°* — done on purpose   *stable* — steady
> *unintentional* — not done on purpose; done by accident   *unstable°* — not steady

On each answer line, write the word from the box that best completes the item.

F. **unintentional°**	G. **uninterested**	H. **unlucky**
I. **unstable°**	J. **unwholesome**	

_____ 6. Most dogs are ___ in vegetables. Unfortunately, so are many children.

_____ 7. Many people eat an ___ diet, filled with fried foods, fatty meats, and sugar, and lacking in vegetables and grains.

_____ 8. "Oh, I'm sorry," said the man who bumped into me. "That was ___."

_____ 9. Many people believe the number thirteen is ___. Some hotels won't even give a room that number.

_____ 10. Our strangely shaped dining-room chairs are so ___ that several people have fallen out of them.

➤ *Final Check*

Read the passages carefully. Then fill in each blank with the word that best fits the context.

A. Big Brothers and Sisters

| A. **appeal** | B. **establish** | C. **potential** | D. **variety** | E. **wholesome** |

This week, the local Big Brother/Big Sister Agency (1)_____ed to the community for volunteers. The organization is looking for men and women who are willing to (2)_____ a new friendship with a young boy or girl from a single-parent home. The only thing required for becoming a volunteer is the desire to become friends with the children, to help them stay in school, and to choose (3)_____ activities that will keep them out of trouble. Volunteers can do a (4)_____ of things with their little "brothers" or "sisters," such as taking them to the park or going out to eat. Whatever activities they choose, volunteers will play an important part in the children's lives, helping them to build their (5)_____ to live full lives and become good citizens.

B. Kevin's First Date

| F. **adequate** | G. **awkward** | H. **customary** | I. **respond** | J. **vanish** |

If you ask Kevin what the most embarrassing time of his life was, he will surely tell you about his first date, which was for an eighth-grade dance. He was so afraid of rejection° when he asked the girl to go with him that he almost didn't notice when she consented° to be his date.

The day of the dance was no better. Between the time he rang her doorbell and the time her father answered, he forgot his date's name—completely. He mumbled something about school (he did remember the school's name), and the girl's father let him in. The man then fired some questions at Kevin, to make sure he was an (6)_____ date for his darling daughter. Kevin could barely (7)_____ to the questions because his nervous thirteen-year-old voice squeaked and cracked so much.

Since it was (8)_____ for boys to bring a corsage of flowers on this special occasion, Kevin had done so. But when his date came down the stairs in a pale pink gown and he opened the florist's box, he became even more nervous. Inside was an excessively° large flower in a bright orange color that didn't go at all with the pink dress. As he pinned the giant blossom onto the gown, he made an (9)_____ movement, stuck his finger, and bled—onto the dress. The girl was so astonished° that her mouth fell open. He wanted to (10)_____ from the face of the earth and never be seen again. He even considered transferring to another school. As it was, he developed such a poor attitude° about dating that he didn't ask another girl out for the next two years.

| *Scores* | Check 2 _____% | Word Work _____% | Word Parts _____% | Final Check _____% |

Enter your scores above and in the vocabulary performance chart on the inside back cover of the book.

brutal	interpret
discipline	propose
eliminate	resort
emphasis	ultimate
furthermore	vague

Ten Words in Context

In the space provided, write the letter of the meaning closest to that of each **boldfaced** word. Use the context of the sentences to help you figure out each word's meaning.

1 brutal
(brōot′l)
– *adjective*

- When we saw the man kicking his dog, we called the police and reported his **brutal** behavior. The dog was taken away and given to a good home.
- In the movie, the actor played a **brutal** criminal. In real life, however, he is a very kind and gentle man.

___*Brutal* means   A. youthful.   B. hardly ever seen.   C. mean.

2 discipline
(dĭs′ə-plĭn)
– *verb*

- The ballplayer was put out of the game for bumping an umpire. He was also **disciplined** with a $10,000 fine.
- José wanted to teach his children to be nonviolent, so he **disciplined** them in gentle ways, such as sending them to their rooms for some quiet "time out."

___*Discipline* means   A. to punish.   B. to leave.   C. to turn to for help.

3 eliminate
(ĭ-lĭm′ə-nāt′)
– *verb*

- If you hang up clothes right after the dryer stops, you can **eliminate** the need to iron many items.
- Because my father has high blood pressure, he's supposed to **eliminate** salt from his diet.

___*Eliminate* means   A. to add to.   B. to remove.   C. to repeat.

4 emphasis
(ĕm′fə-sĭs)
– *noun*

- Brad's father placed a lot of **emphasis** on doing well in sports but gave little attention to doing well in school.
- In my Spanish class, too much **emphasis** was given to reading and not enough to speaking.

___*Emphasis* means   A. delay.   B. addition.   C. importance.

5 furthermore
(fûr′thər-môr′)
– *adverb*

- "I don't believe your story about a flat tire," said Hal's boss. "And **furthermore**, I haven't believed any of your other excuses for being late."
- The Nets will win because they are a talented team. **Furthermore**, they are coached well.

___*Furthermore* means   A. instead.   B. later.   C. also.

6 interpret
(ĭn-tûr′prĭt)
– *verb*

- After Ray had a dental x-ray, the dentist sat down with him to **interpret** it.
- How should I **interpret** the fact that, although we were friendly yesterday, Jean refused to speak to me today?

___*Interpret* means   A. to explain.   B. to suggest.   C. to discover.

7 propose
(prə-pōz')
– *verb*

• Our little brother **proposed** buying our parents a puppy for Christmas this year, but instead we decided to give them a coffee grinder.

• Rafael was obviously too tired to study, so his mother **proposed** that he take a nap and get back to work later.

____ *Propose* means   A. to predict.   B. to remember.   C. to suggest.

8 resort
(ri-zôrt')
– *verb*

• After I'd cooked some spaghetti, I realized I didn't have any spaghetti sauce, so I **resorted** to eating it with ketchup.

• Although school was hard for Tarik, he never **resorted** to cheating.

____ *Resort to* means   A. to explain.   B. to forget about.   C. to turn to.

9 ultimate
(ŭl'tə-mĭt)
– *adjective*

• Chocolate ice cream filled with chocolate chips and topped with fudge sauce—for a chocolate-lover like me, that is the **ultimate** dessert.

• Saying they learned a lot in class is the **ultimate** compliment students can pay a teacher.

____ *Ultimate* means   A. greatest.   B. most interesting.   C. unknown.

10 vague
(vāg)
– *adjective*

• On the essay test, give detailed answers, not **vague** ones.

• Ben had only a **vague** idea of what yeast was. He knew it was used to make bread, but he wasn't sure what it did.

____ *Vague* means   A. general.   B. curious.   C. wrong.

Matching Words with Definitions

Following are definitions of the ten words. **Print** each word next to its definition. If you look closely at each word in context, you will be able to figure out its meaning.

1. _____ Not clear; not exact; not definite

2. _____ To put forward for thinking over or accepting; suggest (an idea)

3. _____ To punish; cause to suffer for doing something wrong

4. _____ To turn or go (to) for help; use for aid

5. _____ Cruel; heartless

6. _____ Special attention; importance given to something

7. _____ In addition; besides

8. _____ To get rid of; do away with

9. _____ To explain the meaning of; make sense of

10. _____ Greatest; highest possible

CAUTION: Do not go any further until you are sure the above answers are correct. Then you can use the definitions to help you in the following practices. Your goal is eventually to know the words well enough so that you don't need to check the definitions at all.

➤ *Check 1*

Using the answer line, complete each item below with the correct word from the box.

A. **brutal**	B. **discipline**	C. **eliminate**	D. **emphasis**	E. **furthermore**
F. **interpret**	G. **propose**	H. **resort**	I. **ultimate**	J. **vague**

_____ 1. Ms. Ramirez took her son's bike away for a week to ___ him after he lied to her.

_____ 2. Your ___ goal is the highest one you hope to reach.

_____ 3. When my grandmother can't think of a word in English, she ___s to saying it in Spanish.

_____ 4. "When I ask my children where they're going," Sheila said, "I don't accept ___ answers. I want to know exactly where they'll be."

_____ 5. Since I didn't understand the results of my blood test, the doctor ___ed it for me.

_____ 6. We encourage our children to ___ weekend activities in which the whole family can participate.

_____ 7. People take aspirin to ___ headaches.

_____ 8. One way to introduce an additional point is with the word "___."

_____ 9. Your boss will put the greatest ___ on the project he or she considers most important.

_____ 10. Someone without mercy can be ___.

NOTE: Now check your answers to these questions by turning to page 239. Going over the answers carefully will help you prepare for the remaining practices, for which answers are not given.

➤ *Check 2*

Using the answer lines, complete each item below with **two** words from the box.

_____
_____ 1–2. "Your answers were too ___," said the teacher. "You should have made them more clear by adding details. ___, you skipped several questions."

_____
_____ 3–4. "I don't want to ___ to sending you to jail," the judge told the young lawbreaker. "Instead, I'm going to ___ you by making you do volunteer work for six weeks."

_____
_____ 5–6. Liz has cut down her smoking to only three cigarettes a day, but her ___ goal is to ___ smoking from her life.

_____
_____ 7–8. Chu's parents had never seen an American-style report card before, so when Chu's teacher met with them, her ___ was on helping them ___ what it said.

_____
_____ 9–10. Gail ___d that we go to the movies instead of attending a boxing match because she feels that boxing is a ___ sport.

➤ *Word Work*

A. In the space provided, write the letter of the choice that most closely relates to the situation in each item.

_____ 1. When I asked a passerby for directions to the post office, she pointed somewhere behind me and said, "It's over there a couple of blocks."

      A. brutal   B. discipline   C. vague

_____ 2. Jasmine hired an accountant to explain her tax forms to her.

      A. discipline   B. interpret   C. propose

_____ 3. A citizens' group will present their idea for a community playground to the town council.

      A. emphasis   B. propose   C. eliminate

_____ 4. The documentary contains scenes of extremely cruel, violent behavior towards animals.

      A. furthermore   B. interpret   C. brutal

_____ 5. Because she came in so late last night, Sharon isn't allowed to go out in the evening for two weeks.

      A. discipline   B. eliminate   C. resort

B. In the space provided, write the letter of the word that best completes each item.

_____ 6. The **ultimate** power in a kingdom belongs to

      A. the weak.   B. the poor.   C. the king.

_____ 7. To give **emphasis** to their words, people often

      A. stutter.   B. speak more loudly.   C. are cruel.

_____ 8. The word **furthermore** can be useful when you want to

      A. repeat yourself.   B. change your mind.   C. add a point to what you've already said.

_____ 9. Politicians sometimes say they want to **eliminate**

      A. voters.   B. schools.   C. hunger.

_____ 10. Many people **resort** to the personal ads for dates. They must believe that the ads are

      A. helpful.   B. harmful.   C. useless.

➤ *Synonyms and Antonyms*

A. Synonyms. Write the letter of the word or phrase that most nearly means the **same** as each boldfaced word.

_____ 1. **emphasis**

   A. flavor
   C. laughter
   B. memory
   D. importance

_____ 2. **furthermore**

   A. on the other hand
   C. also
   B. for instance
   D. instead

_____ 3. **interpret**

   A. punish
   C. resist
   B. memorize
   D. explain

_____ 4. **propose**

   A. suggest
   C. lie
   B. deny
   D. pretend

_____ 5. **resort to**

   A. turn to
   C. suggest
   B. avoid
   D. talk about

B. Antonyms. Write the letter of the word or phrase that most nearly means the **opposite** of each boldfaced word.

_____ 6. **brutal**

   A. firm
   C. quiet
   B. kindly
   D. small

_____ 7. **discipline**

   A. greet
   C. reward
   B. interrupt
   D. drop

_____ 8. **eliminate**

   A. ignore
   C. refuse
   B. hang around
   D. add

_____ 9. **ultimate**

   A. least important
   C. clear
   B. most difficult
   D. medium

_____10. **vague**

   A. needed
   C. trusted
   B. exact
   D. loud

➤ *Final Check*

Read the passages carefully. Then fill in each blank with the word that best fits the context.

A. Differences in a Gym Program

A. **emphasis**	B. **interpret**	C. **propose**	D. **ultimate**	E. **vague**

Last spring, some parents spoke to the school board about the gym program at Walnut Street School. The parents protested the difference in programs offered to boys and girls. The boys were taught a variety° of active sports and given good equipment. They had the chance to join several teams. For girls, however, the (1)_____ in gym was on dancing and exercise. They had no teams and little equipment.

Why were there such big differences between the two programs? The school district's rules about physical education were (2)_____. Since they didn't say exactly what should be taught, each school (3)_____ed the rules in its own way.

The parents (4)_____d allowing both boys and girls to use all the gym equipment at the school. And they appealed° to the school board for some sports teams to be organized for the girls. They pointed out that girls have as much potential° in sports and as much need for physical fitness as boys do. Their (5)_____ goal was to give all the children an equal gym experience.

B. Through a Child's Eyes

F. **brutal**	G. **discipline**	H. **eliminate**	I. **furthermore**	J. **resort**

Babysitting for my five-year-old nephew makes me see things in different ways. For example, last Saturday evening, I was watching an exciting action movie while he played in his room. But then he walked in and began to watch it, too. Suddenly I began to see the movie through his eyes. Instead of exciting, the movie's action seemed cruel and (6)_____. The characters were doing things I'd never want him to (7)_____ to. They frequently demonstrated° selfish, cold-hearted behavior. (8)_____, I'd certainly (9)_____ him if he ever used language like theirs. Now, before I choose a movie to take to his house, I (10)_____ ones that contain violence and bad language. I'm willing to deprive° myself of a few movies in order to set a better example for him.

Scores　Check 2 _____%　Word Work _____%　Synonyms and Antonyms _____%　Final Check _____%

Enter your scores above and in the vocabulary performance chart on the inside back cover of the book.

accustomed	occur
anticipate	particular
linger	reluctant
miserable	revise
misinterpret	version

Ten Words in Context

In the space provided, write the letter of the meaning closest to that of each **boldfaced** word. Use the context of the sentences to help you figure out each word's meaning.

1 accustomed
(ə-kŭs′təmd)
– *adjective*

- Although my grandfather was **accustomed** to sucking a sugar cube while he drank tea, the sugar never seemed to harm his teeth.
- After years of living in sunny Puerto Rico, Alma had trouble becoming **accustomed** to the snowy Minnesota weather.

___*Accustomed to* means   A. uncomfortable with.   B. shocked by.   C. used to.

2 anticipate
(ăn-tĭs′ə-pāt′)
– *verb*

- Lee **anticipated** heavy traffic this morning, so he left for work an hour early.
- Because we **anticipated** a snowstorm, we bought extra groceries in case we couldn't get to the store for several days.

___*Anticipate* means   A. to doubt.   B. to enjoy.   C. to think likely to happen.

3 linger
(lĭng′gər)
– *verb*

- My father has difficulty leaving any social event. He likes to **linger** by the door, chatting on and on with our hosts.
- After the bowling matches are over, we usually **linger** for a while to talk to our friends on the other teams.

___*Linger* means   A. to stare.   B. to stay.   C. to expect.

4 miserable
(mĭz′ər-ə-bəl)
– *adjective*

- The Farrells were **miserable** on their camping trip because the green flies wouldn't stop biting them for a minute.
- Gino is sure to be **miserable** during the allergy season if he doesn't get shots.

___*Miserable* means   A. uncomfortable.   B. not proper.   C. rested.

5 misinterpret
(mĭs′ĭn-tûr′prĭt)
– *verb*

- "Tomorrow, each of you should bring in one interesting fact about Greece," the teacher said. One student **misinterpreted** her instructions and complained, "But I can't think of anything interesting about grease."
- It's clear that Jay **misinterpreted** his wife's request. He brought her flowers for a vase instead of flour for a cake.

___*Misinterpret* means   A. to want.   B. to cause.   C. to understand wrongly.

6 occur
(ə-kûr′)
– *verb*

- A robbery **occurred** at the restaurant just minutes after we left.
- The first moonwalk **occurred** on July 20th, 1969, after Neil Armstrong stepped on the moon and said, "That's one small step for a man, one giant leap for mankind."

___*Occur* means   A. to find.   B. to disappear.   C. to happen.

7 particular
(pər-tĭk′yə-lər)
– *adjective*

- The girl I baby-sit for has dozens of games and toys, but she insists on playing one **particular** game over and over.
- Richie didn't care where he and Elsa ate dinner, but she had a **particular** restaurant in mind, the Mexican restaurant on Fifth Street.

___ *Particular* means   A. daily.   B. rare.   C. special.

8 reluctant
(rĭ-lŭk′tənt)
– *adjective*

- Since we're **reluctant** to have people know our phone number, we keep it unlisted.
- Although the lawyer was **reluctant** to tell his client disappointing news, he had no choice but to do so.

___ *Reluctant* means   A. known.   B. unwilling.   C. excited.

9 revise
(rĭ-vīz′)
– *verb*

- Don't just write a paper out once and hand it in. It's important to **revise** what you write until your paper is in good shape.
- Recent price increases for lumber have made it necessary for carpenters to **revise** their construction charges.

___ *Revise* means   A. to remember.   B. to make changes in.   C. to ignore.

10 version
(vûr′zhən)
– *noun*

- The play *West Side Story* is a modern musical **version** of Shakespeare's *Romeo and Juliet*.
- There have been at least six movies about Frankenstein's monster, but the best is still the 1931 **version**, starring Boris Karloff.

___ *Version* means   A. retelling.   B. suggestion.   C. correction.

Matching Words with Definitions

Following are definitions of the ten words. **Print** each word next to its definition. If you look closely at each word in context, you will be able to figure out its meaning.

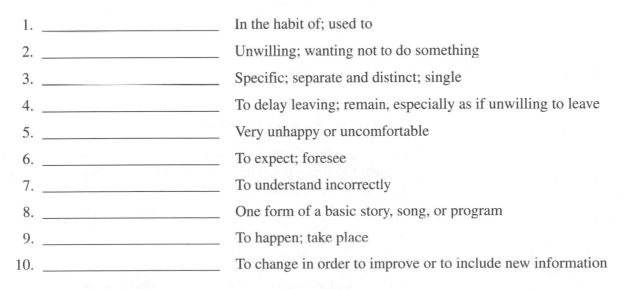

1. _____   In the habit of; used to

2. _____   Unwilling; wanting not to do something

3. _____   Specific; separate and distinct; single

4. _____   To delay leaving; remain, especially as if unwilling to leave

5. _____   Very unhappy or uncomfortable

6. _____   To expect; foresee

7. _____   To understand incorrectly

8. _____   One form of a basic story, song, or program

9. _____   To happen; take place

10. _____   To change in order to improve or to include new information

CAUTION: Do not go any further until you are sure the above answers are correct. Then you can use the definitions to help you in the following practices. Your goal is eventually to know the words well enough so that you don't need to check the definitions at all.

➤ *Check 1*

Using the answer line, complete each item below with the correct word from the box.

| A. **accustomed** | B. **anticipate** | C. **linger** | D. **miserable** | E. **misinterpret** |
| F. **occur** | G. **particular** | H. **reluctant** | I. **revise** | J. **version** |

_____ 1. Could you ___ for a few minutes after the meeting so I can talk privately to you?

_____ 2. We ___ about forty guests at our New Year's Eve party, but we're preparing food for fifty, just in case.

_____ 3. It's about time the city put up a stop sign at that corner. An accident ___s there every month or two.

_____ 4. Although the apartment met our needs, we were ___ to sign a long-term lease.

_____ 5. Dina wrote a ___ of *Romeo and Juliet* that has a happy ending.

_____ 6. When we put out a fresh bowl of jelly beans at home, one ___ kind is gone within a day. My brother eats every red one.

_____ 7. After our cat was run over by a car, the whole family felt ___ for weeks.

_____ 8. For someone brought up in a warm climate, it may take time to become ___ to cold weather.

_____ 9. Another word for "misunderstand" is "___."

_____ 10. Before we present our play to the third-grade class, we will ___ it so it is easier for young children to understand.

NOTE: Now check your answers to these questions by turning to page 239. Going over the answers carefully will help you prepare for the remaining practices, for which answers are not given.

➤ *Check 2*

Using the answer lines, complete each item below with **two** words from the box.

_____
_____ 1–2. When I was in Mexico, I became ___ to having people ___ what I said because I speak Spanish so poorly.

_____
_____ 3–4. Joanne ___d having an boring afternoon at work, so she ___ed in the restaurant to make lunch last as long as possible. She was not at all eager° to return to the office.

_____
_____ 5–6. Jerry wanted one ___ DVD for his birthday—the ___ of *The Sound of Music* that included an interview with the director.

_____
_____ 7–8. No one hates arguments more than Martin; he becomes ___ whenever they ___. Unfortunately, in his household, disputes° are abundant°.

_____
_____ 9–10. I am ___ to show you my story until I've had a chance to ___ it. It needs considerable° changing before it will be ready for you to read.

➤ *Word Work*

A. In the space provided, write the letter of the choice that best completes each item.

_____ 1. Today you are likely to **anticipate**

    A. your birthday party last year.

    B. a phone call your friend promised to make.

    C. an argument you had yesterday.

_____ 2. The person who is most likely to **linger** is

    A. a friend who is in a rush.

    B. a guest at a luncheon.

    C. a person about to get off a bus.

_____ 3. A student might **revise** a paper that

    A. seems perfect.

    B. is too long.

    C. has been handed in to the teacher.

_____ 4. A very **particular** writing assignment would be:

    A. Write a description.

    B. Write about someone you know.

    C. Write a physical description of your oldest living relative.

_____ 5. Most people are **accustomed** to living

    A. in their houses.   B. in the future.   C. at the South Pole.

B. In the space provided, write the letter of the word that most closely relates to the situation in each item.

_____ 6. A strange and wonderful event always happens to me in January.

    A. lingers   B. occurs   C. miserable

_____ 7. A friend says, "Catch you later," but you think he says, "That's our waiter."

    A. anticipate   B. linger   C. misinterpret

_____ 8. Earthquake survivors huddle in the rain, with their houses destroyed and nowhere to go.

    A. miserable   B. revise   C. particular

_____ 9. You know you should visit Great-Uncle Lem over the holidays, but he makes you watch hours of his boring home movies, and you really don't want to go.

    A. accustomed   B. version   C. reluctant

_____10. After the students read the novel *The Grapes of Wrath*, they watched the movie of the same name.

    A. linger   B. version   C. reluctant

➤ *Analogies*

Each item below starts with a pair of words in CAPITAL LETTERS. For each item, figure out the relationship between these two words. Then decide which of the choices (A, B, C, or D) expresses a similar relationship. Write the letter of your choice on the answer line. (All the repeated words in these items are from this unit.)

_____ 1. RELUCTANT : WILLING ::

      A. brutal : kind   B. rapid : fast

      C. anger : argument   D. shy : quiet

_____ 2. MISERABLE : HAPPY ::

      A. awkward° : clumsy   B. bright : shining

      C. current° : old-fashioned   D. famous : brave

_____ 3. LINGER : REMAIN ::

      A. purposely : accidentally   B. complex° : simple

      C. fix : repair   D. wait : depart

_____ 4. ANTICIPATE : EXPECT ::

      A. recollect° : forget   B. cause : effect

      C. explain: understand   D. smash : break

_____ 5. PARTICULAR : GENERAL ::

      A. unfamiliar : nervous   B. eager° : unwilling

      C. shy : quiet   D. bees : honey

_____ 6. OCCUR : HAPPEN ::

      A. run : walk   B. vanish° : disappear

      C. shout : whisper   D. vague° : particular°

_____ 7. REVISE : MISTAKE ::

      A. discipline° : punishment   B. write : print

      C. sing: book   D. eliminate° : error

_____ 8. OBJECTION° : APPROVAL ::

      A. doctor : illness   B. night : moon

      C. emphasis : importance   D. argument : agreement

_____ 9. MISINTERPRET : MISUNDERSTAND ::

      A. penalize° : punish   B. expect : surprise

      C. agree : disagree   D. discipline° : reward

_____ 10. RECOLLECT° : EVENT ::

      A. question : answer   B. interpret° : message

      C. walk : exercise   D. establish° : destroy

➤ *Final Check*

Read the passages carefully. Then fill in each blank with the word that best fits the context.

A. Knowing How to Argue

A. **linger**	B. **misinterpret**	C. **occur**	D. **particular**	E. **reluctant**

Ron and Marlene have a great marriage, and I think one reason is that they know how to argue. Many couples think arguing is bad, but I think they (1)_____ what arguing really is. It can be a good way to settle problems. When couples are (2)_____ to argue, they may not solve their problems, and their angry feelings can (3)_____ for a long time. Ron and Marlene don't hesitate° to argue and get it over with. What's good about the way they argue is that they talk only about the (4)_____ thing that made them angry. For example, if Marlene is angry that Ron isn't doing his share of the housework, that is all she talks about. She doesn't throw in, "And furthermore°, that new friend of yours from work is obnoxious°!" Knowing Ron and Marlene has taught me that arguments (5)_____ in even the best marriages, and that they can make a good relationship stronger.

B. A Change of School, A Change of Heart

F. **accustomed**	G. **anticipate**	H. **miserable**	I. **revise**	J. **version**

Matt and his family were moving, and Matt hated the whole idea. He had lived in Centerville his entire life and had always gone to school with the same group of friends. He had (6)_____d graduating from Centerville High School and then going to Centerville Community College. Now he would have to make an abrupt° change and (7)_____ his whole plan for the future, and he didn't like it a bit. "How can I ever become (8)_____ to a new school?" he asked his parents. "Everyone will already know each other. I'll be solitary°—I'll have no friends."

At first, it seemed that Matt was right. At his new high school, he walked around alone, not smiling or talking to anyone. Finally a friendly teacher advised° him to improve his attitude°. "I know you're feeling lonely and (9)_____," he said. "But you look as though you hate this school and everyone in it. If you'll look a little friendlier, you will find new friends here." Matt decided to try. He began to talk to his classmates and take part in class. He even helped write a funny (10)_____ of *Cinderella* that his Spanish class performed for the rest of the school. By January, Matt was able to tell his parents that he was starting to feel at home in his new school.

Scores	Check 2 _____%	Word Work _____%	Analogies _____%	Final Check _____%

Enter your scores above and in the vocabulary performance chart on the inside back cover of the book.

UNIT TWO: *Review*

The box at the right lists twenty-five words from Unit Two. Using the clues at the bottom of the page, fill in these words to complete the puzzle that follows.

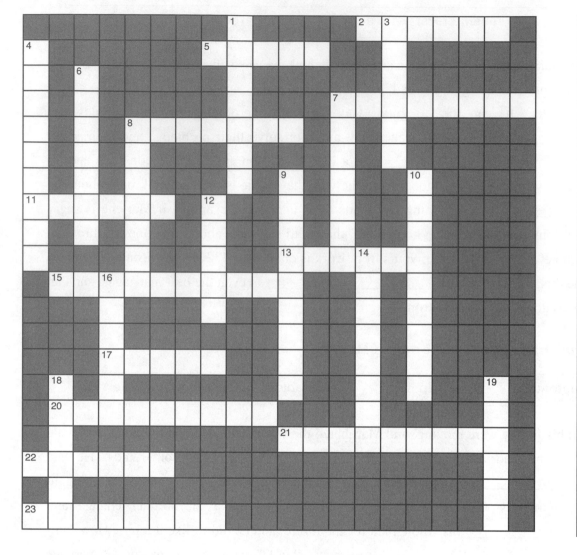

abrupt
advise
astonish
awkward
brutal
consent
current
deprive
eager
eliminate
endure
establish
linger
miserable
objection
occur
particular
potential
reliable
resort
revise
ultimate
vague
vanish
variety

ACROSS

2. Sudden and unexpected
5. Looking forward to with great interest or desire
7. To surprise greatly; amaze
8. Modern; existing now; in general use or practice today
11. To give advice to; recommend
13. To put up with; bear impatiently
15. Specific; separate and distinct; single
17. To happen; take place
20. To bring into being; set up
21. A dislike; feeling of being against something
22. To delay leaving; remain
23. Able to be depended upon

DOWN

1. A number of different kinds; assortment
3. Cruel; heartless
4. To get rid of; do away with
6. To take away from; keep from having or enjoying
7. Clumsy; not graceful
8. To agree to something
9. Very unhappy or uncomfortable
10. A natural ability that may or may not develop; possibility
12. Not clear; not exact; not definite
14. Greatest; highest possible
16. To turn or go to for help; use for aid
18. To change in order to improve or to include new information
19. To disappear from sight

78

UNIT TWO: Test 1

PART A
Choose the word that best completes each item and write it in the space provided.

_____ 1. My parents used to ___ me for misbehaving at the supper table by making me sit on the stairs, where I could hear the conversation but not take part in it.

    A. interpret   B. penalize   C. revise   D. originate

_____ 2. It has been said that the practice of drinking tea ___ in China thousands of years ago when some tea leaves accidentally blew into a pot of boiling water.

    A. originated   B. misinterpreted   C. vanished   D. recollected

_____ 3. That restaurant doesn't accept reservations for small groups. The ___ number of people in your party must be five.

    A. vague   B. complex   C. current   D. minimum

_____ 4. A beginning typist ___ often, while an experienced typist hits the keys rapidly.

    A. advises   B. hesitates   C. occurs   D. endures

_____ 5. My sister-in-law knows a lot about CD players, so I've asked her to ___ me as I decide which one to buy.

    A. cry out   B. deprive   C. recollect   D. advise

_____ 6. I try to ___ my friendship with Sarah, but it's difficult to keep a relationship going when we're separated by so many miles.

    A. maintain   B. revise   C. respond   D. deprive

_____ 7. It used to be taught in schools that George Washington cut down a cherry tree with an ax and then confessed the deed to his father. However, ___ thinking is that the story was invented after Washington died.

    A. horizontal   B. reluctant   C. current   D. vague

_____ 8. Garlic is delicious, but one ___ many people have to it is the way it makes their breath smell.

    A. objection   B. potential   C. version   D. variety

_____ 9. When Mona's children behave badly, she does not spank them; instead, she ___ them of something they enjoy, such as their bicycles or roller skates.

    A. resorts   B. endures   C. proposes   D. deprives

_____ 10. Although Lonnie's car is old, it is still ___; it gets him to work every day.

    A. abrupt   B. reliable   C. miserable   D. ultimate

(Continues on next page)

_____ 11. We stared at the long brownish ___ thing floating in the river, wondering if it was a log or an alligator.

        A. horizontal   B. accustomed   C. adequate   D. wholesome

_____ 12. At the town meeting, several people had ideas about what to do with the empty supermarket building. One woman ___ that it be turned into a skating rink.

        A. vanished   B. resorted   C. endured   D. proposed

_____ 13. Playing outdoors for hours is more ___ than watching TV for hours.

        A. reluctant   B. awkward   C. eager   D. wholesome

PART B
Write **C** if the italicized word is used **correctly**. Write **I** if the word is used **incorrectly**.

_____ 14. "To *misinterpret* my instructions," said the teacher, "listen carefully."

_____ 15. The famous ballet dancer is *awkward*; he moves so lightly his feet never seem to touch the ground.

_____ 16. It was *customary* for people to smile at each other in Laura's small town. Although she now lives in a large city, she still smiles at every stranger that she passes.

_____ 17. I think it is *brutal* to keep chickens in crowded conditions and then cut off their beaks to keep them from pecking one another.

_____ 18. If you want to gain weight, you can *eliminate* more calories in your diet by eating lots of junk food and big desserts.

_____ 19. I'm so *accustomed* to living near the fire department that whenever a siren goes off, I hardly notice.

_____ 20. The angry diner called the restaurant manager and complained that her meal had been cold, *adequate*, and too expensive.

_____ 21. Many people in town were angry when the beautiful old courthouse was *established* in order to make room for an ugly, new shopping center.

_____ 22. The directions Kim gave me to the new apartment were so *vague* that I got very mixed up on my way there.

_____ 23. Because her husband was sick and couldn't work, Corinne *appealed* to their landlady for extra time to pay the rent.

_____ 24. The *ultimate* job in a successful business career would be running errands in a large office.

_____ 25. Our store is well-thought-of because we put an *emphasis* on pleasing customers rather than on making as many sales as possible.

> ***Score***   (Number correct) _____ × 4 = _____%

UNIT TWO: Test 2

PART A

On the answer line, write the word from the box that completes each item below. Use each word once.

A. **abrupt**	B. **anticipate**	C. **classify**	D. **consent**	E. **discipline**
F. **exclaim**	G. **particular**	H. **potential**	I. **recollect**	J. **resort**
K. **revise**	L. **vanish**	M. **variety**		

_____ 1. Every time Robert takes a girl out, he thinks about whether she has the ___ to be a good wife.

_____ 2. Wouldn't it be wonderful if dirt ___ed as easily and completely in real life as it does in the soap ads?

_____ 3. The Four Corners of the World restaurant offers dishes from a ___ of countries, including France, Vietnam, Ethiopia, and Brazil.

_____ 4. To ___ him for writing on the wall of a school bathroom, the principal made Matt paint every bathroom on that floor.

_____ 5. Although Ed has a hot temper, I don't think he would ever ___ to violence.

_____ 6. Because we had ___d eight people for dinner, we were surprised when twelve showed up.

_____ 7. Ronald always shows his short stories to his wife. Then he ___s them after listening to her comments.

_____ 8. When I ask, "What do you need from the grocery store?" it's not helpful to say "Everything." Make me a list of the ___ items you need.

_____ 9. The picnic came to an ___ end when a sudden thunderstorm seemed to come out of nowhere.

_____ 10. In high school, students often ___ one another as belonging to an in-group or an out-group.

_____ 11. "I will ___ to your getting a puppy," Mrs. Anders told her children, "*if* you promise that you will take care of walking, feeding, brushing, and housetraining it."

_____ 12. Sandra didn't want to hurt her boyfriend's feelings when she unwrapped the ugly orange sweater he had bought her, so she ___ed, "Wow, it's so colorful!"

_____ 13. I was very tired last night. Although I ___ that I spoke with John, I can't remember what either of us said.

(Continues on next page)

PART B
Write **C** if the italicized word is used **correctly**. Write **I** if the word is used **incorrectly**.

_____14. When the man shook hands with the child and said, "How do you do?" the child *responded*, "How do I do *what*?"

_____15. Bart was sad when his best friend moved *furthermore* from his house.

_____16. It was fun to go to my first soccer game with Franco. He knows the sport so well that he could *interpret* everything that was happening on the field.

_____17. Rico didn't seem to enjoy the party. He *lingered* before most of the other guests had even shown up.

_____18. The students were *miserable* when their teacher said, "It's such a beautiful day. Let's forget about the math test and go outside to play softball."

_____19. Christmas and New Year's Eve are two holidays that *occur* in December.

_____20. Naturally, most people are *reluctant* to win an all-expenses-paid vacation.

_____21. Which *version* of *The Wizard of Oz* did you like better, the movie with Judy Garland or the one with Diana Ross?

_____22. The speaker *astonished* the audience by opening his speech with, "Good evening, ladies and gentlemen."

_____23. Because the novel is so *complex*, it begins with a chart that lists all the characters and shows how they are related to one another.

_____24. To get through exam week, I had to *endure* several nights without much sleep.

_____25. After hiking for miles with nothing to eat, the friends were *eager* for dinner.

Score	(Number correct) _____	× 4 = _____	%

Enter your score above and in the vocabulary performance chart on the inside back cover of the book.

UNIT TWO: Test 3

PART A: Synonyms
In the space provided, write the letter of the choice that is most nearly the **same** in meaning as the **boldfaced** word.

_____ 1. **advise** A) suggest B) expect C) praise D) forget

_____ 2. **anticipate** A) put up with B) remember C) dislike D) expect

_____ 3. **appeal to** A) ask B) add to C) disappear D) explain

_____ 4. **astonish** A) continue B) surprise C) refuse D) begin

_____ 5. **classify** A) praise B) arrange by type C) begin D) put up with

_____ 6. **deprive** A) suggest B) turn to C) take from D) forget

_____ 7. **discipline** A) punish B) raise up C) continue D) happen

_____ 8. **eliminate** A) add to B) get rid of C) disappear
D) make more difficult

_____ 9. **emphasis** A) least B) importance C) retelling D) possibility

_____10. **endure** A) punish B) demand C) put up with D) explain

_____11. **establish** A) remain B) start C) turn to D) suggest

_____12. **furthermore** A) instead B) later C) in addition D) by the way

_____13. **interpret** A) explain B) depend on C) suggest D) change

_____14. **maintain** A) begin B) continue C) give up on D) cry out

_____15. **misinterpret** A) understand wrongly B) argue C) depend on D) surprise

_____16. **occur** A) begin B) put off C) take place D) remember

_____17. **particular** A) common B) least C) specific D) important

_____18. **potential** A) memory B) feeling C) possibility D) number

_____19. **propose** A) wait B) make worse C) agree D) suggest

_____20. **resort to** A) turn to B) give away C) accept as true D) refuse

_____21. **respond** A) disappear B) answer C) surprise D) remember

_____22. **revise** A) throw out B) remain C) agree D) change

_____23. **ultimate** A) least B) most strange C) greatest D) oldest

_____24. **variety** A) value B) reason C) few D) several different kinds

_____25. **version** A) retelling B) dislike C) assortment D) penalty

(Continues on next page)

PART B: Antonyms
In the space provided, write the letter of the choice that is most nearly **opposite** in meaning to the **boldfaced** word.

_____26. **abrupt**   A) slow   B) willing   C) secret   D) scary

_____27. **accustomed**   A) not exact   B) not similar to   C) not used to   D) not needed

_____28. **adequate**   A) willing   B) not enough   C) not dependable   D) unhappy

_____29. **awkward**   A) up and down   B) polite   C) complicated   D) graceful

_____30. **brutal**   A) well-known   B) shaky   C) gentle   D) dark

_____31. **complex**   A) cheerful   B) simple   C) lucky   D) natural

_____32. **consent**   A) surprise   B) reward   C) appear   D) refuse

_____33. **current**   A) wise   B) old-fashioned   C) unusual   D) common

_____34. **customary**   A) willing   B) most   C) clear   D) unusual

_____35. **eager**   A) not interested   B) not believing   C) ready   D) clear

_____36. **exclaim**   A) refuse   B) forget   C) allow   D) whisper

_____37. **hesitate**   A) ignore   B) suggest   C) rush ahead   D) reward

_____38. **horizontal** A) careless   B) up and down   C) dark   D) square

_____39. **linger**   A) appear   B) insult   C) forget   D) hurry away

_____40. **minimum**   A) unhealthy   B) loud   C) painful   D) most

_____41. **miserable**   A) hard to understand   B) happy   C) willing   D) clear

_____42. **objection**   A) approval   B) joke   C) win   D) loss

_____43. **originate**   A) end   B) explain   C) leave   D) expect

_____44. **penalize**   A) hurry   B) reward   C) give   D) appear

_____45. **recollect**   A) answer   B) ask   C) know   D) forget

_____46. **reliable**   A) not known   B) not enough   C) not usual   D) not dependable

_____47. **reluctant**   A) surprised   B) least   C) willing   D) careless

_____48. **vague**   A) lowest   B) not clumsy   C) clear   D) not exact

_____49. **vanish**   A) expect   B) keep   C) appear   D) wait

_____50. **wholesome**   A) unhealthy   B) simple   C) useful   D) old-fashioned

Score	(Number correct) _____ × 2 = _____%

Enter your score above and in the vocabulary performance chart on the inside back cover of the book.

Unit Three

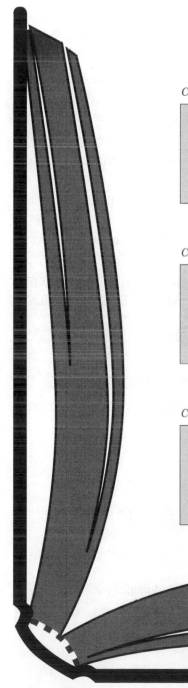

Chapter 11

assume	maximum
conscious	protest
external	remedy
incredible	spectacle
internal	verdict

Chapter 12

artificial	frequency
complicate	represent
conscience	temporary
counsel	transparent
detect	triumph

Chapter 13

agonizing	strive
energetic	substance
foresight	tolerance
interval	trait
prosper	withdraw

Chapter 14

approximately	plea
consistent	practical
cope	random
evaluate	significant
phrase	sole

Chapter 15

authentic	eligible
characteristic	harsh
concept	remote
confront	shallow
disrupt	thrive

assume	maximum
conscious	protest
external	remedy
incredible	spectacle
internal	verdict

Ten Words in Context

In the space provided, write the letter of the meaning closest to that of each **boldfaced** word. Use the context of the sentences to help you figure out each word's meaning.

1 assume
(ə-sōōm′)
– *verb*

• I **assumed** he was telling the truth, but he wasn't.

• We **assumed** the sun would shine during the outdoor wedding. What a mistake! When it comes to weather, one must not take anything for granted.

___*Assume* means   A. to fear.   B. to forget.   C. to believe.

2 conscious
(kŏn′shəs)
– *adjective*

• I don't think Jim is **conscious** that he sometimes seems very rude. Otherwise, he wouldn't be so ill-mannered.

• As Arlene gave her speech to the class, she was **conscious** that people were whispering in the back of the room.

___*Conscious* means   A. pleased.   B. aware.   C. relieved.

3 external
(ĭk-stûr′nəl)
– *adjective*

• The **external** appearances of the two houses were similar, but on the inside, the homes differed quite a bit.

• When my grandmother first came to America, she was given her very first orange. Since no one had told her to remove its **external** layer, she began to eat the peel.

___*External* means   A. final.   B. new.   C. outer.

4 incredible
(ĭn-krĕd′ə-bəl)
– *adjective*

• The moon landing of 1969 was an **incredible** achievement.

• It's **incredible** that a cat could survive forty-three days locked in a crate without food and water, yet it has happened.

___*Incredible* means   A. expected.   B. hard to believe.   C. correct.

5 internal
(ĭn-tûr′nəl)
– *adjective*

• The sofa's covering is torn, but its **internal** condition is fine.

• The car looks terrific, so you'd never guess that some of its **internal** parts—the motor, brakes, and heater—need major repair.

___*Internal* means   A. inside.   B. hard.   C. light in weight.

6 maximum
(măk′sə-məm)
– *adjective*

• The sign told the **maximum** weight the elevator could safely carry.

• Three hundred miles per hour is the **maximum** speed for this airplane; it can go no faster.

___*Maximum* means   A. greatest.   B. worst.   C. longest.

7 protest
(prə-tĕst′)
– *verb*

- When the builder announced plans to pack a hundred homes onto a ten-acre farm, a group called Protect Our Open Spaces showed up to **protest**.
- "Stop it," Billy's mother **protested**. "You can't pour blue food coloring into the mashed potatoes."

___ *Protest* means   A. to ask.   B. to suggest.   C. to complain.

8 remedy
(rĕm′ĭ-dē)
– *noun*

- Grandma's **remedy** for a cold was to wear garlic around her neck. It never cured her cold, but at least no one came close enough to her to catch it.
- There's no quick **remedy** for a broken heart; only time will heal it.

___ *Remedy* means   A. memory.   B. treatment.   C. main cause.

9 spectacle
(spĕk′tə-kəl)
– *noun*

- Circuses are filled with **spectacles**, from chimpanzees riding bicycles to elephants wearing party hats.
- During her temper tantrum in the supermarket, the crying little girl made a **spectacle** of herself by lying down in the middle of the check-out lane and refusing to get up.

___ *Spectacle* means   A. excuse.   B. unusual sight.   C. result.

10 verdict
(vûr′dĭkt)
– *noun*

- The mechanic's **verdict** was that the car was too badly damaged to fix.
- In only ninety minutes, the jury members reached their **verdict**. They found the defendant guilty.

___ *Verdict* means   A. decision.   B. punishment.   C. problem.

Matching Words with Definitions

Following are definitions of the ten words. **Print** each word next to its definition. If you look closely at each word in context, you will be able to figure out its meaning.

1. _____   A cure; something that heals

2. _____   Unbelievable; amazing; extraordinary

3. _____   Aware (of something); noticing (that something is or was happening or existing)

4. _____   Outer; located outside

5. _____   To complain; express dissatisfaction

6. _____   A surprising or unusual sight; a public display or scene

7. _____   To suppose to be true; take for granted

8. _____   A decision or judgment

9. _____   Inner; located inside

10. _____   Most; highest; largest possible

CAUTION: Do not go any further until you are sure the above answers are correct. Then you can use the definitions to help you in the following practices. Your goal is eventually to know the words well enough so that you don't need to check the definitions at all.

➤ Check 1

Using the answer line, complete each item below with the correct word from the box.

A. **assume**	B. **conscious**	C. **external**	D. **incredible**	E. **internal**
F. **maximum**	G. **protest**	H. **remedy**	I. **spectacle**	J. **verdict**

_____ 1. The ___ part of a banana is its sweet, creamy flesh.

_____ 2. The ___ part of a banana is its peel.

_____ 3. The ___ speed allowed here is sixty-five miles an hour.

_____ 4. Do you think there will ever be a ___ for the common cold?

_____ 5. The Grand Canyon is the most ___ sight I've ever seen. It's so huge that it's hard to believe how big it is even when you're looking at it.

_____ 6. As Shelly tried to study, she became ___ of a loud "drip, drip" from the kitchen faucet.

_____ 7. On the day the old hotel was to be knocked down, people came from miles around to watch the ___.

_____ 8. If you don't like a company's policy, why not ___? For example, you could write a strong letter of complaint.

_____ 9. Rather than ___ it would not rain on the outdoor wedding, the bride's family rented a large tent, just in case.

_____ 10. The student smiled happily when she heard the instructor's ___ on her project. "This is excellent work," he said.

NOTE: Now check your answers to these questions by turning to page 240. Going over the answers carefully will help you prepare for the remaining practices, for which answers are not given.

➤ Check 2

Using the answer lines, complete each item below with **two** words from the box.

_____
_____ 1–2. After examining his room, Sean's mother's ___ was that it was too messy to live in. Sean ___ed, saying, "I know exactly where everything is!"

_____
_____ 3–4. Although the accident victim had only a few ___ bruises, he had serious ___ injuries, including damage to his kidneys.

_____
_____ 5–6. It's ___ that penicillin, a ___ for various infections, was discovered by accident after some mold grew in a laboratory dish.

_____
_____ 7–8. The boss had ___d that the workers enjoyed background music, but they said they were not even ___ of it. However, once, when the music ceased°, everyone suddenly became very aware of the silence.

_____
_____ 9–10. College students used to enjoy arranging ___s in which they would crowd the ___ number of people possible into a phone booth.

➤ *Word Work*

A. Write each word next to the examples that best match it.

| A. **assume** | B. **external** | C. **incredible** |
| D. **protest** | E. **remedy** | |

_____ 1. Orange peel
  Book covers
  Gift wrapping

_____ 2. Swallowing sugar to get rid of hiccups
  Holding ice on a bruise to reduce swelling and pain
  Taking antibiotics to clear up an ear infection

_____ 3. The actual invention in 1956 of diapers for birds!
  Glass and brick being made from the same main ingredient: sand!
  The U.S. Army's training bats to drop bombs during World War II!

_____ 4. That most people in your class are right-handed
  That there are lots of people named Smith in your local phone book
  That your friends like pizza with sausage more than pizza with a peculiar° topping such as anchovies

_____ 5. Writing letters to the White House about taxes being too high
  Demanding that a nuclear-power plant be shut down
  Marching in front of a courthouse with signs saying we should eliminate° the death penalty

B. In the space provided, write the letter of the choice that best completes each item.

_____ 6. A popular **spectacle** is

  A. children arriving at school.   B. a Fourth of July fireworks display.   C. a man mowing his lawn.

_____ 7. Because the accident victim suffered **internal** bleeding, he

  A. was bleeding a great deal.   B. was bleeding a little.   C. didn't realize how much blood he had lost.

_____ 8. The judge's **verdict** was

  A. "Guilty."   B. a black robe.   C. a courtroom.

_____ 9. You will usually be fully **conscious** of

  A. a loud noise nearby.   B. your own breathing.   C. a small event taking place one hundred miles away.

_____ 10. The sign on the carnival ride says, "**Maximum** weight for riders is 80 pounds." This means that adults

  A. are the only ones allowed on the ride.   B. must go with children on the ride.   C. are usually not allowed on the ride.

➤ *Word Parts*

A. The prefix *self-* often means "oneself."

Examples: *defense* — protection   *conscious* — aware
                    self-defense — protection of oneself   *self-conscious* — uncomfortably aware of
                                                                                                    oneself

On each answer line, write the word from the box that means the same as the *italicized* words.

A. **self-centered**	B. **self-conscious**	C. **self-control**
D. **self-critical°**	E. **self-educated**	

_____ 1. Corey is so *critical of himself*. He must have a low opinion of himself.

_____ 2. It takes *control of oneself* not to eat too many fresh, warm chocolate-chip cookies.

_____ 3. That writer is so *centered on himself!* After talking about himself for an hour, he said, "But enough about me. What do you think of my writing?"

_____ 4. Irene felt uncomfortably *conscious of herself* because of her new hair color, so she was relieved when most people didn't even notice it.

_____ 5. My grandfather was *educated by himself;* although he never even attended high school, he learned a great deal on his own.

B. The suffix *-ness* means "the quality or state of."

Examples: *wholesome°* — tending to improve the character, mind, or body
                    wholesomeness — the quality of tending to improve the character, mind, or body

                    conscious — aware
                    consciousness — the state of being aware

On each answer line, write the word from the box that best completes the item.

F. **awkwardness°**	G. **consciousness**	H. **eagerness°**
I. **usefulness**	J. **vagueness°**	

_____ 6. With great ___, the family stood in line to enter Disneyland.

_____ 7. The accident victim lost ___ and did not wake up for several days.

_____ 8. Because they are growing so rapidly, many teenagers go through a period of ___ when it seems they are forever tripping over their own feet.

_____ 9. This camping knife is really wonderful for its ___. It provides a screwdriver, toothpick, bottle opener, magnifying glass, and tweezers.

_____ 10. The ___ of the instructions for putting this storage box together is driving me crazy. They are so unclear that I don't even know which side is up.

➤ *Final Check*

Read the passages carefully. Then fill in each blank with the word that best fits the context.

A. Coming Out of a Coma

| A. **external** | B. **incredible** | C. **internal** | D. **remedy** | E. **verdict** |

"Hi, Mom," Francis said. The effort of speaking exhausted him, and he closed his eyes again.

To his mother, these were the best words she had ever heard. The idea that her son was speaking again, after ten weeks in a coma, was (1)_____. He had been gone from this world for so long that it seemed he'd never return. Those ten weeks had been difficult to endure°. Whenever Ms. King had visited Francis at the hospital, he had been completely still. There were no (2)_____ signs that he was thinking or feeling anything. The doctor's (3)_____ was that Francis would never recover. But Ms. King maintained° the hope that he still had some (4)_____ life. Could he, perhaps, hear her words? Could he feel her hand squeezing his? She tried to reach him in any way she could during her daily visits.

Now, although Ms. King knew there was no quick (5)_____ for her son's serious injuries, the simple words "Hi, Mom" gave her hope that he could, someday, live a full life again.

B. The Office Doughnut Contest

| F. **assume** | G. **conscious** | H. **maximum** | I. **protest** | J. **spectacle** |

"Are you telling me there are no doughnuts left? I don't believe it!" Joan said. "How could a huge supply of doughnuts be gone already?"

"I don't know how," Fran responded°. "I just know there aren't any left."

"When I brought three dozen doughnuts in this morning, I (6)_____d I'd get to eat at least one," Joan said. "After all, the (7)_____ number of people who ever work in this place is ten. Today, Sue isn't even here. It's hard to believe that the other eight of you could eat thirty-six doughnuts in less than three hours. I even anticipated° having surplus° doughnuts for tomorrow."

Then Fran and Joan became (8)_____ of laughing in the office next door. When they looked in, the fate of the missing doughnuts became evident°. They could barely believe the (9)_____ that met their eyes: Three grown men were tossing doughnuts across the room, while three other men tried to catch the doughnuts on pencils.

"I don't believe you guys!" Joan (10)_____ed. "Just you wait. Next time it's my turn to bring in the doughnuts, I'll bring in cream-filled and jelly-filled doughnuts, and we'll see how you play your little game then."

| *Scores* | Check 2 _____ % | Word Work _____ % | Word Parts _____ % | Final Check _____ % |

Enter your scores above and in the vocabulary performance chart on the inside back cover of the book.

artificial	frequency
complicate	represent
conscience	temporary
counsel	transparent
detect	triumph

Ten Words in Context

In the space provided, write the letter of the meaning closest to that of each **boldfaced** word. Use the context of the sentences to help you figure out each word's meaning.

1 artificial
(är′tə-físh′əl)
– *adjective*

___*Artificial* means

- My uncle, who lost his left arm in an accident, was recently fitted for an **artificial** arm.
- **Artificial** flowers made of paper or silk last for years.

A. short-term. B. made by humans. C. heavy.

2 complicate
(kŏm′plə-kāt′)
– *verb*

___*Complicate* means

- Cooking for a crowd is difficult enough, so I don't **complicate** the job with fancy dishes. I keep the food simple.
- Don't **complicate** the game with too many rules.

A. to make difficult. B. to find. C. to remember.

3 conscience
(kŏn′shəns)
– *noun*

___*Conscience* means

- After Lena stole the CD, her **conscience** bothered her so much that she couldn't enjoy listening to the music.
- It's strange, but true, that some criminals don't have a **conscience**. They really don't believe that it is wrong to cheat, steal, or even kill.

A. budget. B. plan of action. C. moral sense.

4 counsel
(koun′səl)
– *verb*

___*Counsel* means

- My basketball coach **counseled** me to work at the shoe store fewer hours each week to gain more time to study.
- I **counseled** Angela to break up with her violent boyfriend.

A. to allow. B. to join. C. to suggest to.

5 detect
(dĭ-tĕkt′)
– *verb*

___*Detect* means

- If you **detect** a gas leak, leave immediately and call for help.
- Rachel never actually says that she dislikes Ron, but I **detect** a tone of dislike in her voice.

A. to control. B. to notice. C. to want.

6 frequency
(frē′quən-sē)
– *noun*

___*Frequency* means

- Luis and Adam used to visit each other once or twice a week, but since Adam got married, the **frequency** of their visits has gone down.
- I don't like to watch movies on TV because the **frequency** of ads is so great. I prefer to rent movies and see them without all the interruptions.

A. rate. B. cost. C. action.

7 represent
(rĕp′rĭ-zĕnt′)
– *verb*

- Will you speak for yourself in court, or will a lawyer **represent** you?
- Loretta will **represent** her class at the Student Council meetings.

____ *Represent* means   A. to leave.   B. to hire.   C. to speak for.

8 temporary
(tĕm′pə-rĕr′ē)
– *adjective*

- Mimi used a **temporary** green hair dye just for St. Patrick's Day.
- A **temporary** worker will be hired to fill in for Kwan until she recovers from her injury.

____ *Temporary* means   A. large.   B. short-term.   C. false.

9 transparent
(trăns-pâr′ənt)
– *adjective*

- At first, I thought the glass in the door was **transparent** and that I was seeing someone on the other side. But when I got closer, I realized that it was a mirror and I was looking at myself.
- **Transparent** wrap allows you to see what's inside a container.

____ *Transparent* means   A. able to be seen through.   B. old.   C. thick.

10 triumph
(trī′əmf)
– *noun*

- Our football team's **triumph** over the state's first-place team was the reason for a huge party.
- My brother's good teachers, his understanding parents, and his own hard work all led to his **triumph** over a learning disability.

____ *Triumph* means   A. loss.   B. meeting.   C. win.

Matching Words with Definitions

Following are definitions of the ten words. **Print** each word next to its definition. If you look closely at each word in context, you will be able to figure out its meaning.

1. _____   Allowing light to pass through so that objects on the other side can be seen

2. _____   To give advice or guidance to; advise°

3. _____   The rate at which something occurs; how often something happens

4. _____   To notice; discover that something exists or is present

5. _____   An outstanding or very satisfying success; victory

6. _____   A sense of what is right or wrong in one's behavior

7. _____   To act or speak for

8. _____   To make difficult by adding or involving many parts or details; make complex°

9. _____   Lasting or serving for a limited time only; not permanent

10. _____   Made to imitate something natural

CAUTION: Do not go any further until you are sure the above answers are correct. Then you can use the definitions to help you in the following practices. Your goal is eventually to know the words well enough so that you don't need to check the definitions at all.

➤ *Check 1*

Using the answer line, complete each item below with the correct word from the box.

A. **artificial**	B. **complicate**	C. **conscience**	D. **counsel**	E. **detect**
F. **frequency**	G. **represent**	H. **temporary**	I. **transparent**	J. **triumph**

_____ 1. Beating the first-place team was a greater ___ for the players than winning over the last-place team.

_____ 2. That horror movie must have used gallons of ___ blood.

_____ 3. For how many hours a week would you ___ a student to work?

_____ 4. The ___ of our club's newsletter is about once a month.

_____ 5. If you ___ a job, you make it harder to do.

_____ 6. A person who is cruel must not have much of a ___.

_____ 7. Substitute teachers get ___ job assignments, often for only a day or two at a time.

_____ 8. Elected officials are supposed to ___ the voters—in other words, do what the voters want.

_____ 9. In the winter, we put sheets of ___ plastic over our windows to help keep out the cold.

_____ 10. Although Norah has lived in New York for years, I can still ___ a slight Southern accent in her voice.

NOTE: Now check your answers to these questions by turning to page 240. Going over the answers carefully will help you prepare for the remaining practices, for which answers are not given.

➤ *Check 2*

Using the answer lines, complete each item below with **two** words from the box.

_____
_____ 1–2. To reduce the ___ of infections, people should be ___ed to wash their hands often and well. They should also be advised° to keep counters and cutting boards free of bacteria.

_____
_____ 3–4. If your ___ won't allow you to wear real fur, choose ___ fur instead. Fake fur looks great and feels good, too!

_____
_____ 5–6. I lost ten pounds last year. That was a great victory, but my ___ was only ___. I've gained every ounce of it back.

_____
_____ 7–8. The eyes are sometimes called "the windows of the soul," as if they were ___ and one could ___ what's inside a person's soul by looking into them.

_____
_____ 9–10. The Spruce Street Block Association worked well when it ___ed only the residents of our street. However, it has ___d matters by trying to speak for other parts of the neighborhood, as well.

➤ *Word Work*

A. Write each word next to the examples that best match it.

A. **artificial**	B. **detect**	C. **frequency**
D. **temporary**	E. **triumph**	

_____ 1. Plastic grass
Wax fruit
A glass eye

_____ 2. A neighborhood basketball team wins the city championship.
A student gets all A's on a report card.
You win a citywide talent contest.

_____ 3. Spot a child's chocolate fingerprints on a candy dish
Discover a thief's footprints
Notice fear in someone's voice

_____ 4. Mail delivery: once a day, six days a week
Flu shots: once a year
The Main Street bus: every half hour

_____ 5. Campers' tents set up on the shore of a lake
A place you live in until your new home is ready
Extra salespeople hired for the holiday season

B. In the space provided, write the letter of the choice that best completes each item.

_____ 6. A **transparent** dome on a stadium lets in

    A. rain.   B. sunlight.   C. air.

_____ 7. The school would **complicate** students' lives if it

    A. changed the whole   B. reduced tuition.   C. installed a coffee
    class schedule at midterm.   machine in the library.

_____ 8. Because of your **conscience**, you might

    A. buy silk flowers.   B. apologize to your   C. forget to pay back
                              brother for yelling at him.   a loan.

_____ 9. You might **represent**

    A. a hot summer's day.   B. your neighborhood   C. a good book.
                            in the city council.

_____10. If you wanted to **counsel** friends who had been skipping school, you would

    A. mind your own   B. avoid any contact   C. talk to them about
    business and   with them.   the dangers of
    say nothing,   their behavior.

➤ *Synonyms and Antonyms*

A. Synonyms. Write the letter of the word or phrase that most nearly means the **same** as each boldfaced word.

_____ 1. **conscience**

    A. rate   B. talent

    C. moral sense   D. victory

_____ 2. **counsel**

    A. win   B. make difficult

    C. give advice to   D. imitate

_____ 3. **detect**

    A. act for   B. ignore

    C. disapprove   D. notice

_____ 4. **frequency**

    A. how often something happens   B. allowing light to pass through

    C. difficulty   D. short time

_____ 5. **represent**

    A. imitate   B. discover

    C. speak for   D. succeed

B. Antonyms. Write the letter of the word or phrase that most nearly means the **opposite** of each boldfaced word.

_____ 6. **artificial**

    A. new   B. easy

    C. natural   D. old

_____ 7. **complicate**

    A. lose   B. make easier

    C. ignore   D. pay attention to

_____ 8. **temporary**

    A. easy   B. blocking out light

    C. important   D. lasting forever

_____ 9. **transparent**

    A. blocking out light   B. natural

    C. easy   D. long-lasting

_____ 10. **triumph**

    A. darkness   B. loss

    C. success   D. game

➤ *Final Check*

Read the passages carefully. Then fill in each blank with the word that best fits the context.

A. The People's Choice

A. **conscience**	B. **frequency**	C. **represent**	D. **temporary**	E. **triumph**

Suppose you are a candidate running for a particular° public office—and you win. What a (1)_____! But now consider this: What is the best way to (2)_____ those who voted for you? How do you know what "the people" want? Sometimes the great (3)_____ of letters and phone calls makes you think you know what all the people want. Think again! For most people, interest in what their elected officials are doing is only (4)_____; you will never hear from many of them again. Also, of course, the voters who don't write or call may feel differently from those who do. All right, then, you say, I'll just act according to my own (5)_____ and do what I think is right. Not so fast! Remember that you're supposed to be "the people's choice." So what should you do? If you know the answer to that question, I propose° that you call the politicians in Washington immediately. They've been looking for the answer for over two hundred years.

B. The Christmas Wars

F. **artificial**	G. **complicate**	H. **counsel**	I. **detect**	J. **transparent**

Christmastime is supposed to be peaceful, but in some families it renews old battles. One is the dispute° between those who like a sweet-smelling, natural Christmas tree and those who prefer a shiny (6)_____ tree, with no pine needles to mess up the floor. Another common battle goes on between parents, who seek the best places to hide the gifts until the big day, and children, who search tirelessly to (7)_____ clues about where those hiding places are. No matter what efforts a parent may make to (8)_____ the search by shoving the gifts inside luggage or under three layers of linens, kids soon find them.

Then, of course, because the boxes and packages are not (9)_____, the kids have to resort° to opening a corner of the wrapping. Or they try to determine° what's inside by shaking, bouncing, and rattling the box. Sooner or later, they make enough noise to catch an adult's attention. At this point the kids come out from behind the furnace or under the bed, trying very hard to look innocent. The parents get mad; the kids are in tears. Merry Christmas, everyone! It's hard to know how to (10)_____ parents in this situation. Would the best advice be to ask Grandpa or Grandma to take the kids for a month or so?

Scores	Check 2 _____%	Word Work _____%	Synonyms and Antonyms _____%	Final Check _____%

Enter your scores above and in the vocabulary performance chart on the inside back cover of the book.

agonizing	strive
energetic	substance
foresight	tolerance
interval	trait
prosper	withdraw

Ten Words in Context

In the space provided, write the letter of the meaning closest to that of each **boldfaced** word. Use the context of the sentences to help you figure out each word's meaning.

1 agonizing
(ăg′ə-nī′zĭng)
– *adjective*

• After hours in the blazing sun, the hikers felt an **agonizing** thirst.
• I felt sorry for my sister as she made the **agonizing** decision to end her marriage.

____ *Agonizing* means   A. surprising.   B. normal.   C. very painful.

2 energetic
(ĕn′ər-jĕt′ĭk)
– *adjective*

• The **energetic** soccer game left all the players tired and hungry.
• At the age of 70, my grandmother is still **energetic** enough to go for a long, fast walk every evening after dinner.

____ *Energetic* means   A. short and friendly.   B. lively and active.   C. easy and pleasant.

3 foresight
(fôr′sīt′)
– *noun*

• Jen had the **foresight** to apply to several colleges, knowing that she might not get into the one she wanted most.
• People who are always late show a lack of **foresight**.

____ *Foresight* means   A. wise planning.   B. courage.   C. strength.

4 interval
(ĭn′tər-vəl)
– *noun*

• The **interval** between Christmas and New Year's Day is only a week.
• There was an **interval** of several hours between the births of the twins—in fact, they were born on separate days.

____ *Interval* means   A. happiness.   B. difference in importance.   C. space.

5 prosper
(prŏs′pər)
– *verb*

• The company is so strong that it is expected to **prosper** even though similar companies are going out of business.
• Someone who always jumps from job to job is not likely to **prosper**.

____ *Prosper* means   A. to believe.   B. to do well.   C. to take back.

6 strive
(strīv)
– *verb*

• Many people **strive** to become movie stars, but few succeed.
• Every year, many mountain climbers **strive** to reach the top of Mount Everest.

____ *Strive* means   A. to make a mistake.   B. to make a discovery.   C. to make an effort.

7 substance
(sŭb′stəns)
– *noun*

- Snails leave a trail of a shiny **substance** everywhere they crawl.
- Gold is such a soft **substance** that it can be pounded into a very thin sheet.

___ *Substance* means   A. material.   B. light.   C. force.

8 tolerance
(tŏl′ər-əns)
– *noun*

- The **tolerance** of our neighbors is obvious when you see children of different races playing together at their house.
- Because of the Johnsons' **tolerance**, their son-in-law's different religion is not a problem for the family.

___ *Tolerance* means   A. planning.   B. respect for others.   C. financial success.

9 trait
(trāt)
– *noun*

- My friend's nicest **trait** is her ability to laugh at herself.
- My worst **trait** is always worrying about what people think of me.

___ *Trait* means   A. personal quality.   B. goal.   C. preparation.

10 withdraw
(wĭth-drô′)
– *verb*

- When Warren realized he was working Thursday, he had to **withdraw** his offer to baby-sit for his sister's kids.
- When I saw a large spider in my desk drawer, I **withdrew** my hand and decided to find a pen somewhere else.

___ *Withdraw* means   A. give.   B. find.   C. take back.

Matching Words with Definitions

Following are definitions of the ten words. **Print** each word next to its definition. If you look closely at each word in context, you will be able to figure out its meaning.

1. _____   A quality or feature, as of personality, for which a person is known

2. _____   Respect for the differing views, practices, and characteristics of others; lack of prejudice

3. _____   Lively; spirited; full of energy

4. _____   To take back (something or a statement); remove

5. _____   Causing great physical or mental pain

6. _____   Care in planning or preparing for the future

7. _____   The period of time between two events

8. _____   To try hard

9. _____   To succeed, especially financially

10. _____   A physical material; matter of a particular type

CAUTION: Do not go any further until you are sure the above answers are correct. Then you can use the definitions to help you in the following practices. Your goal is eventually to know the words well enough so that you don't need to check the definitions at all.

➤ *Check 1*

Using the answer line, complete each item below with the correct word from the box.

A. **agonizing**	B. **energetic**	C. **foresight**	D. **interval**	E. **prosper**
F. **strive**	G. **substance**	H. **tolerance**	I. **trait**	J. **withdraw**

_____ 1. I wished I could ___ my angry words, but it was too late.

_____ 2. Don't worry when Paul and Linda raise their voices to each other. "We both like an ___ argument; we aren't really mad," Linda says.

_____ 3. Shelby ___s to do well in all her classes.

_____ 4. Patience is an important ___ for a preschool teacher.

_____ 5. Budgeting requires the ___ to think of future expenses.

_____ 6. Martin Luther King taught that all people should be viewed with ___, no matter what their race or religious beliefs.

_____ 7. Dad went to the emergency room because of ___ pain in his lower back.

_____ 8. There's an ___ of an hour between my last class and the track meet.

_____ 9. The silver-colored ___ inside an old-fashioned thermometer is called mercury.

_____ 10. At first, the Savings Mart didn't do well, but after it lowered its prices and increased its advertising, the store began to ___.

NOTE: Now check your answers to these questions by turning to page 240. Going over the answers carefully will help you prepare for the remaining practices, for which answers are not given.

➤ *Check 2*

Using the answer lines, complete each item below with **two** words from the box.

_____
_____ 1–2. One of Paul's unpleasant ___s is that he has very little ___ for anyone who disagrees with his opinions.

_____
_____ 3–4. People who ___ tend to be individuals who ___ to do their jobs well, spend less than they earn, and save for the future.

_____
_____ 5–6. Lisa loves her ___ workout at the gym, but she also loves the quiet ___ after exercising and before leaving. That's when she sits and talks with friends.

_____
_____ 7–8. The unfortunate man fell asleep on the beach and woke up with an ___ sunburn. He hadn't had the ___ to put on sunblock lotion.

_____
_____ 9–10. One of the sad things about addiction to any ___, such as drugs or alcohol, is that the addiction makes the person ___ from normal life and friendships. The addiction becomes his or her whole life.

➤ *Word Work*

A. In the space provided, write the letter of the choice that best completes each item.

_____ 1. If a person has an **agonizing** injury, he or she would probably
   A. laugh it off.
   B. scream in pain.
   C. limp slightly.

_____ 2. A sign of Rob's **tolerance** is that
   A. he has friends of many different races and religions.
   B. he studies very hard.
   C. he wears expensive clothes.

_____ 3. An especially **energetic** activity is
   A. reading.
   B. resting.
   C. running.

_____ 4. If you and a friend have an argument and you **strive** to understand her point of view, you
   A. don't care what she thinks.
   B. really want to understand her.
   C. know that she is right and you are wrong.

_____ 5. You might **withdraw** a compliment to someone if
   A. you admire that person greatly.
   B. you become angry with that person.
   C. you want to go out with that person.

B. In the space provided, write the letter of the word that most closely relates to the situation in each item.

_____ 6. When my mother travels on a plane, she keeps her pills in her purse, in case the airline loses her luggage.
   A. foresight   B. agonizing   C. tolerance

_____ 7. People who were in on the "ground floor" of the personal computer industry became extremely wealthy.
   A. prosper   B. withdraw   C. energetic

_____ 8. Of the children in our family, my sister is known as the funny one, my brother is the hard-working one, and I am the athletic one.
   A. substance   B. interval   C. trait

_____ 9. Kwan spent a lot of time worrying during the five days between her job interview and the day she learned she was hired.
   A. withdraw   B. substance   C. interval

_____ 10. What is that blob of glowing green stuff on the kitchen table?
   A. tolerance   B. substance   C. trait

➤ *Word Parts*

A. The suffix *-ous* means "full of" or "having much."

> *Examples:* *fury* — violent anger   *prosper* — to succeed financially
> *furious* — full of violent anger   *prosperous* — having much financial success

On each answer line, write the word from the box that best completes the item.

A. **envious**	B. **famous**	C. **furious**
D. **joyous**	E. **prosperous**	

_____ 1. Elvis Presley is still very well known; in fact, he may be more ___ today than he was when he was alive.

_____ 2. After her latest fight with her boyfriend, Jill was so ___ that she wrote him a long, angry letter—and then burned it.

_____ 3. Not many people "get rich quick" by winning the lottery; most of us have to work long and hard to become ___.

_____ 4. The wedding of my eighty-year-old grandmother was a ___ occasion for the family.

_____ 5. It is hard not to feel ___ of Paul, who seems to have everything good in life: a great marriage, a wonderful job, terrific kids, and lots of friends.

B. The suffix *-al* often means "the act of."

> *Examples:* *deny* — to say that something is not true
> *denial* — the act of saying that something is not true
>
> *refuse* — to say "no" to doing, or giving, or accepting something
> *refusal* — the act of saying "no" to something

On each answer line, write the word from the box that best completes the item.

F. **approval**	G. **betrayal°**	H. **denial**
I. **survival**	J. **withdrawal**	

_____ 6. The ___ of one thousand dollars from the man's bank account was unusual. He usually took out only fifty dollars or so.

_____ 7. Giving secret information to an enemy is a ___ of one's country.

_____ 8. My mother strongly believes in the soul's ___ after death, but my father believes there is nothing after death.

_____ 9. Mark's ___ that he had eaten the cookies surprised me because I noticed Oreo crumbs all over his bed.

_____ 10. We can't leave work early without our boss's ___.

➤ *Final Check*

Read the passages carefully. Then fill in each blank with the word that best fits the context.

A. What's Your Type?

A. **agonizing**	B. **prosper**	C. **strive**	D. **tolerance**	E. **trait**

If you find it (1)_____ to be stuck behind a slow-moving car, or if you are often impatient with a friend's progress in completing a task, you may be what researchers classify° as a Type A personality. A (2)_____ shared by Type A people is the desire to make effective use of time. They (3)_____ to accomplish more in an hour than other people do in a day. A typical example of Type A behavior is the man who built a desk onto the front of his exercise bike. Sitting in front of the TV set, he could exercise, watch football, and pay bills all at the same time. Type A's often have little (4)_____ for the calmer Type B people; Type A's feel the Type B's waste a lot of time. Naturally, Type A people often (5)_____ financially, driven as they are to achieve the maximum° success at whatever they do. However, they also suffer from heart disease more often than the more relaxed Type B's. It seems that the Type A's great need for success creates a lot of tension, which causes damage to the body.

B. What a Circus!

F. **energetic**	G. **foresight**	H. **interval**	I. **substance**	J. **withdraw**

I didn't actually volunteer to go to the circus. I was sort of volunteered. My son Tommy was going with his first-grade class, and he told his teacher to sign me up. When I saw how eager° he was for me to accompany° his class, I couldn't (6)_____ the offer.

So there I was, along with a handful of other parents and ninety (7)_____ six- and seven-year-olds. I don't really recollect° a great deal of the circus. What I do remember is the purple (8)_____ that someone spilled on my sneaker, because it never washed off. I remember a lot about the inside of the bathroom, because I took so many children there. I remember washing cotton candy off a lot of faces, since I had the (9)_____ to bring a box of baby wipes along. And I remember the boy who exclaimed°, "Oh, no!" and hid his face in my lap when an acrobat took a scary walk across a high horizontal° wire.

But nothing could spoil the fun those kids had. To them, every act was a wonderful spectacle°. Even when the juggler dropped three of his four bowling pins, the kids thought he was great. Afterward, they were tired. In the brief (10)_____ between our boarding the bus to go home and Tommy's falling asleep, he gave me his verdict°: "That was the bestest circus ever. You were really lucky to get to come along." Looking back at it all, I think I was, too.

Scores	Check 2 _____%	Word Work _____%	Word Parts _____%	Final Check _____%

Enter your scores above and in the vocabulary performance chart on the inside back cover of the book.

approximately	plea
consistent	practical
cope	random
evaluate	significant
phrase	sole

Ten Words in Context

In the space provided, write the letter of the meaning closest to that of each **boldfaced** word. Use the context of the sentences to help you figure out each word's meaning.

1 approximately
(ə-prŏk′sə-mĭt-lē)
– adverb

• A month is **approximately** thirty days long.

• The suspect in the murder case is a dark-haired white woman who is **approximately** forty years old.

____*Approximately* means   A. certainly.   B. never.   C. about.

2 consistent
(kən-sĭs′tənt)
– adjective

• To be rated number one in tennis, a player must be a **consistent** winner, not a winner now and then.

• I would rather work for someone with a **consistent** manner than someone full of praise one day and screaming insults the next.

____*Consistent* means   A. steady.   B. early.   C. surprising.

3 cope
(kōp)
– verb

• The death of a beloved pet is hard to **cope** with.

• I read an interesting article on how to **cope** with difficult people.

____*Cope with* means   A. to value.   B. to predict.   C. to handle.

4 evaluate
(ĭ-văl′yōō-āt′)
– verb

• Reading movie reviews can help you **evaluate** whether a film is worth seeing.

• Several long-distance phone companies make the same promises, so it is hard to **evaluate** which is best.

____*Evaluate* means   A. to ignore.   B. to judge.   C. to remember.

5 phrase
(frāz)
– noun

• The **phrase** "at this point in time" can be reduced to a single word: "now."

• The **phrase** "Tom, Dick, or Harry" means "any member of the general public."

____*Phrase* means   A. puzzle.   B. word group.   C. answer.

6 plea
(plē)
– noun

• The parents of the missing baby made this **plea** to the kidnapper: "We beg you to return our baby to us unharmed!"

• "Please don't cut it too short, the way you did last time!" Martha hoped the hair stylist would listen to her **plea**.

____*Plea* means   A. big joke.   B. urgent request.   C. long story.

7 practical
(prăk′tĭ-kəl)
– *adjective*

- Mom puts old socks to **practical** use as dust rags.
- The two single friends realized it would be **practical** to move in together and split the rent.

___ *Practical* means   A. done for practice.   B. expensive.   C. sensible.

8 random
(răn′dəm)
– *adjective*

- We studied two paintings in art class. One was a clearly organized arrangement of black and white dots; the other seemed to be a **random** collection of spots and streaks of brilliant color.
- The movement of clouds may seem to be **random**, but scientists know that there is a pattern to how they move.

___ *Random* means   A. without order.   B. rare.   C. useful.

9 significant
(sĭg-nĭf′ĭ-kənt)
– *adjective*

- Teron's factory job was hard but worthwhile, because he earned a **significant** part of his college expenses.
- Doctors have found that a good attitude can play a **significant** role in helping people recover from diseases.

___ *Significant* means   A. busy.   B. large.   C. easy.

10 sole
(sōl)
– *adjective*

- After her husband died, the woman was the **sole** support of a large family.
- The **sole** reason my cousin ever calls me is to ask for money.

___ *Sole* means   A. only.   B. friendly.   C. early.

Matching Words with Definitions

Following are definitions of the ten words. **Print** each word next to its definition. If you look closely at each word in context, you will be able to figure out its meaning.

1. _____   Quite large in amount or number; important

2. _____   Almost, but not exactly; more or less

3. _____   Not having a plan, purpose, or pattern; chance

4. _____   To decide on the value of (something)

5. _____   To deal with difficulties; handle

6. _____   Only; being the only one

7. _____   Useful and sensible

8. _____   A request, especially a deeply felt, emotional one; an appeal°

9. _____   Steady; regular

10. _____   A group of words with a meaning; an expression

CAUTION: Do not go any further until you are sure the above answers are correct. Then you can use the definitions to help you in the following practices. Your goal is eventually to know the words well enough so that you don't need to check the definitions at all.

➣ *Check 1*

Using the answer line, complete each item below with the correct word from the box.

A. **approximately**	B. **consistent**	C. **cope**	D. **evaluate**	E. **phrase**
F. **plea**	G. **practical**	H. **random**	I. **significant**	J. **sole**

_____ 1. Rhonda is a ___ student, bringing home B's regularly.

_____ 2. The Murphys have so many pets that they spend a ___ amount of their grocery money to feed them.

_____ 3. The course on "Smart Shopping" teaches people how to ___ the worth of products and services.

_____ 4. Barry begged the waitress to hurry with his meal, but she ignored his ___ and served the other diners first.

_____ 5. I like to take ___ walks, without any plan in mind.

_____ 6. My friends helped me ___ with my father's death.

_____ 7. People just learning English are often puzzled by ___s such as "on the up-and-up" and "You don't say!"

_____ 8. I barely know my neighbor. The ___ conversation we ever have is saying "Good morning" to each other.

_____ 9. White furniture is not ___ for a family with little kids who wear dirty shoes and spill Kool-Aid.

_____ 10. "I'd like you to cut off this much," Eileen told her hairdresser, indicating° ___ two inches.

NOTE: Now check your answers to these questions by turning to page 240. Going over the answers carefully will help you prepare for the remaining practices, for which answers are not given.

➣ *Check 2*

Using the answer lines, complete each item below with **two** words from the box.

_____
_____ 1–2. Dave found an inexpensive, ___ way to ___ with the problem of mice in his house: he got a cat.

_____
_____ 3–4. Pizza is Little Italy's best seller, bringing in ___ 30 percent of the profits, a very ___ part of the restaurant's income.

_____
_____ 5–6. Giving in to her students' ___s, the teacher reluctantly° promised to ___ their projects and tell them their grades before the weekend.

_____
_____ 7–8. The ___ "a chance meeting" refers to a ___ meeting—in other words, one that happens accidentally.

_____
_____ 9–10. The ___ exercise I get is walking—nothing else. But I am ___ about it; I do it every day. I prefer solitary° walks so that I don't have to talk to anyone.

➤ *Word Work*

A. In the space provided, write the letter of the word that most closely relates to the situation in each item.

A. **consistent**	B. **evaluate**	C. **phrase**
D. **random**	E. **significant**	

_____ 1. Our teacher will grade the history projects for originality, neatness, and accuracy.

_____ 2. Kyle is never late for work. He walks in that door at 8:50 every morning, just like clockwork.

_____ 3. You may think my earnings from baby-sitting are small, but they are an important part of my budget. They paid for all my books this semester.

_____ 4. The visitors to the city just wandered up and down the streets, stopping to look at anything that caught their interest.

_____ 5. The line "Make my day!" was made popular by Clint Eastwood.

B. Write each word next to the examples that best match it.

F. **approximately**	G. **cope**	H. **plea**
I. **practical**	J. **sole**	

_____ 6. Buying milk for the family instead of a cola drink
Patching old jeans instead of throwing them out
Getting enough sleep before an important test

_____ 7. A distance of around two miles between the cousins' houses
About 150 people at the meeting
A cost of close to ninety cents a pint for strawberries this summer

_____ 8. "We appeal to you to vote for smoke-free restaurants!"
"Will you buy a box of cookies to support our summer sports program?"
"Please donate your spare change to help a local family whose home has burned down."

_____ 9. Having a flat tire and then putting on a new one
Losing a job and then signing up for a class to learn new job skills
Feeling lonely and then deciding to join a social club

_____ 10. Just one person living on the island
One egg left in the refrigerator
A boy with no brothers or sisters

➤ *Synonyms and Antonyms*

A. Synonyms. Write the letter of the word or phrase that most nearly means the **same** as each boldfaced word.

_____ 1. **cope**

    A. compete with   B. manage

    C. quarrel   D. agree

_____ 2. **evaluate**

    A. judge   B. pay for

    C. see   D. borrow

_____ 3. **plea**

    A. joke   B. abuse

    C. appeal   D. pretend

_____ 4. **phrase**

    A. a practice   B. something useful

    C. a plan   D. a group of words

_____ 5. **sole**

    A. important   B. only

    C. sensible   D. unplanned

B. Antonyms. Write the letter of the word or phrase that most nearly means the **opposite** of each boldfaced word.

_____ 6. **approximately**

    A. well-known   B. exactly

    C. not clear   D. often

_____ 7. **consistent**

    A. having a plan   B. not close

    C. valuable   D. not regular

_____ 8. **practical**

    A. useless   B. valuable

    C. attractive   D. common

_____ 9. **random**

    A. not steady   B. interesting

    C. unknown   D. planned

_____ 10. **significant**

    A. wrong   B. unclear

    C. dull   D. small in amount

➤ *Final Check*

Read the passages carefully. Then fill in each blank with the word that best fits the context.

A. Practicing Kindness

A. **consistent**	B. **evaluate**	C. **phrase**	D. **plea**	E. **random**

Maybe you've heard the (1)_____ or seen the words printed on a bumper sticker. The saying is a (2)_____ for people to do kind things for no particular° reason, with no particular° plan. It goes like this: "Practice (3)_____ acts of kindness and senseless beauty." I don't know where it originated° or who said it first. But I have seen people putting the idea into practice. I've noticed people putting quarters into parking meters so that a stranger's car wouldn't be ticketed. I've heard of someone paying a family's bill in a restaurant, then leaving before the family found out. I know a man who is (4)_____ in not letting a day go by without giving someone a sincere compliment.

Why do these people bother? They probably don't stop to (5)_____ their actions. But if they did, I assume° they would say something like this: Kindness can be catching, just as cruelty can be. When we do something unexpected and nice for another person, who knows where that act of kindness might end?

B. The Stinking Rose

F. **approximately**	G. **cope**	H. **practical**	I. **significant**	J. **sole**

Centuries ago in Rome, it was called "stinking rose." It was then used to flavor food and for such (6)_____ purposes as fighting colds. Today we call it garlic, and we, too, find this wonderful substance° delicious and useful. In fact, in one recent year, Americans bought enough garlic to provide every man, woman, and child with (7)_____ one and a half pounds of the stuff. It is added to a wide variety° of foods, from appetizers to zucchini—even to chocolate peanut butter cups. The unfortunate thing about garlic is that it produces bad breath. One way to (8)_____ with garlic breath is to chew parsley, an excellent natural breath cleaner. Or eat garlic only with others who are also eating it. Being tasty is not the (9)_____ good thing about garlic. It turns out that the ancient Romans were absolutely right about its having health benefits. A (10)_____ number of studies (about 3,000) have been done of the onionlike plant. They suggest that garlic may strengthen the immune system, fight colds, cause a reduction° in blood pressure, and even help prevent cancer.

Scores	Check 2 _____%	Word Work _____%	Synonyms and Antonyms _____%	Final Check _____%

Enter your scores above and in the vocabulary performance chart on the inside back cover of the book.

authentic	eligible
characteristic	harsh
concept	remote
confront	shallow
disrupt	thrive

Ten Words in Context

In the space provided, write the letter of the meaning closest to that of each **boldfaced** word. Use the context of the sentences to help you figure out each word's meaning.

1 authentic
(ô-thĕn′tĭk)
– *adjective*

- Don't be fooled if someone tries to sell you an **authentic** diamond ring for $10.99. The stone in that ring is sure to be fake.
- Several people claim to have saved the little girl from the burning building, so no one knows who is the **authentic** hero.

___*Authentic* means   A. old.   B. qualified.   C. real.

2 characteristic
(kăr′ək-tə-rĭs′tĭk)
– *adjective*

- Leon has his father's **characteristic** warm smile.
- Olive oil, garlic, pasta, and cheese are **characteristic** parts of the Italian diet.

___*Characteristic* means   A. usual.   B. convenient.   C. strange.

3 concept
(kŏn′sĕpt′)
– *noun*

- When asked for her **concept** of heaven, the child said, "A room full of toys and chocolate."
- My sister doesn't understand the **concept** of living within a budget.

___*Concept* means   A. idea.   B. worst fear.   C. memory.

4 confront
(kən-frŭnt′)
– *verb*

- The restaurant manager really should **confront** that waiter and tell him directly about his rude behavior.
- The opposing lawyer plans to **confront** the accused man with a surprise piece of evidence.

___*Confront* means   A. to avoid.   B. to face.   C. to prepare.

5 disrupt
(dĭs-rŭpt′)
– *verb*

- Tina thought it would be fun to sneak her tiny dog into the movie theater. But then the dog got loose and **disrupted** the show.
- Parents who are angry about budget cuts plan to **disrupt** tonight's school board meeting with a noisy demonstration.

___*Disrupt* means   A. to manage.   B. to go to.   C. to upset.

6 eligible
(ĕl′ĭ-jə-bəl)
– *adjective*

- Because of his high grades and his parents' low income, my cousin is **eligible** for some good college scholarships.
- It's not true that any American can become president of the United States. To be **eligible**, you have to be at least thirty-five years old.

___*Eligible* means   A. qualified.   B. known.   C. pleased.

7 harsh
(härsh)
– *adjective*

- The **harsh** ruler decided to punish the entire village for one man's crime.
- The scolding that the children received was too **harsh**. They hadn't done anything all that bad.

___ *Harsh* means   A. fair.   B. rough.   C. wasteful.

8 remote
(rĭ-mōt′)
– *adjective*

- Humans have explored even the most **remote** parts of the planet, areas deep in forests and beneath the seas.
- Some parts of the park are so **remote** that visitors seldom reach them.

___ *Remote* means   A. large.   B. typical.   C. distant.

9 shallow
(shăl′ō)
– *adjective*

- The lifeguard at the pool insists that young children stay at the **shallow** end.
- The cake won't rise very high in that **shallow** pan; you'll need a smaller pan with higher sides.

___ *Shallow* means   A. real.   B. not deep.   C. very wide.

10 thrive
(thrīv)
– *verb*

- African violets like sun, so they should **thrive** in that sunny window.
- In the past, many premature babies died; but with modern medical care, most of them **thrive** and live normal lives.

___ *Thrive* means   A. to do very well.   B. to grow weaker.   C. to need too much care.

Matching Words with Definitions

Following are definitions of the ten words. **Print** each word next to its definition. If you look closely at each word in context, you will be able to figure out its meaning.

1. _____   Not deep

2. _____   To face or oppose boldly

3. _____   To grow very well; improve physically

4. _____   To cause disorder or confusion; upset

5. _____   Qualified to be chosen; desirable as a candidate

6. _____   Unkind or cruel; strict; severe

7. _____   Far away; very distant; hidden away

8. _____   Typical of someone or something

9. _____   A general thought; an idea

10. _____   Real; true; actual

CAUTION: Do not go any further until you are sure the above answers are correct. Then you can use the definitions to help you in the following practices. Your goal is eventually to know the words well enough so that you don't need to check the definitions at all.

➤ *Check 1*

Using the answer line, complete each item below with the correct word from the box.

A. **authentic**	B. **characteristic**	C. **concept**	D. **confront**	E. **disrupt**
F. **eligible**	G. **harsh**	H. **remote**	I. **shallow**	J. **thrive**

_____ 1. The creek was so ___ that the water came up only to my ankles.

_____ 2. Some imitation pearl necklaces are so beautiful that only a jeweler can tell that the pearls are not ___.

_____ 3. When the new employee forgot to lock up the store one night, his boss gave him a ___ warning: "Another mistake like that, Buddy, and you're out of a job!"

_____ 4. The preschool teacher tries to help her little students understand the ___ of sharing.

_____ 5. The student assembly was ___ed by a fire drill.

_____ 6. The weak, sickly child began to ___ after doctors corrected her heart problem.

_____ 7. Professor Liu studies little-known plants in ___ parts of our state forests.

_____ 8. After a man dropped a bag of trash on the ground, another man picked it up and ___ed him, saying, "I think this is yours. Find a trash can."

_____ 9. Students must have at least a B average to be ___ for any of the school sports teams.

_____ 10. Fat, fleshy leaves are ___ of cactus plants.

NOTE: Now check your answers to these questions by turning to page 240. Going over the answers carefully will help you prepare for the remaining practices, for which answers are not given.

➤ *Check 2*

Using the answer lines, complete each item below with **two** words from the box.

_____
_____ 1–2. The two rings looked alike to me, but the jeweler said that only one had the colorful sparkle that is ___ of an ___ diamond.

_____
_____ 3–4. "Tomorrow I'll ___ our neighbors," Alonso said, "and protest° about the way their unleashed dog ___s the children's backyard games."

_____
_____ 5–6. A child who does poorly in school with a ___, bad-tempered teacher might ___ with a teacher who is gentle and caring.

_____
_____ 7–8. Because she is a biologist, Mia is ___ to be part of a research team that will study turtles on a ___ island.

_____
_____ 9–10. Because babies can drown in very little water, the ___ that they are safe in a ___ pool is false. A reliable° adult must watch them every second.

➤ *Word Work*

A. Write each word by the examples that best match it.

A. **authentic**	B. **characteristic**	C. **disrupt**
D. **harsh**	E. **thrive**	

_____ 1. A baby cries during a religious service.
A cat runs onto a baseball field in the middle of a game.
A fire drill occurs° in the middle of a class.

_____ 2. A red stone that a jeweler says is a ruby
An old desk known to be an antique from the seventeenth century
Cave paintings proven to be the work of Stone Age artists

_____ 3. The red color of many barns
The sweet smell of roses
The hot summers of Florida

_____ 4. A clerk who insults all the customers in the store
A boss who forces his employees to work through lunch
A drill sergeant screaming orders at a group of new soldiers

_____ 5. Betsy settles into her new school quickly, makes friends, and earns good grades.
An orphaned kitten grows strong and healthy by drinking formula from a bottle.
A fern hanging in the sunny window grows full and beautiful.

B. In the space provided, write the letter of the word that most closely relates to the situation in each item.

_____ 6. I plan to walk up to my neighbor and tell him that the junk car on his lawn is an eyesore.

A. shallow   B. eligible   C. confront

_____ 7. The idea of infinity—of time and space that have no beginning and no end—is difficult for most people to understand.

A. concept   B. thrive   C. eligible

_____ 8. Any child between the ages of 5 and 9 who is a resident of Ohio may enter a drawing in the art contest.

A. confront   B. disrupt   C. eligible

_____ 9. The hermit lived many miles from town, in a part of the hills that was hard to reach. He wasn't able to cope° very well with the demands of society.

A. confront   B. remote   C. thrive

_____10. That box isn't deep enough—don't you have one that is a better size to hold a salad bowl?

A. shallow   B. authentic   C. harsh

➤ *Analogies*

Each item below starts with a pair of words in CAPITAL LETTERS. For each item, figure out the relationship between these two words. Then decide which of the choices (A, B, C, or D) expresses a similar relationship. Write the letter of your choice on the answer line. (All the repeated words in these items are from this unit.)

_____ 1. AUTHENTIC : REAL ::

    A. lost : found   B. expensive : high-priced

    C. expected : surprising   D. inner : external

_____ 2. EXTERNAL° : INTERNAL° ::

    A. outside : weather   B. sole° : only

    C. agonizing° : pleasant   D. red : bright

_____ 3. HARSH : KIND ::

    A. late : tardy   B. helpful : useful

    C. permanent : temporary°   D. incredible° : amazing

_____ 4. ORANGE : FRUIT ::

    A. cat : dog   B. triumph°: loss

    C. penicillin : remedy°   D. strawberry : cherry

_____ 5. CONFRONT : AVOID ::

    A. strive° : try   B. eligible : qualified

    C. tear : rip   D. prosper° : fail

_____ 6. SHALLOW : DEEP ::

    A. brief: short   B. disrupt : upset

    C. smiling : frowning   D. random° : unplanned

_____ 7. WINDOW : TRANSPARENT° ::

    A. door : doorknob   B. window : curtain

    C. car : highway   D. grass : green

_____ 8. THRIVE : WEAKEN ::

    A. protest° : approve   B. smile : grin

    C. protect : guard   D. spectacle° : watch

_____ 9. TRAIT° : PATIENCE ::

    A. promise : withdraw°   B. substance° : clay

    C. banker : money   D. kindness : intelligence

_____ 10. GIVE : GIFT ::

    A. run : walk   B. detect° : clue

    C. concept : idea   D. verdict° : opinion

➤ *Final Check*

Read the passages carefully. Then fill in each blank with the word that best fits the context.

A. A Modern Fairy Tale

A. **concept**	B. **confront**	C. **disrupt**	D. **eligible**	E. **harsh**

Many fairy tales are versions° of the same story: A prince has his pick of all the (1)_____ women in the kingdom. But the girl he likes best is in big trouble, so the prince bravely rescues her. The girl doesn't do much of anything. She just looks pretty. The stories all end with more or less the same phrase°: "They lived happily ever after."

But one fairy tale, "The Paper Bag Princess," gets rid of the (2)_____ of the brave prince and the helpless girl. In it, Princess Elizabeth is engaged to Prince Ronald. But a dragon (3)_____s their plans by burning the castle and capturing Ronald. Elizabeth decides to rescue him. Since all her pretty clothes have been burned up, she puts on a paper bag. She bravely (4)_____s the dragon and tricks him into using up all his strength on silly tasks. Then she goes into the dragon's cave and finds Ronald.

Instead of being grateful, however, Ronald gives Elizabeth a (5)_____ scolding for being covered with dirt and smoke and for wearing a bag. He tells her to come back when she looks like "a real princess." Elizabeth tells Ronald that though he looks like a real prince, with his fancy clothes and neat hair, he is, in fact, "a bum." The last picture in the book shows Elizabeth dancing happily off into the sunset, with the final line, "They didn't get married after all."

B. Wolf Children

F. **authentic**	G. **characteristic**	H. **remote**	I. **shallow**	J. **thrive**

A tale of children being raised by wolves sounds incredible°. However, though hard to believe, one story about wolf children appears to be (6)_____. In Singapore during the early 1920s, Reverend J. A. L. Singh heard stories of "man-beasts" that were frightening the people of a (7)_____ jungle village. Along with a group of other men, Singh went in search of that hidden village and the strange creatures.

In the village, Singh was taken to a large hill. When he dug a (8)_____ hole in the hill, he quickly discovered a family of wolves. From within the wolves' den, two pale creatures peeked out. Singh's party killed the adult wolves and dug further into the den. There they found two human children curled up with the cubs. The children were captured and brought to the village in bamboo cages.

The children did not speak like other humans; instead, they howled and growled like animals. Their diet was equally wolflike; they preferred raw meat, mice, and cockroaches. And they had the wolf's (9)_____ desire to be active at night, as well as a dislike of the indoors. Sadly, the children did not (10)_____. Both grew weak and died.

Scores Check 2 _____%	Word Work _____%	Analogies _____%	Final Check _____%

UNIT THREE: *Review*

The box at the right lists twenty-five words from Unit Three. Using the clues at the bottom of the page, fill in these words to complete the puzzle that follows.

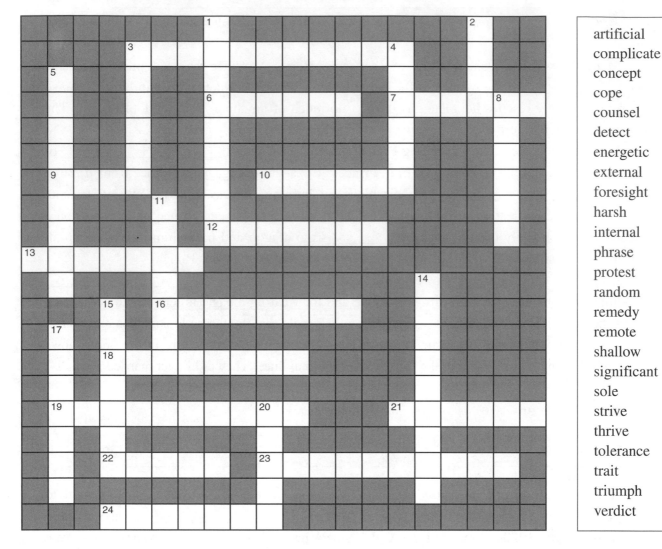

artificial
complicate
concept
cope
counsel
detect
energetic
external
foresight
harsh
internal
phrase
protest
random
remedy
remote
shallow
significant
sole
strive
thrive
tolerance
trait
triumph
verdict

ACROSS

3. Quite large in amount or number
6. Far away; very distant
7. A cure; something that heals
9. Only; being the only one
10. A group of words with a meaning; an expression
12. To give advice or guidance
13. Not deep
16. Outer; located outside
18. Inner; located inside
19. To make difficult by adding or involving many parts or details; make complex
21. Not having a plan, purpose, or pattern; chance
22. Unkind or cruel; strict; severe
23. Made to imitate something natural
24. An opinion or judgment

DOWN

1. Lively; spirited; full of energy
2. To deal with difficulties
3. To try hard
4. To grow very well; improve physically
5. Care in planning or preparing for the future
8. To notice; discover that something exists or is present
11. To complain
14. Respect for the differing views, practices, and characteristics of others
15. An outstanding or very satisfying success; victory
17. A general thought; an idea
20. A quality or feature, as of personality, for which a person is known

116

UNIT THREE: Test 1

PART A
Choose the word that best completes each item and write it in the space provided.

_____ 1. Since my math class was very difficult for me, I consider the B I got for the course to be a great ___.

    A. foresight   B. triumph   C. tolerance   D. trait

_____ 2. The veterinarian's ___ was that our dog was limping because the dog had cracked a bone in her ankle.

    A. verdict   B. conscience   C. tolerance   D. substance

_____ 3. It's hard to believe in a doctor who ___ his patients not to smoke, but who smokes himself.

    A. counsels   B. copes with   C. withdraws   D. prospers

_____ 4. The ___ of Luis's ear infections when he was a little boy was great, but he hasn't had one for years now.

    A. phrase   B. spectacle   C. frequency   D. conscience

_____ 5. "Remember that you ___ all of the people of our city," one man yelled to the mayor, "not just the rich ones."

    A. represent   B. detect   C. protest   D. thrive

_____ 6. It turned out that Peter's interest in collecting stamps was only ___. He forgot about it after a couple of months.

    A. temporary   B. agonizing   C. external   D. transparent

_____ 7. If I ___ a hair in my food, then I can't eat another bite of that food, even after I remove the hair.

    A. strive   B. evaluate   C. assume   D. detect

_____ 8. As much as I would love to skip my chores and go the baseball game, my ___ won't let me.

    A. substance   B. conscience   C. phrase   D. interval

_____ 9. Just because Donald is quiet in class, don't ___ that he is stupid.

    A. assume   B. protest   C. disrupt   D. withdraw

_____ 10. As she read in the living room, Anna became ___ of loud voices coming from her parents' room.

    A. appropriate   B. shallow   C. authentic   D. conscious

_____ 11. My daughter invited some friends over for dinner and then ___ my planning by telling me that one is allergic to eggs, another is allergic to milk, and the third is a vegetarian.

    A. prospered   B. complicated   C. thrived   D. detected

(Continues on next page)

_____ 12. When they visited the coast, the Martins enjoyed a trip in a glass-bottomed boat. They looked through its ___ bottom and saw many fish and other sea creatures.

        A. transparent   B. random   C. remote   D. harsh

_____ 13. The hardware store sells ___ stones made of plastic that you can open and hide a house key in. Then you can hide the key by leaving the "stone" somewhere near your door.

        A. eligible   B. authentic   C. artificial   D. spectacle

PART B
Write **C** if the italicized word is used **correctly**. Write **I** if the word is used **incorrectly**.

_____ 14. After using the *external* part of onions and potatoes in a meal, I use the peels to make broth.

_____ 15. As *incredible* as it seems, the Nile River in Africa has frozen over at least twice.

_____ 16. The house's *internal* appearance is neat, but inside, it's a real mess.

_____ 17. The *maximum* legal driving speed in our state is sixty miles an hour.

_____ 18. My only *spectacle* to my cousin is that spending time with her is more boring than watching paint dry.

_____ 19. The play was so bad that we slipped out of the theater during the *interval* between the first and second acts.

_____ 20. Joan's sickness seemed to be getting better, but over the weekend she had a *remedy* and is now seriously ill.

_____ 21. Instead of looking for a job, my *energetic* brother is spending his summer lying on the couch watching TV.

_____ 22. Knowing that his children often bring home friends after a baseball game, Mr. Hendricks had the *foresight* to make extra hamburgers for dinner.

_____ 23. The chickens *protest* loudly whenever someone takes their eggs out from under them.

_____ 24. I couldn't wait to tell my father the *agonizing* news: I had made the basketball team!

_____ 25. That boss is so *harsh* that he gives every employee an extra day off on his or her birthday.

Score (Number correct) _____ × 4 = _____ %

Enter your score above and in the vocabulary performance chart on the inside back cover of the book.

UNIT THREE: Test 2

PART A

On the answer line, write the word from the box that completes each item below. Use each word once.

A. **approximately**	B. **authentic**	C. **consistent**	D. **cope**	E. **disrupt**
F. **eligible**	G. **phrase**	H. **prosper**	I. **remote**	J. **shallow**
K. **substance**	L. **trait**	M. **withdraw**		

_____ 1. A swarm of bees ___ed the picnic, sending people running and yelling in every direction.

_____ 2. One way to ___ with winter weather is to stay indoors, turn the heat up, play old Beach Boys records, and watch videotapes of Hawaiian hula dancers.

_____ 3. When asked what ___ is most important in a boyfriend or girlfriend, many people answer, "A sense of humor."

_____ 4. In order to have the peace and quiet he needed to finish his book, the writer moved to a ___ cabin where there were no people, no cars, and not even a telephone.

_____ 5. A lemonade stand would ___ on this corner. Hundreds of hot, thirsty people walk by every day.

_____ 6. The librarian complained that someone had returned a book with a strange green ___ all over its cover.

_____ 7. If someone tells you he can sell you an ___ diamond bracelet for twenty dollars, don't believe him.

_____ 8. Do you have to be a high-school graduate to be ___ to join the Army?

_____ 9. The car sells for ___ fifteen thousand dollars; the exact price depends on what "extras" you order, such as power windows or a CD player.

_____ 10. I don't think I'd like to live in a place where the weather is so ___ that there is never any change from day to day.

_____ 11. Don't bury those carrot seeds too deep. Just dig a ___ hole for each one and cover it with a small amount of soil.

_____ 12. I had to ___ my offer to buy my friend's old car when I realized I couldn't afford automobile insurance.

_____ 13. My grandfather usually spoke English, but he always greeted friends with the Spanish ___ "Qué pasa?" which means "What's happening?"

(Continues on next page)

PART B

Write **C** if the italicized word is used **correctly**. Write **I** if the word is used **incorrectly**.

_____14. Manuel is a hard-working person who always *strives* to do his best.

_____15. Amanda was the *sole* person at the table who ate meat. Everyone else was a vegetarian.

_____16. After being put in the sun and watered regularly, the sickly plant soon *thrived*.

_____17. When I asked the traffic cop for directions to the post office, he *evaluated* that it was just down the block.

_____18. Reading a funny story on the bus, Jeremy suddenly burst out laughing. The people around him were surprised by his *plea*.

_____19. My father's blood pressure is so high that he has scheduled a *random* appointment with his doctor.

_____20. The little girl taught herself the *concept* of "right" and "left" by remembering, "I **write** with my **right** hand."

_____21. The families decided it would be too *practical* to eat in an expensive restaurant.

_____22. I keep a couple of quarters in my pocket for *significant* purchases, such as a pack of gum.

_____23. The letters "ski" are a *characteristic* part of many Polish names, such as Kwilinski and Paderewski.

_____24. Because Linda is so shy, she usually *confronts* people rather than daring to face them and actually talk to them.

_____25. It's plain to see from the way Diane quarrels so often with her friends that she has lots of *tolerance* for other people's opinions.

Score   (Number correct) _____ × 4 = _____%

Enter your score above and in the vocabulary performance chart on the inside back cover of the book.

UNIT THREE: Test 3

PART A: Synonyms
In the space provided, write the letter of the choice that is most nearly the **same** in meaning as the **boldfaced** word.

_____ 1. **assume**   A) improve   B) tire   C) manage   D) take for granted

_____ 2. **characteristic**   A) typical   B) strong   C) important   D) amazing

_____ 3. **concept**   A) idea   B) goal   C) period   D) knowledge of right and wrong

_____ 4. **confront**   A) interrupt   B) take away from   C) face boldly   D) succeed

_____ 5. **conscience**   A) respect for others   B) sense of right and wrong   C) feature
          D) how often something happens

_____ 6. **cope with**   A) judge   B) remove   C) believe   D) manage

_____ 7. **counsel**   A) give advice to   B) bring together   C) send away   D) search for

_____ 8. **detect**   A) take from   B) speak for   C) stop briefly   D) discover

_____ 9. **disrupt**   A) upset   B) watch   C) tire   D) complain

_____10. **eligible**   A) important   B) chosen   C) qualified   D) amazing

_____11. **evaluate**   A) judge   B) try   C) grow   D) take back

_____12. **foresight**   A) purpose   B) care in planning   C) cure   D) attention

_____13. **frequency**   A) material   B) goal   C) word group
          D) how often something happens

_____14. **interval**   A) time in between   B) thought   C) system   D) word group

_____15. **phrase**   A) period of time   B) shape   C) group of words   D) amount

_____16. **plea**   A) absence   B) reason   C) request   D) mistake

_____17. **remote**   A) not usual   B) far away   C) believable
          D) able to be seen through

_____18. **represent**   A) speak for   B) feel anger against   C) make smaller   D) send again

_____19. **sole**   A) outer   B) best   C) large   D) only

_____20. **spectacle**   A) angry conversation   B) unusual sight   C) loud noise
          D) embarrassing accident

_____21. **substance**   A) care   B) general thought   C) material   D) knowledge

_____22. **tolerance**   A) win   B) possibility   C) confusion   D) lack of prejudice

_____23. **trait**   A) meeting   B) story   C) plan   D) feature

_____24. **transparent**   A) fake   B) amazing   C) proud   D) able to be seen through

_____25. **verdict**   A) excuse   B) judgment   C) reason   D) fright

(Continues on next page)

121

PART B: Antonyms
In the space provided, write the letter of the choice that is most nearly **opposite** in meaning to the **boldfaced** word.

____26. **agonizing**   A) careless   B) painless   C) hopeless   D) useless

____27. **approximately**   A) always   B) useful   C) exactly   D) properly

____28. **artificial**   A) perfect   B) likeable   C) suitable   D) natural

____29. **authentic**   A) demanding   B) believable   C) sharp   D) fake

____30. **complicate**   A) make easy   B) speed up   C) pass over   D) take advice

____31. **conscious**   A) unqualified   B) unusual   C) unexpected   D) unaware

____32. **consistent**   A) gentle   B) changing   C) rude   D) weak

____33. **energetic**   A) not active   B) necessary   C) lengthy   D) new

____34. **external**   A) useless   B) harmful   C) inner   D) close

____35. **harsh**   A) planned   B) nearby   C) useful   D) kind

____36. **incredible**   A) regular   B) not possible   C) easy to believe   D) disagreeable

____37. **internal**   A) real   B) deep   C) honest   D) outer

____38. **maximum**   A) lowest possible   B) legal   C) exact   D) able

____39. **practical**   A) not useful   B) not inside   C) not easy   D) not possible

____40. **prosper**   A) make easy   B) face   C) grow poor   D) help

____41. **protest**   A) put an end to   B) approve   C) give   D) grow stronger

____42. **random**   A) believable   B) not wanted   C) planned   D) pleasant

____43. **remedy**   A) thought   B) distance   C) purpose   D) disease

____44. **shallow**   A) deep   B) crowded   C) weak   D) least

____45. **significant**   A) not real   B) done on purpose   C) not important   D) not steady

____46. **strive**   A) give advice   B) put in   C) ask for   D) give up

____47. **temporary**   A) long-lasting   B) not qualified   C) weak   D) not typical

____48. **thrive**   A) know   B) argue   C) change   D) grow weak

____49. **triumph**   A) suggestion   B) patience   C) distance   D) loss

____50. **withdraw**   A) erase   B) put back   C) give up   D) forget

Score   (Number correct) _____ × 2 = _____%

Enter your score above and in the vocabulary performance chart on the inside back cover of the book.

Unit Four

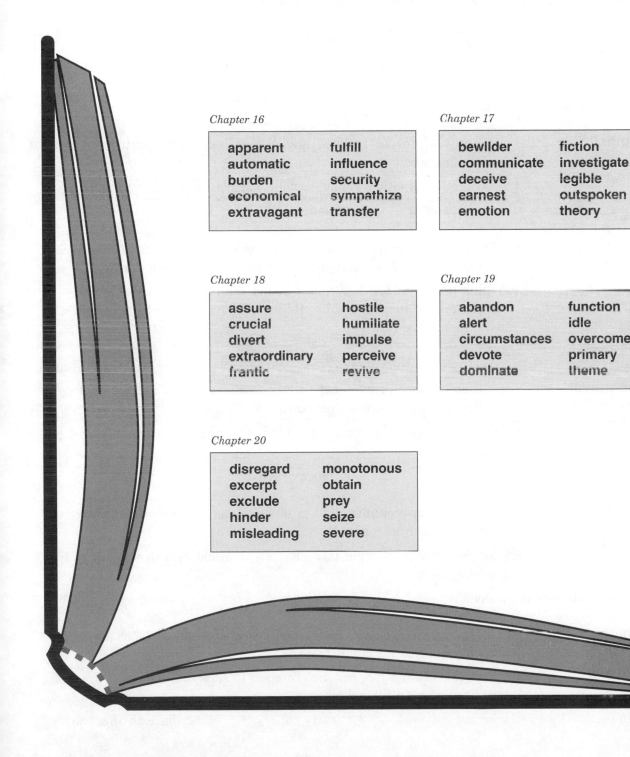

Chapter 16

apparent	fulfill
automatic	influence
burden	security
economical	sympathize
extravagant	transfer

Chapter 17

bewilder	fiction
communicate	investigate
deceive	legible
earnest	outspoken
emotion	theory

Chapter 18

assure	hostile
crucial	humiliate
divert	impulse
extraordinary	perceive
frantic	revive

Chapter 19

abandon	function
alert	idle
circumstances	overcome
devote	primary
dominate	theme

Chapter 20

disregard	monotonous
excerpt	obtain
exclude	prey
hinder	seize
misleading	severe

apparent	fulfill
automatic	influence
burden	security
economical	sympathize
extravagant	transfer

Ten Words in Context

In the space provided, write the letter of the meaning closest to that of each **boldfaced** word. Use the context of the sentences to help you figure out each word's meaning.

1 apparent
(ə-păr′ənt)
– *adjective*

- Marcie's smile made it **apparent** that she had done well on the test.
- It's **apparent** that Leon and Bess have settled their quarrel, since they are dating steadily again.

____*Apparent* means   A. helpful.   B. clear.   C. secret.

2 automatic
(ô′tə-măt′ĭk)
– *adjective*

- Our new coffeemaker is **automatic**. We set it at night, and it turns on by itself in the morning.
- Before the **automatic** washing machine, laundering clothes was not so easy.

____*Automatic* means   A. self-operating.   B. unusual.   C. low in cost.

3 burden
(bûr′dn)
– *noun*

- Although others think raising a handicapped child must be a **burden**, my neighbor says she has found joy, not hardship, in caring for her son.
- At first the lie he had told didn't bother the boy, but after a few days it became a great **burden** to him. He wished he could go back in time and undo what he had done.

____*Burden* means   A. freedom.   B. protection.   C. heavy load.

4 economical
(ĕk′ə-nŏm′ĭ-kəl)
– *adjective*

- It's usually more **economical** to buy food and soap in large packages. Smaller packages cost more per ounce.
- To decide which car is most **economical**, compare prices, gas mileage, and repair costs.

____*Economical* means   A. difficult.   B. money-saving.   C. easy to see.

5 extravagant
(ĭk-străv′ə-gənt)
– *adjective*

- I think it's **extravagant** to buy a prom dress that will be worn only once, so I borrowed one from a friend.
- Rhoda's budget is so tight that she feels it would be **extravagant** to buy herself a ten-dollar pair of earrings.

____*Extravagant* means   A. not effective.   B. obvious.   C. spending too much.

6 fulfill
(fŏŏl-fĭl′)
– *verb*

- One day, Chen hopes to **fulfill** his dream of visiting China again and renewing ties with his family there.
- Jill doesn't like her job, but she promised to stay with it at least one year, and she plans to **fulfill** that promise.

____*Fulfill* means   A. repeat.   B. carry out.   C. have an effect on.

7 influence
(ĭn′flōō-əns)
– *verb*

- My father thinks my friends **influence** me too much. He says they are the reason that I study so little and waste so much time.
- Do advertisements **influence** what you buy?

___*Influence* means   A. delay.   B. protect.   C. affect.

8 security
(sĭ-kyŏŏr′ĭ-tē)
– *noun*

- For nighttime **security**, the owner of the jewelry shop turns on a burglar alarm.
- People with homes near the river like having the **security** of flood insurance.

___*Security* means   A. hardship.   B. expense.   C. safety.

9 sympathize
(sĭm′pə-thīz′)
– *verb*

- The whole town **sympathized** with the family whose house burned down.
- To show he **sympathized** with Mrs. Jackson when her husband died, Scott sent her flowers and a card.

___*Sympathized with*
means   A. felt sorry for.   B. sent for.   C. talked to.

10 transfer
(trăns-fûr′)
– *verb*

- Before I can paint the bookcase, I have to **transfer** all the books into boxes.
- In April, the Army will **transfer** Jamal from a base in South Carolina to one in Virginia.

___*Transfer* means   A. reach.   B. move.   C. see.

Matching Words with Definitions

Following are definitions of the ten words. **Print** each word next to its definition. If you look closely at each word in context, you will be able to figure out its meaning.

1. _____ Costing or spending little; thrifty

2. _____ To move or send from one place to another

3. _____ Moving or operating by itself

4. _____ To have an effect on

5. _____ To feel or express sorrow or pity for

6. _____ To carry out; achieve; do

7. _____ A hardship; something difficult to bear

8. _____ Obvious; easy to see

9. _____ Protection; freedom from danger, fear, or worry

10. _____ Spending much more than is necessary or wise; wasteful

CAUTION: Do not go any further until you are sure the above answers are correct. Then you can use the definitions to help you in the following practices. Your goal is eventually to know the words well enough so that you don't need to check the definitions at all.

➣ *Check 1*

Using the answer line, complete each item below with the correct word from the box.

A. **apparent**	B. **automatic**	C. **burden**	D. **economical**	E. **extravagant**
F. **fulfill**	G. **influence**	H. **security**	I. **sympathize**	J. **transfer**

_____ 1. Sian's boss intends to assign her to another office. In other words, he wants to ___ her there.

_____ 2. A ___ may be a physical or a mental hardship, or both.

_____ 3. Political candidates try to ___ elections with numerous ads.

_____ 4. An ___ person enjoys spending a lot of money.

_____ 5. When we've had the same difficult experience as someone else, it's easier for us to ___ with him or her.

_____ 6. Because Kira was smiling, it was ___ that she was happy about something.

_____ 7. When you make an agreement with people, they expect you to ___ your part of the deal.

_____ 8. After people are robbed, they often feel a greater need for ___.

_____ 9. An ___ person doesn't like to waste money.

_____ 10. Do you think there will ever be a fully ___ car, one that needs no driver?

NOTE: Now check your answers to these questions by turning to page 240. Going over the answers carefully will help you prepare for the remaining practices, for which answers are not given.

➣ *Check 2*

Using the answer lines, complete each item below with **two** words from the box.

_____
_____ 1–2. "Because we are moving," Gina said, "our children will have to ___ to different schools. I can ___ with them because I went through the same experience as a child."

_____
_____ 3–4. ___ yard lights, which go on by themselves at dark, can add to the ___ of a home.

_____
_____ 5–6. Clark had to think of an ___ way to ___ his promise to give each of his twelve nieces and nephews a gift, so he baked them each a pie.

_____
_____ 7–8. From the young hiker's slowed walk, it was ___ that his large backpack had become a ___.

_____
_____ 9–10. Having a credit card has ___d Barry in a sad way. He has become so ___ that he now has a closet full of more clothes than he can wear— and a huge credit-card bill.

➤ *Word Work*

A. Write each word next to the examples that best match it.

A. **automatic**	B. **economical**	C. **extravagant**
D. **security**	E. **sympathize**	

_____ 1. Eating in fancy restaurants every night
Buying two dresses for the same party because you can't decide between them
Purchasing a sterling-silver dog collar

_____ 2. Automobile headlights that turn off when the motor stops running
A door that slides open when a person approaches it
An oven that cleans itself

_____ 3. A burglar alarm
Fire insurance
Armed guards

_____ 4. Sending a card when a friend's mother dies
Hugging a crying child
Taking a friend who is depressed out to dinner

_____ 5. Figure out the best grocery buys
Turn off lights when you leave a room
Use old envelopes for shopping lists

B. In the space provided, write the letter of the choice that most closely relates to the situation in each item

_____ 6. The outside porch light comes on at the same time every evening.

    A. extravagant   B. unfulfilled   C. automatic

_____ 7. To make up for being sick last semester, the student is taking a full load plus two extra classes.

    A. apparent   B. burden   C. transfer

_____ 8. When I saw an ad for chocolate-chip cookies, I decided to go to the kitchen and bake some.

    A. influence   B. automatic   C. burden

_____ 9. I made a New Year's resolution to lose ten pounds, and I'm sticking to it. So I'm not eating any of those chocolate-chip cookies.

    A. transfer   B. burden   C. fulfill

_____ 10. When Jen moved into the attic bedroom, she spent hours carrying her belongings up there.

    A. automatic   B. transfer   C. influence

➢ *Word Parts*

A. The suffix *-ment* often means "the result, state, act, or process of ___."

Examples: *fulfillment* — the result of fulfilling
enjoyment — the state of enjoying

On each answer line, write the word from the box that means the same as the *italicized* words.

A. **astonishment°**	B. **fulfillment**	C. **management**
D. **replacement**	E. **statement**	

_____ 1. The magician's surprising act filled us with a *state of being astonished°*.

_____ 2. The *act of replacing* of our old kitchen floor was not easy. We had to tear the old floor out before the new one could be put in.

_____ 3. It is obvious that the *process of managing* of this company is excellent. The company is very successful, and the workers are very happy.

_____ 4. For me, a small home in the country would be the *result of fulfilling* of a dream.

_____ 5. Kareem likes to study for tests with another person. He says that the *act of stating* of an idea out loud to someone else helps him remember it better.

B. The suffix *-ly* means "in a certain way."

Examples: *economical* — thrifty   *secure* — safe
economically — in a thrifty way   *securely* — in a safe way

On each answer line, write the word from the box that best completes the item.

F. **consistently°**	G. **economically**	H. **exactly**
I. **extravagantly**	J. **securely**	

_____ 6. Ralph may not be the perfect worker, but at least he is steady about one thing: he is ___ late for work each day.

_____ 7. Before leaving on vacation, make sure the doors and windows are closed ___.

_____ 8. Wanting to impress his date, Dan spent money ___ on lobster, champagne, and a hired limousine.

_____ 9. If a math answer is not ___ right, you may not get full credit for it.

_____ 10. The three families got a new lawn mower ___ by buying it together, then sharing it.

➤ *Final Check*

Read the passages carefully. Then fill in each blank with the word that best fits the context.

A. A Mismatched Couple

A. **burden**	B. **economical**	C. **extravagant**	D. **security**	E. **sympathize**

Stacy and Ken have completely different attitudes° toward money. She is (1)_____ to an extreme, always trying to get the best price on even the smallest purchase. Ken, on the other hand, is very (2)_____. He's accustomed° to spending money on anything that catches his eye. If there's a dime in his pocket, he feels that it's a (3)_____, as hard to carry around as a heavy load. He'll find something to spend it on just to be rid of it. Knowing she has money in case of accident or illness gives Stacy a feeling of (4)_____, but Ken doesn't worry about the future. Each is puzzled by the other's "strange" behavior. Stacy sees Ken as wasteful and irresponsible, and Ken calls Stacy "cheap." He can't (5)_____ with her when she's worried about an empty bank account. Since they have very little tolerance° for each other's views on money, no one was surprised when these two got divorced.

B. A Campaign to Become Class President

F. **apparent**	G. **automatic**	H. **fulfill**	I. **influence**	J. **transfer**

In her senior year, Holly wanted very much to be elected class president. But she knew that the other girl who was competing for the office was much better known and had more experience in student government. As a result, Holly began to do all she could to (6)_____ her classmates so that they would vote for her. She listened to every plea° and promised her classmates anything they asked for. "If I'm elected," she told one student, "I will see that the school puts in (7)_____ doors to make it easy to enter when our arms are full of books." To another, she said that a hot tub would be installed in the school gym. She promised a third student that he could (8)_____ to the school across town that his girlfriend attended. As the election drew near, it became (9)_____ that Holly had a good chance of winning. This scared her because she realized that she could not (10)_____ all her promises. Finally, she quit the race, saying she couldn't maintain° her grades and serve as class president, too. She felt foolish for having let her desire to win run away with her good sense.

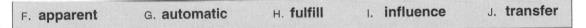

Scores   Check 2 _____%   Word Work _____%   Word Parts _____%   Final Check _____%

Enter your scores above and in the vocabulary performance chart on the inside back cover of the book.

CHAPTER
17

bewilder	fiction
communicate	investigate
deceive	legible
earnest	outspoken
emotion	theory

Ten Words in Context

In the space provided, write the letter of the meaning closest to that of each **boldfaced** word. Use the context of the sentences to help you figure out each word's meaning.

1 bewilder
(bǐ-wǐl′dər)
– *verb*

- The large new school at first **bewildered** Chung, but after a day or two, getting around was no longer confusing to him.
- My grandmother's poor health **bewildered** her doctor until he found out she wasn't taking her medicines.

___ *Bewilder* means A. to calm. B. to puzzle. C. to attract.

2 communicate
(kə-myōō′nǐ-kāt′)
– *verb*

- Alice and I rarely see each other, but we **communicate** often by sending letters and making phone calls.
- Today, many people **communicate** with each other by e-mail.

___ *Communicate* means A. to call. B. to exchange information. C. to visit.

3 deceive
(dǐ-sēv′)
– *verb*

- In order to **deceive** a buyer, a used-car seller sometimes turns back the mileage counter on the car.
- A business owner who tries to **deceive** customers should be reported to the police.

___ *Deceive* means A. to help. B. to find. C. to fool.

4 earnest
(ûr′nǐst)
– *adjective*

- I like our new babysitter because she is very **earnest**; she clearly takes her job very seriously.
- Jimmy seemed **earnest** when he promised to clean the windows by Friday, so I was surprised to see he hadn't done them.

___ *Earnest* means A. confused. B. quiet. C. serious.

5 emotion
(ǐ-mō′shən)
– *noun*

- Stan rarely shows his **emotions**. We have to guess what he is really feeling.
- Many people have trouble talking about their **emotions**, especially anger and fear.

___ *Emotion* means A. feeling. B. explanation. C. movement.

6 fiction
(fǐk′shən)
– *noun*

- One of Mark Twain's most amusing pieces of **fiction** is his story about a Connecticut man who travels back to the time of King Arthur.
- Some newspapers print obvious **fiction**, such as, "Nine-year-old girl has triplets who weigh 100 pounds more than she does!"

___ *Fiction* means A. news. B. made-up writing. C. facts.

130

7 investigate
(ĭn-vĕs′tĭ-gāt′)
– *verb*

• The FBI has been called in to **investigate** the disappearance of some important papers from a government laboratory.

• When I heard a noise downstairs at 3 a.m., I lay still in bed, too frightened to get up and **investigate** the situation.

___*Investigate* means   A. to look into.   B. to delay.   C. to exchange.

8 legible
(lĕj′ə-bəl)
– *adjective*

• My father used to make me rewrite my sloppy homework. "I can barely read this," he would say. "Make it **legible**."

• The fancy script on that new restaurant sign isn't very **legible**. Does it say "Peretti's," "Perelli's," or "Pepetti's"?

___*Legible* means   A. easy to believe.   B. easy to read.   C. easy to prove.

9 outspoken
(out spō′kən)
– *adjective*

• Being **outspoken** doesn't necessarily mean being rude. It's possible to say what you really think without insulting other people.

• The host of the radio call-in show is extremely **outspoken**. She's not afraid to disagree strongly with her callers.

___*Outspoken* means   A. angry but quiet.   B. secretly pleased.   C. open and truthful.

10 theory
(thē′ə-rē)
– *noun*

• According to the **theory** of evolution, plants and animals have developed in ways that help them do well in their environment.

• The police's **theory** was that the killer was a short man with dark hair, but the murderer turned out to be a blonde woman wearing a dark wig.

___*Theory* means   A. action.   B. explanation.   C. question.

Matching Words with Definitions

Following are definitions of the ten words. **Print** each word next to its definition. If you look closely at each word in context, you will be able to figure out its meaning.

1. _____ To exchange or give information

2. _____ To confuse; puzzle

3. _____ Serious and sincere

4. _____ A strong feeling

5. _____ An explanation based on facts; a statement believed to be true

6. _____ Clear enough to be read

7. _____ Literature consisting of imaginary stories; anything made up

8. _____ Direct and open; not shy about stating one's opinion

9. _____ To make (someone) believe something that is not true

10. _____ To explore or examine carefully in order to learn the facts

CAUTION: Do not go any further until you are sure the above answers are correct. Then you can use the definitions to help you in the following practices. Your goal is eventually to know the words well enough so that you don't need to check the definitions at all.

➤ *Check 1*

Using the answer line, complete each item below with the correct word from the box.

A. **bewilder**	B. **communicate**	C. **deceive**	D. **earnest**	E. **emotion**
F. **fiction**	G. **investigate**	H. **legible**	I. **outspoken**	J. **theory**

_____ 1. Every class is made up of a mix of ___ students, very quiet students, and students who are somewhere in between.

_____ 2. Charlotte's sweet smiles don't ___ me. I know that she really dislikes me.

_____ 3. Dolphins ___ with one another through a language of squeaks and grunts.

_____ 4. At first, the many noises, flashing lights, and whirling rides at the fair ___ed the children. They didn't know where to go first.

_____ 5. Murphy has a ___ about life. He believes that everything that can possibly go wrong, will.

_____ 6. When we go on our walks, my dog ___s every bush and tree we come across.

_____ 7. Ten years ago, I carved my initials in a tree. Recently I was surprised to see that they were still ___.

_____ 8. When Gordon begged his boss for another chance, he seemed so ___ that his employer decided to give him his job back.

_____ 9. When I want to relax, I read romances, mysteries, and other kinds of ___.

_____ 10. Which do you think is the more powerful ___, love or hate?

NOTE: Now check your answers to these questions by turning to page 240. Going over the answers carefully will help you prepare for the remaining practices, for which answers are not given.

➤ *Check 2*

Using the answer lines, complete each item below with **two** words from the box.

_____
_____ 1–2. Agatha Christie wrote wonderful works of ___ about Miss Marple, a woman who loved to ___ crimes the police could not solve.

_____
_____ 3–4. Some people believe the ___ that you can teach yourself to write well with either hand, but when I use my left hand, what I write is not ___.

_____
_____ 5–6. The lost little girl spoke no English, so the police officer's attempts to ___ with her only ___ed her more.

_____
_____ 7–8. The man claiming to have lost his wallet seemed so ___ that I believed him and gave him money, but when I saw him doing the same thing a week later, I knew he had ___d me.

_____
_____ 9–10. When her boss tried to fire her, strong ___s made my usually quiet sister quite ___. She stood up to him, told him what she thought of his leadership, and finally said, "I quit."

➢ *Word Work*

A. Write each word next to the examples that best match it.

A. **communicate**	B. **deceive**	C. **fiction**
D. **outspoken**	E. **theory**	

_____ 1. A parent who stands up and complains at a school board meeting
A newspaper editorial that says the police chief should be fired
A neighbor who calls and says, "Your grass is too high. You ought to cut it!"

_____ 2. Pretending to be collecting money for a charity and then keeping the money yourself
Faking an accident in order to collect insurance money
Saying your dog ate your homework when you really didn't do the work

_____ 3. Talking on the phone about a problem
Writing notes about a date to friends
Discussing an assignment with a teacher

_____ 4. "Goldilocks and the Three Bears"
A movie about a talking donkey
An imagined meeting between Abraham Lincoln and Oprah Winfrey

_____ 5. Maybe dinosaurs were wiped out by a meteor that hit the Earth.
The Egyptian pyramids may have been built by aliens from outer space.
Police think the person who stole the jewels may have once worked in the store.

B. In the space provided, write the letter of the choice that best completes each item.

_____ 6. An **earnest** person is likely to tell you

    A. a lie.   B. what he or she thinks you want to hear.   C. the truth.

_____ 7. If math **bewilders** you, that probably means

    A. you are having trouble with math.
    B. you find math easy to do.
    C. the math class was too full and you had to take another class instead.

_____ 8. **Emotions** are likely to be strong during

    A. a nap.   B. an elevator ride.   C. an argument.

_____ 9. A person whose job is mainly to **investigate** is a

    A. pet shop owner.   B. store detective.   C. gardener.

_____ 10. A second-grader whose writing is very **legible** can expect

    A. criticism from his or her teacher.
    B. to be asked to write smaller.
    C. praise from his or her teacher.

➤ *Synonyms and Antonyms*

A. Synonyms. Write the letter of the word or phrase that most nearly means the **same** as each boldfaced word.

____ 1. **bewilder**

    A. make certain   B. release

    C. insist   D. confuse

____ 2. **communicate**

    A. hide   B. make known

    C. remove   D. forget

____ 3. **emotion**

    A. feeling   B. energy

    C. excuse   D. movement

____ 4. **investigate**

    A. puzzle   B. write

    C. inspect   D. fool

____ 5. **theory**

    A. agreement   B. problem

    C. explanation   D. question

B. Antonyms. Write the letter of the word or phrase that most nearly means the **opposite** of each boldfaced word.

____ 6. **outspoken**

    A. modern   B. quiet

    C. graceful   D. tiny

____ 7. **deceive**

    A. stay away from   B. argue

    C. tell the truth to   D. find

____ 8. **earnest**

    A. not sincere   B. unusual

    C. not accurate   D. not perfect

____ 9. **fiction**

    A. justice   B. ability

    C. reason   D. fact

____10. **legible**

    A. not for sale   B. not lasting

    C. not on purpose   D. not readable

➤ *Final Check*

Read the passages carefully. Then fill in each blank with the word that best fits the context.

A. The Famous Detective

A. **deceive**	B. **emotion**	C. **fiction**	D. **investigate**	E. **theory**

One of the most famous characters from the world of (1)_____ is Sherlock Holmes, created by the writer Arthur Conan Doyle. Holmes first appeared in a story Doyle wrote in 1887. It was called "A Study in Scarlet." Holmes was a detective. No criminal, no matter how clever, could (2)_____ him for long. Rather than being affected by (3)_____s such as fear or hate, Holmes used his great powers of thinking to solve crimes. As he (4)_____d crimes, he noticed significant° small details that were not apparent° to others. Then it would not be long before he developed a perfect (5)_____ to explain the crime.

B. Why So Quiet?

F. **bewilder**	G. **communicate**	H. **earnest**	I. **legible**	J. **outspoken**

I still remember my first day in first grade. My first-grade teacher probably does, too. I had grown up in a very large, very noisy family. Everybody yelled, all the time. It wasn't because we were angry. There were just so many of us that we thought it was the only way to (6)_____. I didn't realize that our characteristic° loudness wasn't typical of all families. So by the time I went to school, I was, to say the least, an energetic° and (7)_____ kid. I believed that when you wanted to be heard, the right thing to do was to say what you meant and say it loudly. My teacher was a very gentle person. She talked slowly and never, ever raised her voice. I remember her writing her name on the board in large, (8)_____ letters and saying, "My name is Mrs. Henderson. Can you say 'Mrs. Henderson,' boys and girls?" My shy classmates whispered, "Mrs. Henderson." I shouted, "MRS. HENDERSON!!" at the top of my lungs. (I don't exaggerate°; I was really loud.) Throughout the day, my classmates continued to whisper, and I continued to shout. By the end of the first day, school had totally (9)_____ed me. I was so confused that I thought I had been assigned to the wrong class. I went home and begged my parents to have me placed in a class with people who "talked right." I wasn't kidding; my plea° was completely (10)_____. It took a couple of weeks for me to figure out how to fit in with my quieter classmates.

Enter your scores above and in the vocabulary performance chart on the inside back cover of the book.

CHAPTER
18

assure	hostile
crucial	humiliate
divert	impulse
extraordinary	perceive
frantic	revive

Ten Words in Context

In the space provided, write the letter of the meaning closest to that of each **boldfaced** word. Use the context of the sentences to help you figure out each word's meaning.

1 assure
(ə-shŏor′)
– *verb*

- If you leave jewelry in your hotel room, the hotel cannot **assure** you that it will be safe.
- I asked the salesclerk, "Can you **assure** me that this watch is really waterproof?"

___*Assure* means   A. to remind.   B. to agree with.   C. to promise.

2 crucial
(krōō′shəl)
– *adjective*

- The trial had to stop when a **crucial** witness suddenly disappeared.
- Protein is a **crucial** part of a healthy diet.

___*Crucial* means   A. rare.   B. necessary.   C. useless.

3 divert
(dĭ-vûrt′)
– *verb*

- Traffic had to be **diverted** around the accident for several hours.
- I tried to **divert** Mom's attention from the broken window by saying, "Look at all the windows I didn't break!"

___*Divert* means   A. to keep quiet.   B. to move away.   C. to look at.

4 extraordinary
(ĭk-strôr′dn-ĕr′ē)
– *adjective*

- The restaurant made **extraordinary** attempts to attract new customers, even giving away free meals on certain days.
- The cancer patient inspired others with the **extraordinary** courage she showed in dealing with her illness.

___*Extraordinary* means   A. unfriendly.   B. normal.   C. very unusual.

5 frantic
(frăn′tĭk)
– *adjective*

- The mother robin became **frantic** when we came near her nest, so we quietly backed away.
- Because she thought she was going to miss her plane, Cyndi was **frantic** as she raced to the ticket counter.

___*Frantic* means   A. excited and nervous.   B. warm and friendly.   C. tired and hungry.

6 hostile
(hŏs′təl)
– *adjective*

- The **hostile** crowd threw tomatoes and eggs at the speaker.
- The cat acted **hostile** toward the new kitten, snarling and spitting at it.

___*Hostile* means   A. fearful.   B. unfriendly.   C. embarrassed.

7 humiliate
(hyōō-mĭl′ē-āt′)
– *verb*

- Good teachers do not **humiliate** students for making mistakes by calling them names or holding up their work for everyone to see.
- In dreams, people often **humiliate** themselves by doing things like going outdoors without their clothing on.

___ *Humiliate* means   A. to shame.   B. to protect.   C. to misunderstand.

8 impulse
(ĭm′pŭls′)
– *noun*

- People who go food shopping when they are hungry often get an **impulse** to buy something they don't really need.
- Carmen had planned on staying home alone, but at the last minute she had an **impulse** to phone her new neighbors and invite them to come over that evening for coffee and cake.

___ *Impulse* means   A. unplanned desire.   B. view.   C. fear.

9 perceive
(pər-sēv′)
– *verb*

- I **perceive** from the wonderful smell that someone is barbecuing ribs.
- Hawks have such good eyesight that they can **perceive** a tiny mouse from hundreds of feet in the air.

___ *Perceive* means   A. to remember.   B. to include.   C. to notice.

10 revive
(rĭ-vīv′)
– *verb*

- Even if you've lost all desire to learn history, Mr. Berg, who is a wonderful teacher, can **revive** your interest in that subject.
- No matter how tired our dog is, the question "Want to go for a walk?" will **revive** him.

___ *Revive* means   A. to show.   B. to bring back to life.   C. to embarrass.

Matching Words with Definitions

Following are definitions of the ten words. **Print** each word next to its definition. If you look closely at each word in context, you will be able to figure out its meaning.

1. _____ To make (someone) sure about something; tell with certainty

2. _____ Very excited and anxious; extremely worried, panicked, or fearful

3. _____ To make ashamed; embarrass

4. _____ Extremely important

5. _____ Unfriendly; having or showing ill will

6. _____ To give new energy, spirit, or strength

7. _____ A sudden urge to do something

8. _____ Beyond the ordinary; special

9. _____ To turn aside from a course or direction; draw away attention

10. _____ To be or to become aware of through one's senses; see, hear, feel, taste, or smell

CAUTION: Do not go any further until you are sure the above answers are correct. Then you can use the definitions to help you in the following practices. Your goal is eventually to know the words well enough so that you don't need to check the definitions at all.

➤ *Check 1*

Using the answer line, complete each item below with the correct word from the box.

A. **assure**	B. **crucial**	C. **divert**	D. **extraordinary**	E. **frantic**
F. **hostile**	G. **humiliate**	H. **impulse**	I. **perceive**	J. **revive**

_____ 1. Bullies ___ other people in order to make themselves feel powerful.

_____ 2. Engineers are trying to ___ the river to the west, so that it will not flood the town when it overflows.

_____ 3. My boss ___s me that I will definitely get a raise soon.

_____ 4. The flowers in the garden were beginning to droop in the dry weather, but a heavy rain shower soon ___d them.

_____ 5. Grocery-store managers often place candy bars, combs, and other small, inexpensive items near the checkout, hoping that shoppers will have an ___ to buy them.

_____ 6. To succeed at a job interview, it is ___ that you arrive on time.

_____ 7. Because parents know their children so well, they can often ___ that the children are not feeling well just by looking at them.

_____ 8. Two of my coworkers are very ___ toward each other. They glare at each other and argue at staff meetings.

_____ 9. "I've lost my purse!" my mother cried. After a ___ ten-minute search, she realized she had left it in our car.

_____ 10. The newspaper carried a story about an ___ woman who is a terrific tennis player, even though she uses a wheelchair.

NOTE: Now check your answers to these questions by turning to page 240. Going over the answers carefully will help you prepare for the remaining practices, for which answers are not given.

➤ *Check 2*

Using the answer lines, complete each item below with **two** words from the box.

_____
_____ 1–2. When Len's boss ___d him in front of his coworkers, he felt a sudden ___ to grab the man's necktie and snip it off with scissors.

_____
_____ 3–4. Once I ___d the aroma of fried chicken, I stopped doing my homework because my attention was ___ed by the wonderful smell.

_____
_____ 5–6. The builders know it is ___ that the bathroom be finished before our visitors arrive next week, and they have ___d us the work will be done.

_____
_____ 7–8. When Sandra got the chance to work with an ___ coach—one who had coached many champions—it ___d her childhood dream of someday competing in the Olympics.

_____
_____ 9–10. The more ___ the angry, impatient bus driver became, the more ___ he made the little girl who had lost her bus ticket.

➤ *Word Work*

A. In the space provided, write the letter of the choice that best completes each item.

_____ 1. A common **hostile** comment is

    A. "Nice to meet you."   B. "Mind your own business."   C. "See you later."

_____ 2. A little child would probably become **frantic** if

    A. he couldn't find his mother in a store.
    B. someone gave him a kitten.
    C. he had just learned to ride a bicycle.

_____ 3. Something that might **divert** the attention of a person studying late at night is

    A. a textbook.   B. a dripping faucet.   C. coffee.

_____ 4. While eating pizza for dinner, Chang **perceived**

    A. the events of his day.
    B. a thought about his girlfriend.
    C. a dash of hot pepper in the sauce.

_____ 5. The company president **assured** the workers that

    A. there would be no layoffs.
    B. the company might be for sale.
    C. there might be pay cuts at the end of the year.

B. In the space provided, write the letter of the word that most closely relates to the situation in each item.

_____ 6. These beautiful paintings are the work of a nine-year-old artist with amazing talent.

    A. frantic   B. revive   C. extraordinary

_____ 7. "I've got an idea!" said Nelson, jumping up from his desk. "Let's take a break and all go get some ice cream."

    A. hostile   B. perceive   C. impulse

_____ 8. After talking for a while to the prettiest girl at the dance, the boy glanced in a mirror and realized he had a large piece of spinach stuck in his teeth.

    A. assure   B. crucial   C. humiliate

_____ 9. The first two years of life greatly affect the mental and emotional development of a child.

    A. crucial   B. perceive   C. hostile

_____10. Aisha came home from work feeling tired, but a short nap made her refreshed and energetic.

    A. perceive   B. revive   C. extraordinary

➤ *Word Parts*

A. The suffix *-ity* means "the quality or state of being ___."

Examples: *brutal* — cruel   *rare* — unusual
             brutality — the quality of being cruel   *rarity* — the state of being unusual

On each answer line, write the word from the box that best completes the item.

| A. **brutality**° | B. **generosity** | C. **hostility** |
| D. **rarity** | E. **security**° | |

_____ 1. Mrs. Lee likes the ___ of living in an apartment that's on the tenth floor, where no thieves can enter through the windows.

_____ 2. Everyone was amazed by the ___ of the man who won a huge lottery prize and then gave it all away to charity.

_____ 3. There are laws to protect animals from ___; it is against the law to beat or otherwise harm them.

_____ 4. Ever since Margo asked Rose's boyfriend out on a date, there has been ___ between the two women.

_____ 5. There are only a few white tigers known to exist. Because of their ___, thousands of people go to see them in zoos.

B. The suffixes *-able* and *-ible* can mean "able to be ___."

Examples: *perceive* — to notice through one's senses
          perceptible — able to be noticed through use of the senses

On each answer line, write the word from the box that best completes the item.

| F. **manageable** | G. **perceptible** | H. **readable** |
| I. **transferable** | J. **usable** | |

_____ 6. Nadia's handwriting is so bad that it is usually not even ___.

_____ 7. If you decide to leave one college and go to another one, you may lose some credits. Some of your credits may not be ___.

_____ 8. I have tons of homework to do this weekend, but it is ___. If I use my time well, I can handle it.

_____ 9. The odor of fried fish is ___ in the house even hours after we've had dinner.

_____ 10. These bananas are too ripe, but they are still ___ for banana bread. You could also freeze them and utilize° them later in fruit drinks.

➤ *Final Check*

Read the passages carefully. Then fill in each blank with the word that best fits the context.

A. Fear of Speaking

A. **divert**	B. **frantic**	C. **hostile**	D. **humiliate**	E. **impulse**

Some people are afraid of spiders. Others fear heights. But for many people, the scariest thing of all is having to speak in front of a group of strangers. Even people who are ordinarily quite outspoken° can become (1)_____ with fear at the idea of facing an audience. They often imagine that the audience will be (2)_____, even when it is actually friendly. Because they are so sure that they will (3)_____ themselves, they usually manage to do just that. They are so awkward° when they walk to the front of the room that they almost trip over their own feet. When they begin to speak, their hands flutter, causing the papers they are holding to shake loudly. This annoying noise (4)_____s the attention of the audience from what the speakers are trying to say. Embarrassed by their poor performance, the unfortunate speakers have to fight the (5)_____ to crawl under a chair and hide. One of the best things people like this can do for themselves is take a course in public speaking. Even if they never learn to love public speaking, they can learn to face an audience without feeling frightened.

B. Do You Believe in Magic?

F. **assure**	G. **crucial**	H. **extraordinary**	I. **perceive**	J. **revive**

Have you ever wondered how magic tricks work? Magicians work hard to make their tricks look like authentic° magic. But no other magician has done what Horace Goldin did to make a trick look real. Goldin performed the well-known act in which a volunteer from the crowd is placed in a box, cut in half, and then reconnected right in front of the audience. But Goldin's trick was (6)_____ because of a special added twist. After the victim was sawed in half and reconnected, the audience was (7)_____d that the volunteer was fine and could return to his seat. When the man stood up, however, the top half of his body seemed to separate and fall to the floor. Meanwhile, the bottom half also fell, but then it (8)_____d, got up, and ran off the stage! The trick totally bewildered° the audience.

How did Goldin do it? The secret was the volunteer, a close friend of Goldin's. The volunteer had a twin brother who had no legs. What the audience (9)_____d as the volunteer's upper half was really the legless twin. The separate walking legs were just a very short person hidden inside full-length pants. In 1921, however, the legless twin brother demanded a higher salary. When Goldin refused to pay, the twin quit the act. With a (10)_____ part of the act gone, Goldin had to stop performing the trick.

Scores	Check 2 _____%	Word Work _____%	Word Parts _____%	Final Check _____%

Enter your scores above and in the vocabulary performance chart on the inside back cover of the book.

CHAPTER 19

abandon	function
alert	idle
circumstances	overcome
devote	primary
dominate	theme

Ten Words in Context

In the space provided, write the letter of the meaning closest to that of each **boldfaced** word. Use the context of the sentences to help you figure out each word's meaning.

1 abandon
(ə-băn′dən)
– *verb*

- When it got dark out, the players had to **abandon** their search for the lost softball.
- Because they ran out of money, the scientists had to **abandon** their research project.

___*Abandon* means   A. to begin.   B. to sell.   C. to quit.

2 alert
(ə-lûrt′)
– *adjective*

- If you are riding a bicycle on a busy city street, you need to be **alert** at all times.
- Many people need a cup of coffee in the morning to make them feel really **alert**.

___*Alert* means   A. bad-tempered.   B. well dressed.   C. fully awake.

3 circumstances
(sûr′kəm-stăns′əz)
– *noun*

- My sister and brother-in-law had a big argument about something yesterday, but I do not know the exact **circumstances**.
- Here are the main **circumstances** of the robbery: A man wearing a Santa Claus mask took some money from a toy store.

___*Circumstances* means   A. facts.   B. answers.   C. people.

4 devote
(dĭ-vōt′)
– *verb*

- The kids **devoted** the entire evening to playing video games.
- Professor Morales **devoted** her life to the study of ancient Egypt.

___*Devote* means   A. to look at.   B. to give attention to.   C. to win over.

5 dominate
(dŏm′ə-nāt′)
– *verb*

- McDonald's and Burger King seem to **dominate** the country's burger market.
- My brother likes to dream about a time when his favorite team will be so good that it will **dominate** football.

___*Dominate* means   A. to take pity on.   B. to be a leader in.   C. to lose interest in.

6 function
(fŭngk′shən)
– *noun*

- A waiter's **function** is to take the diners' orders and then to bring them their food.
- What is the **function** of that red button on the front of the VCR?

___*Function* means   A. purpose.   B. subject.   C. length of time.

7 idle
(īd′l)
– *adjective*

- After being at home for a week with the flu, I was sick of being **idle**, and I was happy to get back to work.
- When the boss is out of town, many of the workers in this store are **idle** much of the time.

____ *Idle* means   A. not busy.   B. outside.   C. in a group.

8 overcome
(ō′vər-kŭm′)
– *verb*

- My brother had to **overcome** a learning disability to become a successful student.
- With the help of swimming lessons, I **overcame** my fear of water.

____ *Overcome* means   A. to know.   B. to write about.   C. to beat.

9 primary
(prī′mĕr′ē)
– *adjective*

- My sister's **primary** interest in life seems to be playing basketball. She practices day and night.
- The **primary** reason for the family reunion is to celebrate Grandma's ninetieth birthday.

____ *Primary* means   A. easiest.   B. forgotten.   C. main.

10 theme
(thēm)
  noun

- The writing assignment is a five-hundred-word paper on the **theme** "a surprising event."
- *Romeo and Juliet* and *West Side Story* share the same **theme**: young lovers separated by the hatred of others.

____ *Theme* means   A. answer.   B. rule.   C. idea.

Matching Words with Definitions

Following are definitions of the ten words. **Print** each word next to its definition. If you look closely at each word in context, you will be able to figure out its meaning.

1. _____   Most important; major

2. _____   To win in a struggle over; defeat

3. _____   To stop trying to continue; discontinue; quit; let go of

4. _____   To give one's time or attention completely to something or someone

5. _____   The expected activity of a person or thing; purpose; role

6. _____   Wide-awake and watchful; highly aware

7. _____   Not doing anything; inactive

8. _____   To have a leading place or position in; be at the head of

9. _____   Condition or facts of a particular situation or event

10. _____   The main subject; the topic around which something is organized

CAUTION: Do not go any further until you are sure the above answers are correct. Then you can use the definitions to help you in the following practices. Your goal is eventually to know the words well enough so that you don't need to check the definitions at all.

➤ *Check 1*

Using the answer line, complete each item below with the correct word from the box.

A. **abandon**	B. **alert**	C. **circumstances**	D. **devote**	E. **dominate**
F. **function**	G. **idle**	H. **overcome**	I. **primary**	J. **theme**

_____ 1. An ___ person is wide-awake and very much aware of his or her surroundings.

_____ 2. It is clear that the ___ reason my aunt's boyfriend likes her is her money.

_____ 3. When the boss is just staring out the window, she may look ___, but she is really trying to figure out a problem.

_____ 4. Dances often have a special ___, such as "Winter Wonderland."

_____ 5. Before Cara can visit her grandparents in Italy, she needs to ___ her fear of flying in an airplane.

_____ 6. When a friend called to ask if I wanted to go to the movies, I quickly ___ed my ironing and got ready to go out.

_____ 7. The young skater ___s five hours each day to practicing.

_____ 8. At first I thought Jorge was unfriendly, but when I learned the ___ of his life—he is a single parent who is also caring for his elderly father—I understood that he doesn't have much time to chat.

_____ 9. A pen and a pencil have the same ___.

_____ 10. Coca Cola and Pepsi ___ the cola market.

NOTE: Now check your answers to these questions by turning to page 240. Going over the answers carefully will help you prepare for the remaining practices, for which answers are not given.

➤ *Check 2*

Using the answer lines, complete each item below with **two** words from the box.

_____
_____ 1–2. During the Depression of the 1930s, ___ were so bad that many young people had to ___ their education and go to work full-time.

_____
_____ 3–4. Some bosses get angry when they see workers taking a long break. "Your ___ is to get work done," they snap, "not to sit around ___!"

_____
_____ 5–6. "You'll have to read carefully to find the ___ of this story," our teacher said. Then he assured° us, "But if you are ___ and pay attention to every clue, I think you can figure out what the author is actually writing about."

_____
_____ 7–8. Some women's ___ interest is their careers, and some ___ themselves entirely to their families; others manage to do both.

_____
_____ 9–10. There are many true stories of very successful people who have ___ serious physical problems and gone on to ___ a sport.

➤ *Word Work*

A. In the space provided, write the letter of the choice that best completes each item.

_____ 1. Today at the store, the other salespeople and I were **idle** most of the day because
  A. there were so many customers to take care of.
  B. there were very few customers.
  C. we didn't have time for a lunch break.

_____ 2. If someone says that Mindy always tries to **dominate** the conversation, you can guess that Mindy
  A. doesn't let anyone else speak much.   B. is very funny.
  C. is too shy to speak up.

_____ 3. Your **primary** goal in life is
  A. something that doesn't matter much to you.
  B. the goal you would say is second or third in importance.
  C. your most important goal.

_____ 4. A student might **abandon** her homework one night if she
  A. really needed a good grade.
  B. had a friend who wanted to study with her.
  C. suddenly felt sick.

_____ 5. "Look **alert**!" my father sometimes said to us. He meant
  A. Quiet down and go to sleep this minute!   B. Pay attention!
  C. Comb your hair!

B. Write each word next to the examples that best match it.

A. **circumstances**	B. **devote**	C. **function**
D. **overcome**	E. **theme**	

_____ 6. Wheelchair users compete in tennis and basketball.
  Someone gets over a stutter to become a fine public speaker.
  An alcoholic stays sober for many years.

_____ 7. People spend many hours with and for their children.
  People put a lot of time and energy into their jobs.
  People contribute much effort to the cause of civil rights.

_____ 8. Cheating as the topic of a student paper
  A book about how to survive a divorce
  A circus cake, circus decorations, and a clown at a kid's birthday party

_____ 9. The details of Anna's financial situation
  Living conditions in Betsy's house
  The realities of life in Cory's neighborhood

_____ 10. Of a bathroom scale: to measure people's weight
  Of the red light on the dashboard: to let you know the oil is low
  Of a traffic police officer: to control traffic

➤ *Synonyms and Antonyms*

A. Synonyms. Write the letter of the word or phrase that most nearly means the **same** as each boldfaced word.

_____ 1. **circumstances**

    A. conditions   B. jobs

    C. activities   D. abilities

_____ 2. **dominate**

    A. lead   B. follow

    C. be active   D. leave

_____ 3. **devote**

    A. get rid of   B. win over

    C. hide from   D. give attention to

_____ 4. **function**

    A. subject   B. fact

    C. purpose   D. rule

_____ 5. **theme**

    A. fact   B. safety

    C. use   D. subject

B. Antonyms. Write the letter of the word or phrase that most nearly means the **opposite** of each boldfaced word.

_____ 6. **abandon**

    A. leave   B. continue with

    C. lose   D. work badly

_____ 7. **alert**

    A. sleepy   B. curious

    C. complete   D. late

_____ 8. **idle**

    A. new   B. stiff

    C. active   D. grateful

_____ 9. **overcome**

    A. win   B. follow

    C. continue   D. give in to

_____ 10. **primary**

    A. least expensive   B. least important

    C. not enough   D. not prepared

➤ *Final Check*

Read the passages carefully. Then fill in each blank with the word that best fits the context.

A. The Miracle Runner

| A. **devote** | B. **dominate** | C. **idle** | D. **primary** | E. **overcome** |

Glenn Cunningham was one of the most famous and extraordinary° athletes of the 1930s. To succeed, he had to (1)_____ difficulties that might have stopped anyone else. When Glenn was eight years old, he and his older brother, Floyd, were trapped in a burning building. Floyd was killed, and Glenn was badly burned. The fire had eaten deep into his legs, and the toes of one foot were gone. In fact, doctors advised° his parents to have Glenn's legs taken off. Glenn lay in bed for months, his legs thin as sticks. He hated being (2)_____, so he struggled to learn to stand and then to take a few steps. Then he began to run. At first, his (3)_____ goal in running was just to get rid of his limp. Then he discovered that he was a very good runner.

At age 13, Glenn entered a mile race at a local fair and won easily. From then on, he (4)_____d himself to running—and to winning. Nothing diverted° him from his goal. In high school, then in college, and later when he was a member of the United States Olympic team, he (5)_____d his sport. He set a world-record time for running the mile: 4 minutes, 4.4 seconds. And this was someone who had been told he would never walk again!

B. One of Those Days

| F. **abandon** | G. **alert** | H. **circumstances** | I. **function** | J. **theme** |

My poor brother! Last Friday, he had one of those days whose (6)_____ seemed to be "things that go wrong." He is taking some college classes, and his class began at 8 a.m. But his alarm clock did not perform its (7)_____; it didn't make a sound. When he finally woke up, he had no time to eat. But because he was sleepy, he made a cup of coffee to help him feel more (8)_____. When he poured milk into the coffee, though, he found that the milk was sour. Yuck! So he (9)_____ed his effort to have a cup of coffee, grabbed his car keys, and ran out. A minute later he remembered that his car was in the shop for repairs. The last I saw of him, he was racing to catch the bus.

Later, he told me the rest of the story. Just as he got to the bus stop, the bus drove off. By then he was so frantic° that he could hardly think. Desperate° to get to school, he decided to continue on foot, so he began running again. Then along came a car that hit a deep puddle and splashed him with mud from head to foot.

At school, he told his instructor the (10)_____ that had made him late, muddy, and out of breath. Looking annoyed that he had disrupted° the class, she told him to hand in his assignment. At that point, he discovered he had brought the wrong textbook and notebook. I think the next time my brother oversleeps, he should just stay in bed!

| *Scores* | Check 2 _____% | Word Work _____% | Synonyms and Antonyms _____% | Final Check _____% |

disregard	monotonous
excerpt	obtain
exclude	prey
hinder	seize
misleading	severe

Ten Words in Context

In the space provided, write the letter of the meaning closest to that of each **boldfaced** word. Use the context of the sentences to help you figure out each word's meaning.

1 disregard
(dĭs′rĭ-gärd′)
– *verb*

- I suggested that Patty put some of her money in a savings account, but she **disregarded** my idea and spent it all.
- The drive with Luis was frightening. Even though the road was icy, he **disregarded** the speed limit and drove seventy miles an hour.

___*Disregard* means   A. to follow.   B. to ignore.   C. to get in the way of.

2 excerpt
(ĕk′sûrpt′)
– *noun*

- The *New York Times* printed all of the President's speech, but most newspapers printed only brief **excerpts** from it.
- Previews advertise films by showing several **excerpts**, short scenes that will make people want to come see the whole movie.

___*Excerpt* means   A. part.   B. price.   C. speech.

3 exclude
(ĭk-sklo͞od′)
– *verb*

- When you preserve pickles, you must be sure to **exclude** air from the jars. Otherwise, the pickles will spoil.
- The little boy ran crying to his teacher after other children **excluded** him from their game.

___*Exclude* means   A. to watch.   B. to invite.   C. to keep out.

4 hinder
(hĭn′dər)
– *verb*

- Not having computer skills **hindered** Jane in her search for an office job.
- Bad weather **hindered** the climbers on their hike up the mountain.

___*Hinder* means   A. to get in the way of.   B. to cheer up.   C. to find.

5 misleading
(mĭs-lē′dĭng)
– *adjective*

- The fact that the two close friends happen to have the same last name is **misleading**. Many people think they are really sisters.
- My cousin may appear rich, but his fancy car and nice clothes are **misleading**. In reality, he owes thousands of dollars on his credit card.

___*Misleading* means   A. hard to find.   B. recent.   C. giving the wrong idea.

6 monotonous
(mə-nŏt′n-əs)
– *adjective*

- The child in the supermarket kept up a **monotonous** request: "I want some candy. I want some candy. I want some candy."
- My days had become **monotonous**. I got up, went to school, came home, slept, then did it all over again.

___*Monotonous* means   A. dull.   B. pleasant.   C. messy.

7 obtain
(əb-tān′)
– *verb*

- After completing the driver's education class, Maria **obtained** a driver's license.
- The soldier **obtained** a three-day pass in order to attend his sister's wedding.

____ *Obtain* means   A. to grab.   B. to get.   C. to give away.

8 prey
(prā)
– *noun*

- Because a cat's **prey** includes mice, farmers like to keep cats in their barns.
- Movie stars are the **prey** of thoughtless photographers who will do anything to get a photo.

____ *Prey* means   A. those that are hunted.   B. part of a whole.   C. sickness.

9 seize
(sēz)
– *verb*

- The woman screamed when a thief **seized** her pocketbook.
- Before anyone could stop him, the baby **seized** the cat's tail and pulled.

____ *Seize* means   A. to laugh at.   B. to grab.   C. to know.

10 severe
(sə-vîr′)
– *adjective*

- A **severe** storm hit our area, causing great damage and several deaths.
- Patients with the most **severe** illnesses are kept in a separate part of the hospital, where they receive special care.

____ *Severe* means   A. fair.   B. dangcrous.   C. boring.

Matching Words with Definitions

Following are definitions of the ten words. **Print** each word next to its definition. If you look closely at each word in context, you will be able to figure out its meaning.

1. _____   A creature or creatures that are hunted by another animal; the victim or victims of an attack

2. _____   A part of a whole work (such as a book, speech, or film)

3. _____   To pay no attention to

4. _____   To refuse to allow in; not include

5. _____   To get something through planning or effort

6. _____   Leading to a mistake in thought or action

7. _____   Boring because of lack of change or differences; repetitious; always the same

8. _____   Causing great physical or mental suffering; very serious

9. _____   To take hold of suddenly or with force

10. _____   To stop or slow down (someone or something); block; interfere with

CAUTION: Do not go any further until you are sure the above answers are correct. Then you can use the definitions to help you in the following practices. Your goal is eventually to know the words well enough so that you don't need to check the definitions at all.

➤ *Check 1*

Using the answer line, complete each item below with the correct word from the box.

A. **disregard**	B. **excerpt**	C. **exclude**	D. **hinder**	E. **misleading**
F. **monotonous**	G. **obtain**	H. **prey**	I. **seize**	J. **severe**

_____ 1. Cynthia's bright smile is ___; actually, she is feeling quite angry.

_____ 2. The robbers' usual ___ were newlyweds, whose houses might contain expensive wedding gifts.

_____ 3. My aunt is a vegetarian and ___s all meat from her house.

_____ 4. A huge snowstorm ___ed Thanksgiving travelers.

_____ 5. Although the car wasn't damaged much in the crash, the driver had ___ injuries.

_____ 6. No matter how much you like your favorite food, having it at every meal would soon become ___.

_____ 7. Members of the Environmental Club went door-to-door to ___ signatures for their request to set up a recycling center in town.

_____ 8. There are a number of "Best of *Saturday Night Live*" videos. They contain funny ___s from the long-running comedy show.

_____ 9. When she realized her train would leave in just an hour, Rita ___d her suitcase from the shelf and quickly began stuffing clothes into it.

_____ 10. Phil lost his money when he ___ed the "Out of Order" sign and put two quarters in the jukebox.

NOTE: Now check your answers to these questions by turning to page 240. Going over the answers carefully will help you prepare for the remaining practices, for which answers are not given.

➤ *Check 2*

Using the answer lines, complete each item below with **two** words from the box.

_____
_____ 1–2. It is striking to see a hawk drop out of the sky and ___ a field mouse, then fly away with its ___ in its claws.

_____
_____ 3–4. When my uncle had a ___ illness, the doctor ___ed everyone from his hospital room except my aunt.

_____
_____ 5–6. The TV ads for the movie were ___. They used an ___ from the film that was funny, even though the movie was not a comedy at all.

_____
_____ 7–8. Yolanda wanted to ___ tickets by phone for a very special concert, but the large volume of callers ___ed her from placing the order.

_____
_____ 9–10. Because Wendy is so shy, she ___s invitations to go out. As a result, she stays home night after night and leads a very ___ life.

➤ *Word Work*

A. In the space provided, write the letter of the choice that best completes each item.

_____ 1. If someone **seizes** a book from you, then probably
    A. you gave that person the book.
    B. the person took the book without permission.
    C. the person bought the book from you.

_____ 2. One way to **hinder** a friend who is housecleaning is to
    A. hide the vacuum cleaner.
    B. hire a cleaning company.
    C. do the dusting for him or her.

_____ 3. A job that is **monotonous** will involve
    A. danger.   B. no boss.   C. the same duties day after day.

_____ 4. An animal goes looking for **prey** when the animal is feeling
    A. sleepy.   B. hungry.   C. playful.

_____ 5. A person who **disregards** a "No Smoking" sign
    A. will wait and smoke somewhere else.
    B. will put the sign in his or her pocket and leave.
    C. will smoke in spite of the sign.

B. Write each word next to the examples that best match it.

A. **excerpt**	B. **exclude**	C. **misleading**
D. **obtain**	E. **severe**	

_____ 6. An ad for a broken-down old car that says, "Classic antique; needs just a little work"
A store window sign that says "Reductions up to 80 percent!" when only several items are reduced 80 percent
A letter that says in big type, "You have won the grand prize!" and in tiny type, "if you have the winning number"

_____ 7. A chapter from a novel
A scene from a movie
A paragraph from a short story

_____ 8. Earning a high-school diploma
Getting a job
Getting a license to drive a school bus

_____ 9. A hailstorm that breaks car windows and destroys crops
A fever of 104 degrees
A loss of electrical power that lasts for three days

_____ 10. A diet that contains no salt
A club that does not allow everyone to join
A bar that does not let underage people in

➤ *Analogies*

Each item below starts with a pair of words in CAPITAL LETTERS. For each item, figure out the relationship between these two words. Then decide which of the choices (A, B, C, or D) expresses a similar relationship. Write the letter of your choice on the answer line. (All the repeated words in these items are from this unit.)

_____ 1. MONOTONOUS : EXCITING ::

    A. healthy : strong   B. film : camera
    C. five : fifteen   D. hinder : help

_____ 2. PREY : VICTIM ::

    A. artist : painting   B. baby : infant
    C. security° : lock   D. doctor : patient

_____ 3. SEVERE : MILD ::

    A. painful : pleasant   B. angry : frowning
    C. harmful : dangerous   D. loud : noisy

_____ 4. COMMUNICATE° : TELEPHONE ::

    A. fiction° : book   B. divert° : attention
    C. sweep : broom   D. screwdriver : nail

_____ 5. EXTRAORDINARY° : COMMON ::

    A. assure° : promise   B. chew : gum
    C. mask : face   D. hostile° : friendly

_____ 6. DISREGARD : IGNORE ::

    A. recall : remember   B. important : silly
    C. protect : reveal   D. sing : choir

_____ 7. ECONOMICAL° : EXTRAVAGANT° ::

    A. country : map   B. earnest° : sincere
    C. pitch : ball   D. calm : worried

_____ 8. PRETTY : UGLY ::

    A. friendly : nice   B. frantic° : calm
    C. important : crucial°   D. difficult : burden°

_____ 9. SEIZE : TAKE ::

    A. exclude : include   B. humiliate° : embarrass
    C. pull : push   D. shout : whisper

_____ 10. PERCEIVE° : SENSES ::

    A. lazy : idle°   B. song : music
    C. write : letter   D. run : legs

➤ *Final Check*

Read the passages carefully. Then fill in each blank with the word that best fits the context.

A. The All-Too-Common Cold

A. **excerpt**	B. **exclude**	C. **hinder**	D. **misleading**	E. **severe**

Your throat feels a little scratchy. Your nose is a little stuffy. And then—"Ah-CHOO!" Yes, it's certain; you have a cold. It's no wonder we call it the "common" cold, for almost no one is (1)_____d from experiencing this pesky disease. The average child catches a cold six to eight times a year; the average adult, two to four times a year.

What causes the common cold? First, let's talk about what *doesn't* cause it. It's true that people catch colds more often in the winter, but it's (2)_____ to think that cold weather *causes* colds. It doesn't. This (3)_____ from a website about the common cold explains the real connection: "More people catch colds when the weather is cold than when it is warm outside because they tend to be inside more often and longer . . . in closer, prolonged contact with other people who have colds." In addition, the viruses that cause colds thrive° in dry conditions, such as heated buildings, where the air is typically very dry.

There are some things you can do to (4)_____ the spread of the common cold. Wash your hands frequently with soap. Avoid being close to people who have colds. When you are around infected people, avoid touching your eyes, nose, or mouth, so you don't introduce the virus into your own body.

Most colds are mild and go away on their own. If a cold is (5)_____, however, it can lead to other complications. If you develop a high fever, sinus pain, or a cough that won't go away, see a doctor. Maybe your "common cold" has turned into something less common.

B. A Criminal with a Tail

F. **disregard**	G. **monotonous**	H. **obtain**	I. **prey**	J. **seize**

One of the best known, most extraordinary° criminals ever sentenced to Pennsylvania's Graterford Prison was not a thief, a murderer, or a cheat. In fact, he was not even human. Prisoner #C2559, also known as Pep, was a dog who was (6)_____d by police in 1924 and forced to spend the rest of his days behind bars. Pep got into trouble by attacking his neighbor's cat one hot summer afternoon. Unfortunately for Pep, his furry (7)_____ happened to belong to Gifford Pinchot, the governor of Pennsylvania. The angry governor (8)_____ed the fact that Pep was a dog and ordered an immediate trial. Without the ability to speak or (9)_____ a lawyer for himself, Pep was sent to jail for life.

In prison, however, Pep was treated more kindly. His fellow prisoners were very fond of him. Even though he had to live in a cell, Pep was allowed to transfer° from one cell to another whenever he wanted. His furry face and wagging tail were a welcome change in the otherwise (10)_____ world of the prison, where each day seemed like the one before it. When he died six years later, Pep was the most popular inmate in the entire prison.

Scores	Check 2 _____%	Word Work _____%	Analogies _____%	Final Check _____%

Enter your scores above and in the vocabulary performance chart on the inside back cover of the book.

UNIT FOUR: Review

The box at the right lists twenty-five words from Unit Four. Using the clues at the bottom of the page, fill in these words to complete the puzzle that follows.

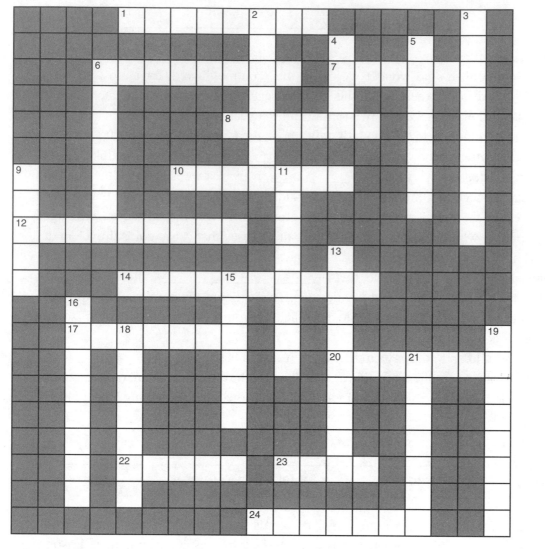

abandon
alert
apparent
automatic
bewilder
crucial
deceive
divert
dominate
emotion
exclude
fulfill
function
hinder
hostile
humiliate
idle
impulse
influence
legible
monotonous
prey
security
seize
theory

ACROSS

1. Obvious; easy to see
6. The expected activity of a person or thing; purpose
7. To turn aside from a course or direction
8. To stop or slow down; block
10. To discontinue; quit
12. To have an effect on
14. Boring because of lack of change or differences
17. To refuse to allow in; not include
20. Clear enough to be read
22. Wide-awake and watchful
23. A creature or creatures that are hunted by another animal
24. Unfriendly; having or showing ill will

DOWN

2. A strong feeling
3. Moving or operating by itself
4. Not doing anything; inactive
5. To make (someone) believe something that is not true
6. To carry out; achieve; do
9. To take hold of suddenly or with force
11. To have a leading place or position in; be at the head of
13. To make ashamed; embarrass
15. A statement that explains events or facts
16. Protection; freedom from danger, fear, or worry
18. Extremely important
19. To confuse; puzzle
21. A sudden urge to do something

154

UNIT FOUR: Test 1

PART A
Choose the word that best completes each item and write it in the space provided.

_____ 1. It's not surprising that Lisa does well on the debate team. She is a naturally ___ person, with strong opinions on many issues.

    A. primary   B. legible   C. alert   D. outspoken

_____ 2. In my dream, my family had suddenly started speaking a foreign language, which I didn't understand at all. Naturally, I was ___.

    A. bewildered   B. obtained   C. communicated   D. revived

_____ 3. Letters are still my favorite way to ___ with faraway friends and family.

    A. fulfill   B. seize   C. communicate   D. humiliate

_____ 4. Mel kept his wife from knowing he had lost his job. He ___ her by leaving the house each morning as if he were going to work.

    A. alerted   B. fulfilled   C. devoted   D. deceived

_____ 5. To show how ___ he was about wanting the job, Ira offered to work for no pay for a week.

    A. automatic   B. primary   C. hostile   D. earnest

_____ 6. A raised voice can mean one of several ___: anger, excitement, happiness, or surprise.

    A. emotions   B. preys   C. burdens   D. fictions

_____ 7. It is hard for a right-handed person to write a ___ message using his or her left hand.

    A. severe   B. frantic   C. legible   D. primary

_____ 8. Not satisfied with the way the local police were handling the murder case, the victim's family hired a detective to ___ it.

    A. revive   B. influence   C. investigate   D. exclude

_____ 9. When my daughter said, "There is a monster under my bed," her story was not pure ___: there was a large spider hiding there.

    A. fiction   B. burden   C. function   D. excerpt

_____ 10. I used to believe that all dog lovers were nice people. But Doreen proved that my ___ was wrong. She is very nice to dogs, but nasty to human beings.

    A. prey   B. theme   C. function   D. theory

_____ 11. To increase her feeling of ___ when she walks home from the bus stop at night, Elena learned karate.

    A. security   B. circumstances   C. burden   D. impulse

(Continues on next page)

_____ 12. It's ___ that your shoes are muddy—you're leaving dirty footprints on the carpet.

      A. extravagant   B. hostile   C. apparent   D. crucial

_____ 13. Although many of our neighbors have gardens, Mr. Soo's is really ___. He grows thirty-pound watermelons, tomatoes as big as softballs, and flowers as beautiful as anything in a flower shop.

      A. hostile   B. extraordinary   C. misleading   D. monotonous

PART B

Write **C** if the italicized word is used **correctly**. Write **I** if the word is used **incorrectly**.

_____ 14. Because my sister skipped assignments and classes, it's hard for me to *sympathize* with her disappointment over failing algebra.

_____ 15. Mario's boss *fulfilled* his request for a day off, saying, "No, you've had too much time off already."

_____ 16. Someday I'd like to replace my old-fashioned camera with a new *automatic* one that does everything by itself, even advancing the film.

_____ 17. Fay is so *extravagant* that she purposely finds fault with waiters so that she can refuse to leave them a tip.

_____ 18. Some parents worry that Barbie dolls, with their impossibly long legs and tiny waists, can *influence* little girls, making them feel bad about their own bodies.

_____ 19. Dan is worried about his math test because he knows it is *crucial* to his grade for the course.

_____ 20. It is more *economical* to buy a six-pack of sodas for $1.99 than to buy six single sodas at 50 cents each.

_____ 21. Since he was a little boy, Jon has *devoted* himself to becoming a pilot. He reads constantly about airplanes and flying, and he saves all his money for flying lessons.

_____ 22. I feel so tired that instead of getting up this morning, I would love just to *transfer* in bed.

_____ 23. Having our grandfather live with us is not a *burden*. He is easy to live with, and he is also very helpful around the house.

_____ 24. I was really excited when my parents *humiliated* me with a plane ticket to visit my sister in England.

_____ 25. As Dan studied for his test, his family tried to *divert* his attention by turning off the TV and keeping the house quiet and peaceful.

    Score   (Number correct) _____ × 4 = _____ %

UNIT FOUR: Test 2

PART A

On the answer line, write the word from the box that completes each item below. Use each word once.

A. **abandon**	B. **circumstances**	C. **disregard**	D. **function**	E. **hinder**
F. **hostile**	G. **misleading**	H. **monotonous**	I. **perceive**	J. **prey**
K. **revive**	L. **seize**	M. **severe**		

_____ 1. It is the ___ of advertising to persuade you that you will be happier and better off if only you will buy a certain product.

_____ 2. When Della's voice teacher said she had no talent, Della didn't ___ her efforts to become a singer; instead, she got a new teacher.

_____ 3. When children get chicken pox, the disease is just a minor problem, but for adults, chicken pox can be a ___ illness.

_____ 4. Paula's parents live in unusual ___; although they have been divorced for years, they continue to live in separate parts of the same house.

_____ 5. Our Morrisville address is ___. We actually live much closer to the town of Hendrix.

_____ 6. I prefer a job that takes a lot of effort to one that is easy but ___, with little or no change from hour to hour and day to day.

_____ 7. Foolishly, Randy ___ed the fact that he is allergic to seafood, ate a lobster, and ended up in the hospital.

_____ 8. Before I could take a bite of my grilled cheese sandwich, a hungry dog ___d it, pulling it out of my hand and gulping it down.

_____ 9. Eduardo does not let his lack of a car ___ him from getting to work; he rides his bicycle.

_____ 10. Early in the season, the baseball team's chance of getting to the World Series was not good. But then the team ___d its hopes by winning eight games in a row.

_____ 11. Long before I entered the house, I could ___ that Mom was making her famous spaghetti sauce. Its wonderful smell was the clue.

_____ 12. To catch its ___, the anteater sticks its tongue into an anthill.

_____ 13. Never run up to pat a dog you don't know. Move toward it slowly until you are sure it is not ___.

(Continues on next page)

PART B
Write **C** if the italicized word is used **correctly**. Write **I** if the word is used **incorrectly**.

_____14. I will let my cousin move into my apartment only if he *assures* me it will be for no more than a week.

_____15. Mr. Henderson does everything according to *impulse*. For example, when he decided to buy a car, he spent months comparing models and prices, reading articles in car magazines, and visiting car dealers.

_____16. Anitra is the most *idle* one in her family. She does all of the cooking and cleaning by herself.

_____17. Every group of friends seems to have one especially *frantic* member who helps keep the others calm and peaceful.

_____18. In 1998, one film—*Titanic*—*dominated* the Academy Awards, winning eleven Oscars.

_____19. The videotapes of the robbery showed that as it was going on, the night watchman was *alert* and snoring in his office.

_____20. Although Marla was abused as a child, she has *overcome* that terrible experience and is a kind, loving parent herself.

_____21. The sweater has bits of blue and green in it, but its *primary* color is red.

_____22. Have you ever really had to write a paper on the *theme* "How I Spent My Summer Vacation"?

_____23. I read *excerpts* from the book but did not take the time to read the entire book.

_____24. "No bacon for me, thank you," said Ahmed. "We Muslims *exclude* pork from our diet."

_____25. Scientists are working on a treatment that will help people *obtain* the virus that causes AIDS.

Score   (Number correct) _____ × 4 = _____ %

Enter your score above and in the vocabulary performance chart on the inside back cover of the book.

UNIT FOUR: Test 3

PART A: Synonyms
In the space provided, write the letter of the choice that is most nearly the **same** in meaning as the **boldfaced** word.

_____ 1. **assure** A) argue with B) promise C) run from D) reach out to

_____ 2. **automatic** A) operating by itself B) money-saving C) clear D) ashamed

_____ 3. **bewilder** A) discontinue B) hide C) confuse D) examine

_____ 4. **circumstances** A) feelings B) situation C) hardships D) enemies

_____ 5. **communicate** A) take seriously B) make strong C) pay for D) talk

_____ 6. **devote** A) slow down B) turn away C) get rid of D) give one's time

_____ 7. **divert** A) turn away B) point toward C) get near D) make better

_____ 8. **emotion** A) movement B) victim C) hardship D) feeling

_____ 9. **excerpt** A) sudden decision B) effect C) part of a work D) whole

_____10. **fulfill** A) hurry B) embarrass C) search for D) carry out

_____11. **function** A) knowledge B) hardship C) topic D) use

_____12. **humiliate** A) shame B) give energy to C) send D) calm

_____13. **impulse** A) position B) sudden desire C) heartbeat D) difficulty

_____14. **influence** A) say B) activity C) get D) have an effect on

_____15. **investigate** A) examine B) ignore C) punish D) lose

_____16. **misleading** A) proper B) aware C) giving the wrong idea D) unfriendly

_____17. **obtain** A) protect B) explore C) move D) get

_____18. **perceive** A) notice B) grab C) ignore D) lie to

_____19. **prey** A) hardship B) subject C) victim D) struggle

_____20. **primary** A) small B) main C) moving by itself D) aware

_____21. **seize** A) grab B) tell C) puzzle D) convince

_____22. **sympathize** A) ignore B) slow down C) leave out D) feel pity

_____23. **theme** A) difficulty B) condition C) main topic D) hardship

_____24. **theory** A) explanation B) effect C) activity D) choice

_____25. **transfer** A) puzzle B) study closely C) win D) move

(Continues on next page)

PART B: Antonyms
In the space provided, write the letter of the choice that is most nearly **opposite** in meaning to the **boldfaced** word.

_____26. **abandon**   A) make clear   B) surprise   C) lose   D) continue

_____27. **alert**   A) patient   B) sleepy   C) serious   D) special

_____28. **apparent**   A) not proper   B) hidden   C) difficult   D) unfriendly

_____29. **burden**   A) truth   B) something easy to handle   C) something usual
D) thought

_____30. **crucial**   A) not real   B) not important   C) not clear   D) not wanted

_____31. **deceive**   A) tire   B) give away   C) tell the truth to   D) let go of

_____32. **disregard**   A) know   B) throw away   C) make fun of   D) pay attention to

_____33. **dominate**   A) accept as true   B) lie to   C) argue with
D) have a low position

_____34. **earnest**   A) weak   B) dishonest   C) not fearful   D) not important

_____35. **economical**   A) exciting   B) expected   C) expert   D) expensive

_____36. **exclude**   A) set free   B) support   C) lose to   D) include

_____37. **extraordinary**   A) friendly   B) careless   C) usual   D) important

_____38. **extravagant**   A) troubled   B) money-saving   C) confident   D) not serious

_____39. **fiction**   A) action   B) idea   C) subject   D) truth

_____40. **frantic**   A) unclear   B) relaxed   C) important   D) fast

_____41. **hinder**   A) give away   B) help   C) change   D) lose

_____42. **hostile**   A) not sincere   B) brave   C) not boring   D) friendly

_____43. **idle**   A) busy   B) valuable   C) not proper   D) brave

_____44. **legible**   A) not boring   B) unreadable   C) untruthful   D) not easy

_____45. **monotonous**   A) unusual   B) interesting   C) true   D) easy to understand

_____46. **outspoken**   A) least important   B) friendly   C) exact   D) silent

_____47. **overcome**   A) continue   B) lose to   C) have faith in   D) find fault with

_____48. **revive**   A) make clear   B) pay attention   C) listen carefully
D) make weak

_____49. **security**   A) relief   B) activity   C) anger   D) danger

_____50. **severe**   A) sad   B) fast   C) new   D) mild

> _Score_   (Number correct) _____ × 2 = _____ %

Enter your score above and in the vocabulary performance chart on the inside back cover of the book.

Unit Five

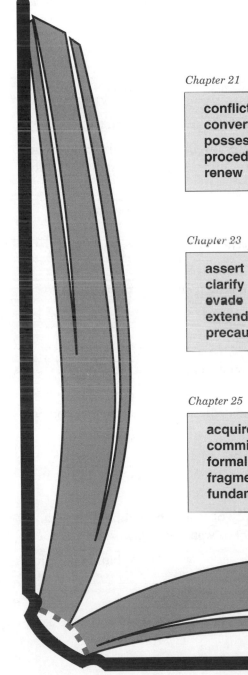

Chapter 21

conflict	resources
convert	stress
possess	unanimous
procedure	vary
renew	vicinity

Chapter 22

abolish	precise
corrupt	promote
decay	reform
expand	tendency
nevertheless	vast

Chapter 23

assert	preconception
clarify	resemble
evade	rigid
extend	senseless
precaution	vertical

Chapter 24

anxious	illustrate
comprehend	impression
convince	inferior
dramatic	overwhelm
frank	thorough

Chapter 25

acquire	precede
commitment	resent
formal	solemn
fragment	spite
fundamental	symbolize

conflict	resources
convert	stress
possess	unanimous
procedure	vary
renew	vicinity

Ten Words in Context

In the space provided, write the letter of the meaning closest to that of each **boldfaced** word. Use the context of the sentences to help you figure out each word's meaning.

1 conflict
(kŏn′flĭkt′)
– *noun*

- When the **conflict** between the two diners became noisy, the restaurant manager asked them to settle their quarrel outside.
- Marsha's children often have an angry **conflict** about whose turn it is to put out the trash.

___ *Conflict* means   A. fight.   B. joke.   C. duty.

2 convert
(kən-vûrt′)
– *verb*

- Cold can turn water into ice, while heat can **convert** it into steam.
- Scientist George Washington Carver was the first to **convert** peanuts into peanut butter. He also used them in more than three hundred other products, including glue, ink, and dyes.

___ *Convert* means   A. to buy.   B. to change.   C. to copy.

3 possess
(pə-zĕs′)
– *verb*

- I can't understand the desire to **possess** very expensive cars and jewelry. If I had more money, I'd spend it on travel.
- People who spend time with young children need to **possess** plenty of patience.

___ *Possess* means   A. to have.   B. to know.   C. to see.

4 procedure
(prə-sē′jər)
– *noun*

- What **procedure** should I follow to become a citizen?
- Even kindergarten students can learn the **procedure** for reporting an emergency: Dial 911, give your name and address, and describe the problem.

___ *Procedure* means   A. answer.   B. steps.   C. support.

5 renew
(rĭ-nōo′)
– *verb*

- After helping to pay for their children's education, many parents barely have time to **renew** their savings in time for retirement.
- We need a good rain to **renew** the supply of water throughout this area. In the meantime, people are being asked not to water their lawns.

___ *Renew* means   A. to change.   B. to upset.   C. to build up again.

6 resources
(rē′sôrs′əs)
– *noun*

- West Virginia's natural **resources** include coal and timber.
- A country's **resources** include its workers—the people who help to keep the economy strong.

___ *Resources* means   A. plans.   B. expenses.   C. wealth.

7 stress
(strəs)
– *noun*

- My doctor said my headaches were caused by **stress**. He suggested that I think of ways to reduce the tension in my life.
- Troy and Angie are experiencing a lot of **stress**. Angie's mother is very sick, Troy lost his job, and they just learned that Angie is going to have twins.

___ *Stress* means   A. relief.   B. pressures.   C. details.

8 unanimous
(yōō-năn′ə-məs)
– *adjective*

- The vote electing Wayne president of the book club was **unanimous**. In fact, there was no other candidate to vote for.
- The jury's decision was **unanimous**. Every juror believed that the woman on trial had robbed the beauty parlor after getting her hair cut.

___ *Unanimous* means   A. showing full agreement.   B. uncertain.   C. hard to understand.

9 vary
(vâr′ē)
– *verb*

- There are often great changes in weather along the coast. In one day, the temperature can **vary** by as much as forty degrees.
- Joan's lunches never **vary**. Every day, she eats a peanut butter and celery sandwich, pretzels, and a banana.

___ *Vary* means   A. to begin.   B. to change.   C. to disappear.

10 vicinity
(vĭ-sĭn′ĭ-tē)
– *noun*

- In the **vicinity** of the elementary school, the speed limit is fifteen miles an hour.
- The Johnsons decided not to buy the house when they learned that there was a nuclear power plant in the **vicinity**.

___ *Vicinity* means   A. yard.   B. building.   C. neighborhood.

Matching Words with Definitions

Following are definitions of the ten words. **Print** each word next to its definition. If you look closely at each word in context, you will be able to figure out its meaning.

1. _____ Whatever makes up the present and future wealth of a country, state, etc., including natural supplies and labor force

2. _____ To fill up again; replace; start up again

3. _____ The area near or around a place

4. _____ A quarrel or fight; disagreement

5. _____ Showing full agreement

6. _____ Mental or emotional tension; strain

7. _____ To experience change; become different

8. _____ To make something change completely; transform

9. _____ To own; have

10. _____ A method; the way in which something is done

CAUTION: Do not go any further until you are sure the above answers are correct. Then you can use the definitions to help you in the following practices. Your goal is eventually to know the words well enough so that you don't need to check the definitions at all.

➤ *Check 1*

Using the answer line, complete each item below with the correct word from the box.

A. **conflict**	B. **convert**	C. **possess**	D. **procedure**	E. **renew**
F. **resources**	G. **stress**	H. **unanimous**	I. **vary**	J. **vicinity**

_____ 1. A country's ___ include all of its minerals, such as coal, gold, and silver.

_____ 2. If there is no disagreement among jurors, we say that their decision is ___.

_____ 3. Whether two people or groups are fighting with words or weapons, we can say they are having a ___.

_____ 4. If someone lives in the ___ of your home, you would call that person a neighbor.

_____ 5. If you are always patient, we can say that you ___ lots of patience.

_____ 6. Roses ___ greatly in color, size, and shape.

_____ 7. A ___ is a process that often involves a series of steps.

_____ 8. The beach artist ___ed a pile of wet sand into a statue of a giant turtle.

_____ 9. To ___ my supply of clean towels, I'll have to do my laundry tonight.

_____ 10. Anything that puts pressure on our emotions, bodies, or minds can be called ___.

NOTE: Now check your answers to these questions by turning to page 240. Going over the answers carefully will help you prepare for the remaining practices, for which answers are not given.

➤ *Check 2*

Using the answer lines, complete each item below with **two** words from the box.

_____
_____ 1–2. The ongoing ___ between the Millers and Smiths—an argument over the Smiths' noisy parties—has caused the Millers so much ___ that they are thinking of moving.

_____
_____ 3–4. My father feels lucky that there is a surgeon in our ___ who has developed a special ___ for doing the type of operation that he needs.

_____
_____ 5–6. The natural ___ of the United States ___, depending upon the part of the country. For example, the Midwest is rich in farmland, and the Northeast has more coal.

_____
_____ 7–8. The city council's ___ decision was to ___ the vacant lot into a community softball field.

_____
_____ 9–10. According to one fairy tale, a king ___es a magic box full of gold coins; whenever the box becomes empty, it ___s its supply of coins.

➢ *Word Work*

A. In the space provided, write the letter of the word that most closely relates to the situation in each item.

_____ 1. When you arrive at the doctor's office, tell the receptionist your name and sign the check-in chart.

    A. procedure   B. vary   C. vicinity

_____ 2. Rita uses her blender to turn old, dry bread into bread crumbs.

    A. stress   B. convert   C. conflict

_____ 3. A hard day at work and a flat tire on the way home left Lou with a pounding headache.

    A. renew   B. resources   C. stress

_____ 4. All the judges agreed that Evelyn should be named winner of the talent contest.

    A. unanimous   B. renew   C. possession

_____ 5. The state has attracted investors because of its mineral rights and its well-trained workers.

    A. conflict   B. resources   C. vicinity

B. In the space provided, write the letter of the choice that best completes each item.

_____ 6. The roommates have a **conflict** over housecleaning. They

    A. agree on how clean the room should be.
    B. hire someone else to clean the room.
    C. disagree over how clean the room should be.

_____ 7. The boss's mood **varies**, so the boss's employees

    A. never know what kind of mood he will be in.
    B. know that he is always in a good mood.
    C. think that he is usually in a good mood.

_____ 8. Because our house is in the **vicinity** of many great restaurants, we

    A. have to travel a long way to find a good restaurant.
    B. don't have to travel far to find a good restaurant.
    C. can't find any good restaurants.

_____ 9. A quality that Tony **possesses** is a good sense of humor. Tony

    A. finds it hard to see the funny side of things.
    B. is easily able to laugh at things.
    C. gets angry when people laugh at him.

_____ 10. The store's supply of milk was **renewed** today. The store

    A. is out of milk.
    B. no longer sells milk.
    C. has a fresh supply of milk.

➤ *Word Parts*

A. The suffix *-ful* mean "producing ___" or "full of ___."

> ***Examples:*** *stress* — tension   *joy* — great happiness
>   *stressful* — producing tension   *joyful* — full of great happiness

On each answer line, write the word from the box that means the same as the *italicized* words.

A. **beautiful**	B. **playful**	C. **stressful**
D. **thankful**	E. **wasteful**	

_____ 1. "All you can eat" restaurants encourage people to be *producing waste*, piling far more food on their plates than they really want or need.

_____ 2. Although the outside of an oyster shell is rather ugly, the inside is *full of beauty*, with its pale, milky rainbow of colors.

_____ 3. When Glenn's car broke down on a dark road far from his home, he was *full of thanks* that a police officer quickly arrived and offered him a ride to town.

_____ 4. Most people find it *producing stress* to have to speak in front of a large group.

_____ 5. That boss may seem overly serious. But when she's not busy, she can be quite *full of play*, laughing and telling jokes.

B. The prefixes *com-* and *con-* mean "with" or "together."

> ***Examples:*** *conflict* — a quarrel with someone
>   *communicate°* — to exchange information together

On each answer line, write the word from the box that best completes the item.

F. **communicate°**	G. **complicate°**	H. **conflict**
I. **confront°**	J. **contrast°**	

_____ 6. Thelma had a ___ with her neighbors over their dogs' getting into her garbage cans.

_____ 7. The more people you invite, the more you will ___ our job of preparing for the party.

_____ 8. There's a big ___ between the two Williams brothers. One is very outgoing and friendly, and the other is quite shy.

_____ 9. When the Carveys didn't pay their rent for the third month in a row, the landlord actually came to their door to ___ them.

_____ 10. In the 1800s, it must have been very difficult to ___ with people who lived far away. Today, many people stay in touch by using cell phones and e-mail.

➤ *Final Check*

Read the passages carefully. Then fill in each blank with the word that best fits the context.

A. Traveling with Children

A. **conflict**	B. **stress**	C. **unanimous**	D. **vary**	E. **vicinity**

Whether I'm driving in the (1)_____ of home or farther away, the trip seems to last longer if my kids are in the car. The minute we're on the road, the baby begins to cry, and the older children start a major (2)_____. These fights (3)_____ from time to time, but they often have something to do with one of four primary° complaints:

1. One kid is in the front seat when it's another kid's turn.

2. Someone who had a window seat last time got one again.

3. One of the kids hates the music that another has turned on. (No single radio station has won the (4)_____ approval of all the children.)

4. One child thinks another "is looking at me funny."

Now that I think about it, maybe I can preserve° the peace and lower the level of (5)_____ in my life. I'll make my kids take a bus!

B. Saving Earth's Natural Supplies

F. **convert**	G. **possess**	H. **procedure**	I. **renew**	J. **resources**

Once some of Earth's valuable (6)_____ are used up, it will be impossible to (7)_____ them. For example, coal will someday be used up and gone forever.

We do, however, (8)_____ other important supplies that can be used over and over. We can (9)_____ paper, metal, plastics and glass into new products by means of recycling. If we don't recycle, who knows what severe° shortages and garbage problems will result? It's up to each of us to have the interest and foresight° to learn about the recycling methods in our communities and then to follow those (10)_____s.

Scores   Check 2 _____%   Word Work _____%   Word Parts _____%   Final Check _____%

Enter your scores above and in the vocabulary performance chart on the inside back cover of the book.

abolish	precise
corrupt	promote
decay	reform
expand	tendency
nevertheless	vast

Ten Words in Context

In the space provided, write the letter of the meaning closest to that of each **boldfaced** word. Use the context of the sentences to help you figure out each word's meaning.

1 abolish
(ə-bŏl'ĭsh)
– *verb*

- With our advanced farming methods, why can't we **abolish** hunger?
- One way for a school to raise students' test scores is to **abolish** summer vacation and hold classes all year round.

___*Abolish* means   A. to make longer.   B. to get rid of.   C. to pay for.

2 corrupt
(kə-rŭpt')
– *adjective*

- A **corrupt** police officer went to prison for selling the drugs he took in a raid.
- The country was run by a **corrupt** ruler, who robbed the rich and poor alike.

___*Corrupt* means   A. not honest.   B. respected.   C. poor.

3 decay
(dĭ-kā')
– *verb*

- Teeth that are brushed and flossed regularly are not likely to **decay**.
- Leaves fall from the trees, **decay**, and become part of the forest floor.

___*Decay* means   A. to increase.   B. to bend.   C. to rot.

4 expand
(ĭk-spănd')
– *verb*

- The grocery is buying the shop next door so that it can **expand** enough to double its space.
- During a heavy rain, that little creek **expands** into a fast-moving river.

___*Expand* means   A. to bend.   B. to break down.   C. to grow.

5 nevertheless
(nĕv'ər-thə-lĕs')
– *adverb*

- Too much sun can cause skin cancer; **nevertheless**, many people want a deep suntan.
- The doll is old and tattered, but the little boy loves it **nevertheless**.

___*Nevertheless* means   A. rarely.   B. because of that.   C. in spite of that.

6 precise
(prĭ-sīs')
– *adjective*

- In baking, it is important to be **precise** when measuring ingredients.
- We found the house easily, thanks to our host's **precise** directions.

___*Precise* means   A. exact.   B. busy.   C. strong.

7 promote
(prə-mōt′)
– *verb*

- The dentist visited the classroom to **promote** good dental care at home.
- Mr. Sanchez won't let his kids watch movies that seem to **promote** violent behavior.

___ *Promote* means   A. to support.   B. to attack.   C. to prevent.

8 reform
(rĭ-fôrm′)
– *verb*

- Does serving time in prison **reform** people or only keep them off the streets?
- Training classes can **reform** dogs so that they don't pull on their leashes and jump on people.

___ *Reform* means   A. to annoy.   B. to make better.   C. to confuse.

9 tendency
(tĕn′dən-sē)
– *noun*

- Fishermen have a **tendency** to tell big stories about the fish they almost caught.
- I have a bad **tendency** to put off doing work until the last minute.

___ *Tendency* means   A. hard work.   B. limit.   C. habit.

10 vast
(văst)
– *adjective*

- Lake Superior is so **vast** that you could easily mistake it for an ocean.
- The library has a **vast** collection of books for adults, but not so many for children.

___ *Vast* means   A. well-known.   B. gradual.   C. very big.

Matching Words with Definitions

Following are definitions of the ten words. **Print** each word next to its definition. If you look closely at each word in context, you will be able to figure out its meaning.

1. _____ To spread out; get larger

2. _____ To break down gradually; rot

3. _____ In spite of that; even so; despite that

4. _____ Dishonest; crooked

5. _____ To cause or persuade to behave better

6. _____ To put an end to

7. _____ Exact; correct; accurate

8. _____ A leaning toward thinking or behaving in a certain way

9. _____ Very large in size, amount, or area

10. _____ To speak for or work toward something; encourage; help make happen

CAUTION: Do not go any further until you are sure the above answers are correct. Then you can use the definitions to help you in the following practices. Your goal is eventually to know the words well enough so that you don't need to check the definitions at all.

➤ *Check 1*

Using the answer line, complete each item below with the correct word from the box.

A. **abolish**	B. **corrupt**	C. **decay**	D. **expand**	E. **nevertheless**
F. **precise**	G. **promote**	H. **reform**	I. **tendency**	J. **vast**

_____ 1. I don't know Uncle Hank's ___ age, but I guess he's in his mid-fifties.

_____ 2. The sun is shining brightly; ___, it is quite chilly outside.

_____ 3. The house is beginning to ___. Its windows are broken, and its paint is peeling off.

_____ 4. The high school is going to ___ by adding more classrooms.

_____ 5. To ___ reading in the community, the banks have started a "Bucks for Books" program. The bank managers actually pay kids to read.

_____ 6. Scholars, writers, and researchers from all over the world visit the Library of Congress in Washington, D.C., to make use of its ___ collection of books and papers on every topic imaginable.

_____ 7. Former employees told reporters about ___ practices in the supermarket, such as soaking spoiling hams in bleach to get rid of the bad smell.

_____ 8. Eli used to answer the phone by yelling, "Who is this?" But a few lessons in phone manners ___ed him so that he now politely says, "Hello?"

_____ 9. I have a ___ to talk loudly and quickly when I am nervous.

_____ 10. The restaurant's owner decided to ___ the smoking section and make the entire restaurant smoke-free.

NOTE: Now check your answers to these questions by turning to page 240. Going over the answers carefully will help you prepare for the remaining practices, for which answers are not given.

➤ *Check 2*

Using the answer lines, complete each item below with **two** words from the box.

_____
_____ 1–2. Elena has a ___ to be careless and messy at home; ___, she is always neat and careful at work.

_____
_____ 3–4. Many people feel that to ___ politicians and improve politics, it is necessary to ___ all gifts of money from groups that wish to influence° lawmakers.

_____
_____ 5–6. The housing project is so ___ that you can get lost walking around in it, and it's so poorly cared for that the buildings are starting to ___.

_____
_____ 7–8. At his trial, it was revealed that the ___ mayor had used city funds to ___ his automobile collection. While in office, he bought two Rolls-Royces and a Ferrari.

_____
_____ 9–10. The new principal promised to ___ better teacher-parent communication. But he didn't explain the ___ ways that he would do that.

➤ *Word Work*

A. In the space provided, write the letter of the word that most closely relates to the situation in each item.

_____ 1. The world's largest desert, the Sahara, covers 3½ million square miles of North Africa.

    A. vast   B. corrupt   C. promote

_____ 2. Some people put their food scraps in a compost heap, where the food slowly rots and turns into rich fertilizer for the garden.

    A. precise   B. expand   C. decay

_____ 3. Because the speeding driver gave him fifty dollars, the police officer who stopped him did not write a ticket.

    A. tendency   B. vast   C. corrupt

_____ 4. Randy, who believes in the benefits of health foods, is trying to persuade his brother and sister to eat tofu and raw vegetables.

    A. corrupt   B. promote   C. expand

_____ 5. I usually wait until the last minute before beginning a project.

    A. tendency   B. reform   C. expand

B. In the space provided, write the letter of the choice that best completes each item.

_____ 6. If a school **abolishes** its football team, the football players will probably

    A. be upset.   B. be more popular.   C. win more games.

_____ 7. A business is likely to **expand** when it is

    A. not honest.   B. closing.   C. doing very well.

_____ 8. I love chocolate ice cream; **nevertheless,**

    A. I am not going to have any.
    B. I am going to take a large helping.
    C. it is my favorite flavor.

_____ 9. An example of a **precise** measurement of time is

    A. a few minutes.   B. several hours.   C. forty-three seconds.

_____ 10. A thief who **reforms** himself

    A. commits more thefts.
    B. stops stealing.
    C. begins hurting people as well as stealing.

➤ *Synonyms and Antonyms*

A. Synonyms. Write the letter of the word or phrase that most nearly means the **same** as each boldfaced word.

_____ 1. **reform**

    A. make better   B. make more difficult

    C. make sure   D. get bigger

_____ 2. **tendency**

    A. thought   B. habit of acting in a certain way

    C. fear   D. making something larger

_____ 3. **decay**

    A. build   B. continue

    C. leave   D. spoil

_____ 4. **precise**

    A. helpful   B. unclear

    C. dishonest   D. exact

_____ 5. **nevertheless**

    A. because   B. perhaps

    C. despite that   D. sometimes

B. Antonyms. Write the letter of the word or phrase that most nearly means the **opposite** of each boldfaced word.

_____ 6. **corrupt**

    A. small   B. helpless

    C. honest   D. stiff

_____ 7. **promote**

    A. discourage   B. anger

    C. pay   D. hide

_____ 8. **vast**

    A. many   B. broken

    C. incorrect   D. tiny

_____ 9. **expand**

    A. grow stronger   B. get smaller

    C. break   D. build

_____10. **abolish**

    A. end   B. become used to

    C. like   D. create

➤ *Final Check*

Read the passages carefully. Then fill in each blank with the word that best fits the context.

A. More Fat, Anyone?

A. **decay**	B. **expand**	C. **nevertheless**	D. **precise**	E. **vast**

We know that fatty and sugary foods are bad for us. (1)_____, we love to eat them. There's a high demand for food with (2)_____ amounts of fat and sugar.

To meet the demand for fat, many fast-food giants offer more and bigger high-fat menu items. Pizza Hut sells its Triple Decker Pizza, a health nightmare with as much fat as a stick and a half of butter! McDonald's offers a super-fat triple cheeseburger. And Taco Bell sells a variety° of fatty bacon products. To make matters worse, the fast-food chains offer sugar-filled ice cream, shakes, sodas, pies, cakes, and cookies that make us fatter. These foods also cause our teeth to (3)_____ and get cavities. Although fat and sugar are not wholesome° for the customer, they are certainly good for the financial health of the fast-food chains.

Why do we disregard° what science teaches us about a good diet? Researchers cannot explain the (4)_____ reasons why we ignore what we know about healthy eating, but one thing is certain. As long as our appetite for fat and sugar continues to increase, our waistlines will also continue to (5)_____.

B. Is Prison Effective?

F. **abolish**	G. **corrupt**	H. **promote**	I. **reform**	J. **tendency**

There's a lot of disagreement about how to (6)_____ criminals and make them good citizens. Today, most of them are sent to prison. But many people believe that serving time in prison does not really make a person less likely to commit another crime. They point out that in prison, a person may spend months or years in the company of more hardened criminals. Will a prisoner in such company come out of jail with a (7)_____ to be honest? Not likely, they say. Instead, the prisoner will probably learn only how to be more (8)_____.

In addition, many people want to (9)_____ the death penalty. They believe it is just as wrong to kill a killer as it was for him or her to commit murder in the first place.

Even if you agree with these points, the question remains of how to deal with people who harm others. Some people want to convert° prisons from places where people are just locked up to places where prisoners can obtain° an education, job training, and counseling. They want to see the system adjust to a prisoner's needs, rather than treat everyone the same. They want prisons to be places that (10)_____ positive values, instead of only punishing criminals.

Scores	Check 2 _____%	Word Work _____%	Synonyms and Antonyms _____%	Final Check _____%

Enter your scores above and in the vocabulary performance chart on the inside back cover of the book.

assert	preconception
clarify	resemble
evade	rigid
extend	senseless
precaution	vertical

Ten Words in Context

In the space provided, write the letter of the meaning closest to that of each **boldfaced** word. Use the context of the sentences to help you figure out each word's meaning.

1 assert
(ə-sûrt′)
– *verb*

- The mayor **asserted** in court that he never took bribes, but the jury did not believe him.
- Every once in a while, the newspapers sold in supermarkets **assert** that Elvis Presley is alive and hiding somewhere.

___*Assert* means   A. to doubt.   B. to fear.   C. to state strongly.

2 clarify
(klăr′ə-fī′)
– *verb*

- Mr. Patel is a great math teacher. He can **clarify** even the hardest problems so that everyone can understand.
- Todd didn't understand his health insurance plan, so he asked someone at the insurance company to **clarify** it for him.

___*Clarify* means   A. to explain.   B. to create.   C. to stop.

3 evade
(ĭ-vād′)
– *verb*

- Our dog will do anything to **evade** a bath. Once we get him near the tub, we have to shut the bathroom door, or he will escape.
- In my favorite cops-and-robbers movie, the robbers tried to **evade** the police by leaving through a hole in the roof. However, their plan failed; the police were waiting on the roof!

___*Evade* means   A. to break down.   B. to get away from.   C. to find.

4 extend
(ĭk-stĕnd′)
– *verb*

- We had so much fun camping that we **extended** our vacation one more day.
- "Because many students are having trouble finishing this project on time," said the instructor, "I will **extend** the deadline by one more week."

___*Extend* means   A. to make longer or later.   B. to make clear.   C. to escape.

5 precaution
(prĭ-kô′shən)
– *noun*

- We took the **precaution** of having the car tuned up before we began our long trip.
- If you walk in the woods, wear long pants as a **precaution** against poison ivy.

___*Precaution* means   A. cure for a problem.   B. something stated.   C. step taken to be safe.

6 preconception
(prē′kən-sĕp′shən)
– *noun*

- From her voice on the phone, I had a **preconception** of my brother's girlfriend as being rather unfriendly.
- Our **preconception** that the party would be boring was completely wrong. Once we got there, we had a great time.

___*Preconception* means   A. wish.   B. judgment made without experience.   C. statement of fact.

7 **resemble**
   (rǐ-zěm′bəl)
   – *verb*

- A certain worthless mineral is known as "fool's gold" because it **resembles** real gold. Both minerals are shiny yellow.
- Eating wild mushrooms can be dangerous because a poisonous mushroom sometimes **resembles** one that is safe.

___ *Resemble* means   A. to be better than.   B. to look the same as.   C. to be easier to find than.

8 **rigid**
   (rǐj′ǐd)
   – *adjective*

- Modeling clay is **rigid** when it is cold, but once it warms in your hands, it becomes softer and easier to work with.
- The guards outside the palace stood stiffly—they looked as **rigid** as poles.

___ *Rigid* means   A. not heavy.   B. hard to beat.   C. not bending.

9 **senseless**
   (sěns′lǐs)
   – *adjective*

- Building a new high school seems **senseless** to me. I think the school we have is perfectly fine.
- Leo loves desserts. In his opinion, it's **senseless** to fill up on vegetables.

___ *Senseless* means   A. silly.   B. possible.   C. smart.

10 **vertical**
   (vûr′tǐ-kəl)
   – *adjective*

- Clothes with **vertical** stripes generally make the wearer look taller and thinner.
- The dark **vertical** lines of the telephone poles looked striking against the background of the snowy field.

___ *Vertical* means   A. very clear.   B. curving.   C. up-and-down.

Matching Words with Definitions

Following are definitions of the ten words. **Print** each word next to its definition. If you look closely at each word in context, you will be able to figure out its meaning.

1. _____   An opinion formed before having enough information or experience

2. _____   To look like or be similar to; be like

3. _____   To make clear or easy to understand

4. _____   Something done in advance to avoid a problem

5. _____   Foolish; not making good sense

6. _____   To state positively, often without proof

7. _____   To escape or avoid through clever action

8. _____   In a straight, up-and-down line; upright

9. _____   Stiff; not bending

10. _____   To make longer in time or later in time; continue

CAUTION: Do not go any further until you are sure the above answers are correct. Then you can use the definitions to help you in the following practices. Your goal is eventually to know the words well enough so that you don't need to check the definitions at all.

➤ Check 1

Using the answer line, complete each item below with the correct word from the box.

A. assert	B. clarify	C. evade	D. extend	E. precaution
F. preconception	G. resemble	H. rigid	I. senseless	J. vertical

_____ 1. A good math teacher can ___ a difficult problem.

_____ 2. The people who want to build the mall ___ that it will mean more business for local stores, but the local stores owners do not believe them.

_____ 3. The children found a ___ board to use as a bridge over the creek.

_____ 4. Eli was a poor worker. He ___d responsibility whenever possible.

_____ 5. The teacher ___ed the test so everyone had time to finish.

_____ 6. Before tasting spinach, many kids have the ___ they will not like it.

_____ 7. Expensive silk roses ___ real roses.

_____ 8. "Everyone is doing it" is a ___ reason to do anything.

_____ 9. Remember to put on sunblock lotion as a ___ against sunburn.

_____ 10. As we got closer to New York City, we saw the ___ shape of the tall Empire State Building against the bright summer sky.

NOTE: Now check your answers to these questions by turning to page 240. Going over the answers carefully will help you prepare for the remaining practices, for which answers are not given.

➤ Check 2

Using the answer lines, complete each item below with **two** words from the box.

_____
_____ 1–2. It was ___ of the town to open a swimming pool without taking the ___ of hiring a lifeguard first.

_____
_____ 3–4. Because Krista ___s her sister physically, I had the ___ that she would have a similar personality, but the two girls are actually very different.

_____
_____ 5–6. A reporter said the mayor's views on taxes were unclear, and he asked the mayor to ___ her ideas. However, the mayor ___d the question by saying, "Who can think about taxes when our basketball team is about to win the state championship?"

_____
_____ 7–8. The new advertisements for the motor oil ___ that using the oil is guaranteed to ___ the life of your car.

_____
_____ 9–10. To build a playhouse, Mac began with four thick, ___ pieces of wood. He stuck one end of each deep in the ground, so that each piece of wood was in a ___ position.

➤ *Word Work*

A. In the space provided, write the letter of the choice that best completes each item.

_____ 1. After someone **clarifies** a problem, it should be

A. a mystery.

B. easier to understand.

C. even more troubling.

_____ 2. Because a snowstorm arrived during the furniture sale, the sale was **extended**, so people

A. had more time to shop during the sale.

B. could not buy furniture.

C. had to pay full price for the furniture.

_____ 3. A **precaution** against slipping on your icy sidewalk is

A. an injury, such as a broken bone.

B. an ice storm.

C. spreading plenty of sand or salt over the ice.

_____ 4. Two people who are likely to **resemble** one another physically are

A. best friends.

B. members of the same soccer team.

C. brothers.

_____ 5. People **evade** questions that they

A. are happy to answer truthfully.

B. did not hear.

C. do not want to answer.

B. In the space provided, write the letter of the word that most closely relates to the situation in each item.

_____ 6. A hotel clerk claims that she has been offered a part in a Hollywood movie.

A. assert   B. extend   C. clarify

_____ 7. Before it is cooked, spaghetti is hard and breaks instead of bending.

A. evade   B. senseless   C. rigid

_____ 8. When the phone rang, the mother ran into the house to answer it, leaving her two-year-old alone outside.

A. vertical   B. clarify   C. senseless

_____ 9. In the middle of his fifth-grade year, Ben began to think that he was going to have a terrible time in sixth grade.

A. precaution   B. preconception   C. resemble

_____ 10. The sunflower grew six feet tall, straight up into the air.

A. evade   B. vertical   C. clarify

➤ *Word Parts*

A. The prefix *ex-* can mean "beyond" or "out."

> *Examples:* *extraordinary°* — beyond the ordinary
> *excerpt°* — a part that is taken out of a whole work

On each answer line, write the word from the box that best completes the item.

A. **excerpt°**	B. **exclude°**	C. **extend**
D. **external°**	E. **extraordinary°**	

_____ 1. Since so many people had something to say, the meeting was ___ed another thirty minutes.

_____ 2. A TV show titled *That's Entertainment* included ___s from many wonderful musical films.

_____ 3. When the children play, they prefer to ___ Hank because he is such a bully.

_____ 4. You are supposed to cut off the ___ layer of the kiwi fruit before eating it.

_____ 5. Mrs. Martin is an ___ woman. She has brought up four wonderful children by herself and also built a fine career at a bank where she is now a vice president.

B. The prefix *pre-* often means "before."

> *Examples:* *precaution* — something done beforehand to avoid a problem
> *preserve°* — to protect or keep in good condition, before there's a problem

On each answer line, write the word from the box that best completes the item.

F. **preconception**	G. **preheat**	H. **prepare**
I. **preserve°**	J. **pretest**	

_____ 6. To ___ for the trip, I have to wash and pack a lot of clothes.

_____ 7. Sometimes teachers give students a ___ to help them see if they are ready for the real test.

_____ 8. The brownie recipe says to ___ the oven to 350 degrees.

_____ 9. To ___ her wedding dress for her daughter, Mrs. Henry keeps it covered in plastic and in a box.

_____ 10. New college students often have the ___ that instructors will remind them about assignments and tests. But in college, students must keep track of such things themselves.

➣ *Final Check*

Read the passages carefully. Then fill in each blank with the word that best fits the context.

A. She Changed My Mind

A. **clarify**	B. **extend**	C. **preconception**	D. **resemble**	E. **rigid**

When I entered a Catholic school as a third-grader, I was very scared. The teachers were nuns, and although I had never known any nuns myself, I had a (1)_____ of what a nun would be like. I pictured a hostile° woman dressed in a strange robe and sitting stiffly, as (2)_____ as the ruler in her hand, and frowning when I forgot the answers to her questions. I imagined her deciding to (3)_____ my school day by several hours after everyone else went home.

By the time I actually arrived in the classroom, I would not have been surprised if the teacher had had fire coming out of her nostrils. Imagine my surprise, then, when I saw an attractive young woman standing at the front of the classroom. "Good morning!" she said cheerily. "My name is Sister Mary Elizabeth." I stared at her in surprise. She (4)_____d my favorite aunt. Her face was not cold as I had expected, but warm and smiling. When she stopped by my desk later that morning to (5)_____ an arithmetic problem, she knelt beside me and gave my ponytail a gentle, playful tug. One day in class was adequate° for me to fall in love with Sister Mary Elizabeth and to realize how little I had really known about nuns.

B. So Sue Me

F. **assert**	G. **evade**	H. **precaution**	I. **senseless**	J. **vertical**

"I'll sue!" This threat is all too often carried out. Americans have a strong tendency° to bring one another to court.

Take the case of the teenager who walked down the street, listening to music through the headphones of his personal stereo. He came to a curb and stepped into the street. A car running through a red light nearly hit him. Because he was listening to music, he had not heard the car coming. Did he sue the driver? No; he sued the maker of the stereo. He claimed the stereo should have come with a note telling him to take the (6)_____ of removing the head-phones when he crossed a street. Such a claim is a (7)_____ waste of court time.

Another well-known case involved a similar circumstance°. A woman sued a fast-food chain for serving her coffee that was too hot. She spilled the coffee in her own lap, burned herself, and (8)_____ed that the restaurant was to blame.

What is next? Should ice-cream cones carry warning labels saying, "Keep the cone in a (9)_____ position or else the ice cream might fall off"? It seems that suing someone else has become yet another way for people to (10)_____ responsibility for their own actions.

Scores	Check 2 _____%	Word Work _____%	Word Parts _____%	Final Check _____%

Enter your scores above and in the vocabulary performance chart on the inside back cover of the book.

anxious	illustrate
comprehend	impression
convince	inferior
dramatic	overwhelm
frank	thorough

Ten Words in Context

In the space provided, write the letter of the meaning closest to that of each **boldfaced** word. Use the context of the sentences to help you figure out each word's meaning.

1 anxious
(ăngk′shŭs)
– *adjective*

- Dean was **anxious** about his new job. He worried about doing well and whether he would like his supervisor.
- You seemed **anxious** before the test, but you look more relaxed now.

___ *Anxious* means   A. sure.   B. troubled.   C. late.

2 comprehend
(kŏm′prĭ-hĕnd′)
– *verb*

- Although my Japanese friend knew English pretty well when she came to this country, she did not **comprehend** such slang terms as "cool" and "gross."
- I cannot **comprehend** how a computer works, but at least I understand how to use one for writing papers and e-mail.

___ *Comprehend* means   A. to believe.   B. to remember.   C. to understand.

3 convince
(kən-vĭns′)
– *verb*

- The lawyer is sure she can **convince** the jury that her client is innocent.
- Cindy tried to **convince** her roommate that she had not stolen her necklace, but her roommate still did not believe her.

___ *Convince* means   A. to learn from.   B. to cause to believe.   C. to keep from.

4 dramatic
(drə-măt′ĭk)
– *adjective*

- To hold our interest, our gym teacher used **dramatic** movements, such as waving her arms or jumping.
- Mr. Johnson prefers not to be noticed when he enters a room, but Mrs. Johnson enjoys making **dramatic** entrances, such as by swirling a bright purple cape around her shoulders.

___ *Dramatic* means   A. distant.   B. usual.   C. attracting attention.

5 frank
(frăngk)
– *adjective*

- Mrs. Robins told her doctor, "Please be **frank** with me. If you know what is wrong with me, please tell me the truth."
- "To be **frank**," my sister said to me, "your new hairdo looks as if you had stuck your finger into an electrical socket."

___ *Frank* means   A. careful.   B. honest.   C. worried.

6 illustrate
(ĭl′ə-strāt′)
– *verb*

- Whenever Mrs. Fine wanted to teach us a new word, she **illustrated** its use in a sentence.
- Pastor Gibson **illustrated** his point about forgiving by telling a story about one victim who learned to forgive his attacker.

___ *Illustrate* means   A. to explain with an example.   B. to change.   C. to make difficult.

7 impression
(ĭm-prĕsh′ən)
– *noun*

- My first **impression** of Leroy was that he was loud and rude, but spending time with him showed me that under all the noise was a warm, friendly person.
- I had the **impression** that Vicky was coming on the ski trip, but at the last minute I learned that she had never really planned to come.

____ *Impression* means   A. argument.   B. rule.   C. opinion.

8 inferior
(ĭn-fîr′ē-ər)
– *adjective*

- Silver is considered to be **inferior** to gold, but I still prefer silver jewelry.
- Joan's basketball skills are **inferior** to those of the other team members, but the coach believes that Joan will improve quickly.

____ *Inferior to* means   A. just like.   B. worse than.   C. new to.

9 overwhelm
(ō′vər-hwĕlm′)
– *verb*

- You will **overwhelm** children if you give too many instructions at one time.
- A group of bystanders **overwhelmed** the purse-snatcher, holding him down until the police could arrive.

____ *Overwhelm* means   A. to encourage.   B. to overpower.   C. to watch.

10 thorough
(thûr′ō)
– *adjective*

- After a **thorough** search of every corner of my apartment, I finally found my glasses—in my pocket.
- Before signing up their children at a day-care center, parents should do a **thorough** check of how kind and well-trained the staff are.

____ *Thorough* means   A. quick.   B. careful.   C. exciting.

Matching Words with Definitions

Following are definitions of the ten words. **Print** each word next to its definition. If you look closely at each word in context, you will be able to figure out its meaning.

1. _____   Honest and open; sincere

2. _____   Lower in value or quality

3. _____   Complete; very carefully done

4. _____   To understand completely

5. _____   To make clear by using an example, picture, or demonstration°

6. _____   Worried; troubled; fearful about what might happen

7. _____   Having very exciting, interesting qualities; striking; very noticeable

8. _____   A belief, opinion, or feeling—often based on little information

9. _____   To persuade by argument or proof

10. _____   To make mentally, emotionally, or physically helpless with too much of something; overpower

CAUTION: Do not go any further until you are sure the above answers are correct. Then you can use the definitions to help you in the following practices. Your goal is eventually to know the words well enough so that you don't need to check the definitions at all.

➣ *Check 1*

Using the answer line, complete each item below with the correct word from the box.

A. **anxious**	B. **comprehend**	C. **convince**	D. **dramatic**	E. **frank**
F. **illustrate**	G. **impression**	H. **inferior**	I. **overwhelm**	J. **thorough**

_____   1. If you say that you ___ a math problem, it means you understand it well.

_____   2. A grade of C is ___ to a B.

_____   3. Your first ___ of people may change as you get to know them better.

_____   4. Too much confusing work would ___ anyone.

_____   5. It usually takes more time to do a ___ job than an incomplete one.

_____   6. A news report that is frightening or troubling makes people ___.

_____   7. A ___ outfit is unusual and will attract attention.

_____   8. A ___ person is likely to tell you just what he or she thinks of your new hairdo, instead of giving you false compliments.

_____   9. It should take a great deal of proof to ___ a jury that someone is guilty.

_____   10. A good way to make an idea more clear is to ___ it in some way. To do so, you might use an example or a picture.

NOTE: Now check your answers to these questions by turning to page 240. Going over the answers carefully will help you prepare for the remaining practices, for which answers are not given.

➣ *Check 2*

Using the answer lines, complete each item below with **two** words from the box.

_____
_____   1–2. Karla's bright lipstick, false eyelashes, and ___ red dress gave me the ___ that she wanted everyone to notice her.

_____
_____   3–4. Many people would feel ___ about moving to a foreign country, especially if they did not ___ the language.

_____
_____   5–6. That boss is so ___ that she will often tell stories about her own mistakes to ___ her instructions.

_____
_____   7–8. A mother in the shoe store was trying to ___ her child not to choose a certain pair of shoes. "You like them because they have your favorite cartoon character on them," she explained. "But they are so ___ to this other pair that they will fall apart in a month."

_____
_____   9–10. "Don't let this big exam ___ you," said the instructor. "We've done a ___ job of reviewing the material, and I'm sure you will all do well."

➤ *Word Work*

A. In the space provided, write the letter of the word that most closely relates to the situation in each item.

A. **anxious**	B. **dramatic**	C. **frank**
D. **illustrate**	E. **inferior**	

_____ 1. As Tri Lee described how North and South Vietnam were once divided, he drew a map of the country on the blackboard.

_____ 2. Sara chewed her nails and tapped her foot as she waited to learn if she had passed the test.

_____ 3. I bought these two shirts on the same day. One still looks like new, but the other has faded and is tearing at the seams.

_____ 4. "I think I should tell you that I've been in prison," said Tom. "I hope you will still consider me for the job."

_____ 5. In the movie *Aladdin*, Prince Ali makes a grand entrance into the city, surrounded by soldiers, elephants, dancers, and musicians.

B. In the space provided, write the letter of the choice that best completes each item.

_____ 6. Hana did a **thorough** job of cleaning her room. Hana

    A. dusted the room a little.
    B. spent a long time carefully cleaning.
    C. cleaned the room once a month.

_____ 7. The magician **convinced** the audience that he could read minds. The audience

    A. believed the magician.
    B. laughed at the magician.
    C. paid no attention to the magician.

_____ 8. On the first day of school, all the new faces and instructions **overwhelmed** Emmy. Emmy

    A. was pleased with the new experience.
    B. was confused by being faced with so much that was new.
    C. gained a better view of herself.

_____ 9. Paul quickly **comprehended** the instructions for building the model. When it comes to building models, it seems that Paul is

    A. not interested.
    B. not experienced.
    C. skillful.

_____ 10. Ivan's main **impression** of his girlfriend's father was that he had a pleasant smile. Ivan and his girlfriend's father

    A. were close friends.
    B. had seen each other only briefly.
    C. had never met face to face.

➤ *Synonyms and Antonyms*

A. Synonyms. Write the letter of the word or phrase that most nearly means the **same** as each boldfaced word.

____ 1. **convince**

    A. point out   B. study

    C. persuade   D. fear

____ 2. **dramatic**

    A. helpful   B. striking

    C. confusing   D. not well-known

____ 3. **illustrate**

    A. have faith   B. work hard

    C. give examples   D. argue

____ 4. **impression**

    A. belief   B. proof

    C. news   D. honesty

____ 5. **overwhelm**

    A. delay   B. make clear

    C. overpower   D. overwork

B. Antonyms. Write the letter of the word or phrase that most nearly means the **opposite** of each boldfaced word.

____ 6. **anxious**

    A. calm   B. forgetful

    C. busy   D. lonely

____ 7. **comprehend**

    A. pretend   B. know

    C. find   D. misunderstand

____ 8. **frank**

    A. certain   B. expert

    C. humorous   D. dishonest

____ 9. **inferior**

    A. far away   B. well-known

    C. better   D. simple

____10. **thorough**

    A. truthful   B. risky

    C. sensible   D. incomplete

➤ *Final Check*

Read the passages carefully. Then fill in each blank with the word that best fits the context.

A. Fear of Public Speaking

A. **anxious**	B. **convince**	C. **inferior**	D. **overwhelm**	E. **thorough**

I get (1)_____ even thinking about getting up in front of the whole class to give my history report. I don't know why I'm so worried. I guess I'm afraid that I will humiliate° myself. I have done a (2)_____ job of preparing my report; I don't think I've left out anything important. I guess I compare myself with others and worry about whether my work is (3)_____ to theirs. I hope that my fears won't be so strong that they (4)_____ me and prevent me from doing a good job. I'll just have to (5)_____ myself that as long as I have made an effort, my report will be OK.

B. Mrs. Thornton's Condition

F. **comprehend**	G. **dramatic**	H. **frank**	I. **illustrate**	J. **impression**

Adults should be honest with children. I can (6)_____ this point by telling how I and my fellow first-graders suffered when our teacher had a baby. It wasn't that we didn't like babies or that we didn't like Mrs. Thornton. Most of us loved them both. The problem was that we did not realize she was pregnant, so her (7) _____ growth frightened us. Could that happen to us some day? Would we balloon up for no reason? Also, we were worried about her. But even when we made our concern evident° by asking what was happening to her, she gave us only senseless° answers, like "I guess I ate too much breakfast!"

Finally, one day she didn't appear at school. Our principal simply announced, "Mrs. Thornton will not be your teacher anymore." We were left with the (8)_____ that something awful had happened to her. We were fearful and sad. Fortunately, the substitute teacher who took Mrs. Thornton's place sympathized° with us. When she saw our tearful faces, she realized we did not (9)_____ the situation. She explained that Mrs. Thornton had just had a baby and that she was fine and very happy. But we could have been saved a great deal of worry and fear if the adults in our lives had just been more (10)_____ with us and had clarified° the situation—instead of hiding the truth.

Scores	Check 2 _____%	Word Work _____%	Synonyms and Antonyms _____%	Final Check _____%

Enter your scores above and in the vocabulary performance chart on the inside back cover of the book.

CHAPTER

25

acquire	precede
commitment	resent
formal	solemn
fragment	spite
fundamental	symbolize

Ten Words in Context

In the space provided, write the letter of the meaning closest to that of each **boldfaced** word. Use the context of the sentences to help you figure out each word's meaning.

1 acquire
(ə-kwīr′)
– *verb*

- While living in England, Brad **acquired** a little bit of an English accent.
- Before going on the trip, I **acquired** a good pair of hiking boots.

___*Acquire* means   A. to appreciate.   B. to get.   C. to do without.

2 commitment
(kə-mĭt′mənt)
– *noun*

- Nita has made a **commitment** to stop smoking this year.
- The Greens made a **commitment** to give 5 percent of their income to charity.

___*Commitment* means   A. promise.   B. piece.   C. symbol.

3 formal
(fôr′məl)
– *adjective*

- Because the boss is a rather **formal** person, people in the office never call him by his first name or try to joke with him.
- A **formal** wedding can be very expensive, so Julie and Ed have decided on a casual wedding in the park.

___*Formal* means   A. interesting.   B. traditional and proper.   C. full of hope.

4 fragment
(frăg′mənt)
– *noun*

- Don't go into the kitchen barefoot. I broke a glass, and there may still be a **fragment** on the floor.
- Scientists digging up an ancient city found a piece of pottery which they think is a tiny **fragment** of a bowl.

___*Fragment* means   A. whole.   B. copy.   C. small part.

5 fundamental
(fŭn′də-mĕn′tl)
– *adjective*

- A **fundamental** rule of water safety is this: Don't go swimming alone.
- One must learn the **fundamental** operations of arithmetic before going on to algebra.

___*Fundamental* means   A. based on fun.   B. unusual.   C. needing to be learned first.

6 precede
(prĭ-sēd′)
– *verb*

- Do you think that friendship **precedes** love in a relationship? Or does love come first?
- On the East Coast, the 11 o'clock news **precedes** the *Tonight Show*, which begins at 11:35 p.m.

___*Precede* means   A. to come before.   B. to be part of.   C. to stand for.

7 resent
(rĭ-zĕnt′)
– *verb*

- The voters **resent** the fact that the mayor made promises he did not keep after his election.
- People often **resent** being given advice they did not ask for.

___ *Resent* means   A. to feel bitter about.   B. to feel good about.   C. to feel frightened by.

8 solemn
(sŏl′əm)
– *adjective*

- The fire chief told some jokes to get the children's attention. But when he began to speak about not playing with matches, he became **solemn**.
- The group of laughing children became **solemn** when they heard that their friend had been injured.

___ *Solemn* means   A. hard to understand.   B. silly.   C. serious.

9 spite
(spīt)
– *noun*

- Turning against her former friend, the girl said with **spite** in her voice, "Everyone thinks you're a real loser."
- The disk jockeys' **spite** toward each other was obvious. Each of them said nasty things about the other on the air.

___ *Spite* means   A. puzzlement.   B. hate.   C. sense of humor.

10 symbolize
(sĭm′bə-līz′)
– *verb*

- In ancient Egypt, a picture of a small circle with a dot in the middle **symbolized** the sun.
- During World War II, holding two fingers up in a V stood for victory; during the 1960s, it **symbolized** peace.

___ *Symbolize* means   A. to be like.   B. to stand for.   C. to point toward.

Matching Words with Definitions

Following are definitions of the ten words. **Print** each word next to its definition. If you look closely at each word in context, you will be able to figure out its meaning.

1. _____   Proper; not casual; according to custom or tradition

2. _____   A promise to do something; pledge

3. _____   To get through one's own actions; gain something as one's own

4. _____   Basic; forming a foundation; essential

5. _____   A small piece broken off something whole

6. _____   To feel angered and injured by

7. _____   An unfriendly feeling that causes one to want to hurt or shame another

8. _____   To stand for; be a symbol of; represent°

9. _____   Serious and respectful

10. _____   To come before

CAUTION: Do not go any further until you are sure the above answers are correct. Then you can use the definitions to help you in the following practices. Your goal is eventually to know the words well enough so that you don't need to check the definitions at all.

➤ *Check 1*

Using the answer line, complete each item below with the correct word from the box.

| A. **acquire** | B. **commitment** | C. **formal** | D. **fragment** | E. **fundamental** |
| F. **precede** | G. **resent** | H. **solemn** | I. **spite** | J. **symbolize** |

_____ 1. When I dropped the blue china vase, it broke into ___s.

_____ 2. The neighbors' ___ to keep their street beautiful shows in their neat lawns and lovely flower gardens.

_____ 3. Instead of having a ___ class, the instructor and students held a picnic.

_____ 4. Every year, the library ___s about two hundred new books.

_____ 5. The soap-opera character is famous for her ___. In almost every episode, she is planning to do something nasty to someone she dislikes.

_____ 6. Crystal ___s the way her roommate cooks late-night snacks and then leaves dirty dishes for her to clean up.

_____ 7. When I go to a movie theater, I try to get there early enough so that I can see the ads that ___ the film.

_____ 8. Jerome is usually lighthearted, but he becomes ___ when he talks about his brother's struggle with mental illness.

_____ 9. There are lots of rules about good manners, but the ___ idea behind them all is this: Treat people the way you wish they would treat you.

_____ 10. After the attacks on the World Trade Center and the Pentagon, many people wore small American flags to ___ their sympathy and patriotism.

NOTE: Now check your answers to these questions by turning to page 240. Going over the answers carefully will help you prepare for the remaining practices, for which answers are not given.

➤ *Check 2*

Using the answer lines, complete each item below with **two** words from the box.

_____
_____ 1–2. To remind themselves of why they are saving money, Sam and Chris ___d a dollhouse to ___ the real house they hope to buy someday.

_____
_____ 3–4. Everyone was very ___ at the much-loved doctor's funeral. Many people expressed their ___ to carrying on his good works and keeping his memory alive.

_____
_____ 5–6. Graduation day begins with the principal's speech, which ___s the handing out of diplomas. His speech is always very ___. But afterward, one of the teachers gives a casual, funny talk.

_____
_____ 7–8. When Ray was ordered to share his toy with his sister, he showed his ___ by breaking the toy into pieces and handing the ___s to the girl.

_____
_____ 9–10. Maya ___s the fact that Will told her secret to other people. By doing that, he broke a ___ rule of friendship.

➤ *Word Work*

A. In the space provided, write the letter of the choice that best completes each item.

_____ 1. The cosmetic company has made a **commitment** never to test its products on animals. The company

    A. never used to test its products on animals, but now does.
    B. is looking into the idea of testing its products on animals.
    C. has promised not to test its products on animals.

_____ 2. The mood in the courtroom was **solemn**. People in the courtroom had heard something very

    A. exciting.   B. serious.   C. funny.

_____ 3. Somehow or other, the reporter **acquired** a copy of the secret memo. The reporter had

    A. lost a copy of the memo. B. sold a copy of the memo. C. gotten a copy of the memo.

_____ 4. Since their discussion, Ana has **resented** Mark. Ana

    A. is angry about what Mark said.
    B. agrees with what Mark had to say.
    C. forgot what Mark said.

_____ 5. Devon's voice was full of **spite** as he spoke to his teammate. Devon

    A. admired his teammate.
    B. was angry with his teammate.
    C. was entertained by his teammate.

B. Write each word next to the examples that best match it.

| A. **formal** | B. **fragment** | C. **fundamental** |
| D. **precede** | E. **symbol** | |

_____ 6. A dance at which the men wear tuxedos and the women wear long dresses
    Bowing to the queen
    Standing up when an older person enters the room

_____ 7. A bit of broken glass
    A piece of an old dish
    A scrap of torn-up paper

_____ 8. A before B
    January before February
    President George Washington before President Abraham Lincoln

_____ 9. The color red means anger.
    In a letter, a row of *XXX*'s means kisses.
    The bald eagle stands for the United States.

_____ 10. Spanish I
    The ABCs
    Food, shelter, clothing

➤ *Analogies*

Each item below starts with a pair of words in CAPITAL LETTERS. For each item, figure out the relationship between these two words. Then decide which of the choices (A, B, C, or D) expresses a similar relationship. Write the letter of your choice on the answer line. (All the repeated words in these items are from this unit.)

_____ 1. PRECEDE : FOLLOW ::

    A. hurry : rush   B. earlier : later

    C. speak : talk   D. bother : annoy

_____ 2. SPITE : BITTERNESS ::

    A. insult : compliment   B. abolish° : keep

    C. love : hate   D. friendship : affection

_____ 3. ACQUIRE : OWN ::

    A. get : possess°   B. clarify° : confuse

    C. locate : lose   D. buy : sell

_____ 4. SOLEMN : PLAYFUL ::

    A. funny : laughter   B. fun : party

    C. ugly : talented   D. boring : exciting

_____ 5. FRAGMENT : WHOLE ::

    A. law school : lawyer   B. fixed : broken

    C. dog : German shepherd   D. page : book

_____ 6. HONEST : CORRUPT° ::

    A. early : late   B. fundamental : basic

    C. start : begin   D. symbolize : flag

_____ 7. OIL : RESOURCES° ::

    A. hate : love   B. give : gift

    C. uncle : relatives   D. coal : mine

_____ 8. SENSELESS° : MEANINGFUL ::

    A. old : ancient   B. ball : bat

    C. food : grapes   D. peace : war

_____ 9. VERTICAL° : FLAGPOLE ::

    A. convert° : change   B. flat : table

    C. cold : summer   D. gray : black

_____10. EXTEND° : SHORTEN ::

    A. frank° : honest   B. easy : difficult

    C. precise° : exact   D. wear : necklace

➤ *Final Check*

Read the passages carefully. Then fill in each blank with the word that best fits the context.

A. Wacky Weddings

A. **commitment**	B. **formal**	C. **fundamental**	D. **precede**	E. **symbolize**

The ingredients needed for a wedding are pretty basic. They include two people who have decided to get married and someone qualified to marry them. But from the same (1)_____ ingredients, people create an amazing variety° of ceremonies. Some weddings are very (2)_____. In those, the bride and groom wear traditional outfits—a fancy white dress for her, a tuxedo for him—and have bridesmaids and groomsmen. During such customary° weddings, the groom (3)_____s the bride down the aisle, and afterward, they leave hand in hand. But some people like their weddings to be playful rather than traditional. One man and woman got married while dressed as clowns. Another couple were married while riding a roller coaster. Yet others have said "I do" while they were doing something energetic°, like skydiving or ice skating.

Is an offbeat wedding any less meaningful than a traditional one? The couples that choose unusual weddings say "no." They say the most important thing is the (4)_____ that they are making to one another. In the case of the two clowns, they said that their unusual wedding (5)_____d their desire to keep fun in their marriage.

B. The Cost of Hatred

F. **acquire**	G. **fragment**	H. **resent**	I. **solemn**	J. **spite**

An old story illustrates° the nature of (6)_____ and the terrible effects such meanness can have on people. There were two merchants in a village. They had grown up together, and each always (7)_____ed what the other did. No one could remember why the two men had first quarreled. But by the time they were middle-aged, their hatred of one another influenced° their lives greatly. Neither could bear to see the other happy or successful. If one of them (8)_____d a new house, the other had to get a bigger, better one. If one man's shop did well, the other was furious until his did better. One day, one of the men dropped on old jar that had been sitting on a shelf for years. It broke into (9)_____s. Immediately, a mighty genie appeared. "Oh, lucky man!" said the genie. "You have a great opportunity, for I will grant you any wish. But first I must give you one small warning. Whatever you wish for yourself, your enemy will receive in double measure. If you wish for a million dollars, he will receive two million. If you ask for a golden castle, he will have two." The man became (10)_____ and thought deeply. There were many wonderful things he could ask for, but he could not bear to think of his lifelong enemy receiving twice as much as he did. Finally he thought of an answer to his problem. An evil smile spread over his face as he made his wish. "I wish, Genie," he said, "that you would beat me half to death."

Scores Check 2 _____%	Word Work _____%	Analogies _____%	Final Check _____%

Enter your scores above and in the vocabulary performance chart on the inside back cover of the book.

UNIT FIVE: Review

The box at the right lists twenty-five words from Unit Five. Using the clues at the bottom of the page, fill in these words to complete the puzzle that follows.

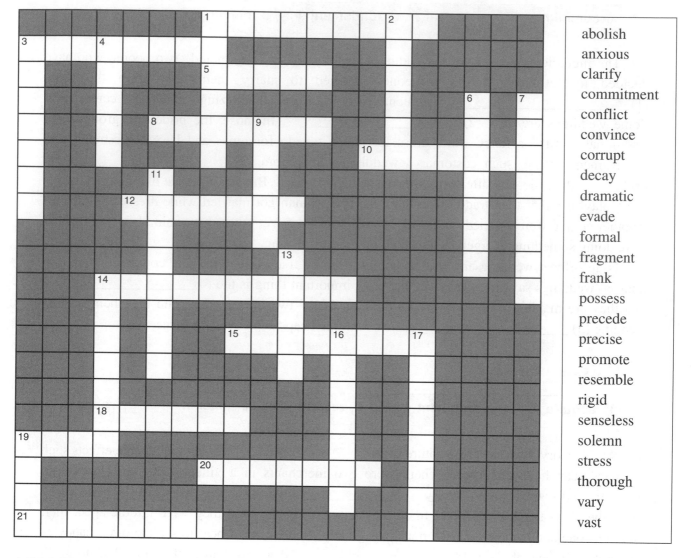

abolish
anxious
clarify
commitment
conflict
convince
corrupt
decay
dramatic
evade
formal
fragment
frank
possess
precede
precise
promote
resemble
rigid
senseless
solemn
stress
thorough
vary
vast

ACROSS

1. Foolish; not making good sense
3. A quarrel or fight; disagreement
5. Stiff; not bending
8. To own; have
10. Worried; troubled; fearful about what might happen
12. To come before
14. A promise to do something
15. Having very exciting, interesting qualities; striking; very noticeable
18. Proper; not casual; according to custom or tradition
19. To experience change; become different
20. Exact; correct; accurate
21. Complete; very carefully done

DOWN

1. Mental or emotional strain
2. Serious and respectful
3. Dishonest; crooked
4. Honest and open; sincere
6. To speak for or work toward something; encourage
7. To look like or be similar to
9. To escape or avoid through clever action
11. A small piece broken off something whole
13. To gradually break down; rot
14. To make clear or easy to understand
16. To put an end to
17. To persuade by argument or proof
19. Very large in size, amount, or area

UNIT FIVE: Test 1

PART A
Choose the word that best completes each item and write it in the space provided.

_____ 1. Some of the new ___ for treating cancer are quicker and less unpleasant than older ones.

    A. vicinities   B. fragments   C. conflicts   D. procedures

_____ 2. In court, the decision of the jury must be ___. If even one juror has a different opinion, the decision doesn't count.

    A. senseless   B. vertical   C. solemn   D. unanimous

_____ 3. When we lived in the ___ of a railroad, we got so used to the noise of trains that we stopped noticing it.

    A. resources   B. vicinity   C. precaution   D. tendency

_____ 4. Marie's moods ___ with the weather. She's cheerful when the sun shines and gloomy when it's cloudy.

    A. decay   B. precede   C. abolish   D. vary

_____ 5. Even good events can create ___ in people's lives. For example, researchers have found that there's even more strain in getting married than in being fired from one's job.

    A. fragment   B. stress   C. resource   D. precaution

_____ 6. To ___ how much smell affects taste, our teacher had us eat a banana while smelling an onion.

    A. evade   B. illustrate   C. resent   D. overwhelm

_____ 7. Emily went through life feeling ___ to her brother, who she believed was more intelligent and talented than she could ever be.

    A. inferior   B. senseless   C. thorough   D. formal

_____ 8. The new principal wants to ___ report cards. The kids love the idea of having no report cards, but the teachers do not.

    A. abolish   B. corrupt   C. overwhelm   D. expand

_____ 9. When Jared's father asked, "What time did you come in last night?" Jared tried to ___ the question by answering, "I wasn't wearing a watch."

    A. comprehend   B. resent   C. evade   D. symbolize

_____ 10. When I take jeans off the clothesline, they often feel ___, so I shake them or put them in the clothes dryer for a few minutes to make them soft again.

    A. anxious   B. dramatic   C. fundamental   D. rigid

(Continues on next page)

_____ 11. Myrna's purple and black living room is certainly ___, but I prefer something a little less showy.

        A. corrupt   B. fundamental   C. precise   D. dramatic

_____ 12. From the smile on Rico's face, you might have the ___ that he has no problems. The truth is, however, that his parents are both quite ill, and he lost his job two weeks ago.

        A. commitment   B. precaution   C. impression   D. fragment

_____ 13. The Masons were not very happy when their daughter ___ a nose-ring.

        A. extended   B. reformed   C. acquired   D. preceded

PART B
Write **C** if the italicized word is used **correctly**. Write **I** if the word is used **incorrectly**.

_____ 14. I used to be *anxious* about going to the dentist, but then I started going to Dr. Craine. He's so funny and nice that I just can't feel afraid of him.

_____ 15. Ms. Acosta is respected for being a *corrupt* teacher. She'll make you work hard, but you'll gain a lot from her course.

_____ 16. The former friends are certainly not nice to each other now. At the party, they *promoted* each other all evening.

_____ 17. Because I missed the first fifteen minutes of the movie, I didn't really *comprehend* the rest of the story.

_____ 18. Soaking cucumbers in vinegar will *convert* them into pickles.

_____ 19. Parties at the Schroeders' house are rather *formal*, with guests taking off their shoes, helping themselves to food from the refrigerator, and generally acting at home.

_____ 20. I was *frank* enough to tell Edna that she looked lovely in her new purple dress, even though I really thought it made her look like an eggplant.

_____ 21. After angrily tearing up her boyfriend's letter, Elaine wanted to read it again, so she glued the *fragments* back together.

_____ 22. Whenever Mr. Fletcher goes for a walk, he *precedes* his dog. The dog runs ahead, pulling Mr. Fletcher by the leash.

_____ 23. Mac did a *thorough* job of cleaning our windows; they seem almost invisible.

_____ 24. The natural *resources* of South Africa include gold and diamonds.

_____ 25. The teacher wanted to *overwhelm* his new students, so he gave them just a little homework at first.

Score   (Number correct) _____ × 4 = _____%

UNIT FIVE: Test 2

PART A
On the answer line, write the word from the box that completes each item below. Use each word once.

A. **assert**	B. **conflict**	C. **convince**	D. **decay**	E. **expand**
F. **fundamental**	G. **precaution**	H. **precise**	I. **renew**	J. **resemble**
K. **solemn**	L. **symbolize**	M. **tendency**		

_____ 1. Two robins in the yard were having a noisy ___ over a worm that they both wanted to eat.

_____ 2. In a forest, fallen trees ___ until they become part of the earth on the forest floor.

_____ 3. If you're making a pair of pants, you have to be ___ in your measurements if you want the pants to fit well.

_____ 4. Small dogs are quick and lively; large dogs have a ___ to be quiet and slow-moving.

_____ 5. The TV ad ___s that this little eight-pound vacuum cleaner does a better job than many full-size vacuums.

_____ 6. When Buck plans to eat a big dinner, he wears a pair of pants with a waist that ___s.

_____ 7. Ella is so worried about a house fire that every time she leaves home, she takes the ___ of unplugging all the lamps, the toaster, and the TV.

_____ 8. In my opinion, the smell of blue cheese ___s the smell of an old running shoe.

_____ 9. Even though I had homework to do, Raoul ___d me that I should go skating with him instead. He said, "The exercise will wake up your brain."

_____ 10. My parents were not strict about housekeeping, but they did have two ___ rules: we had to make our beds every morning, and we were never allowed to leave unwashed dishes overnight.

_____ 11. Some paper companies are taking steps to ___ the forests they are cutting down, so that in the future, the forests will still be there.

_____ 12. Although everyone was ___ at my grandfather's funeral, there was laughter at the luncheon afterward, when people began telling loving, funny stories about him.

_____ 13. In many stories and pictures, the dove is used to ___ peace.

(Continues on next page)

PART B
Write **C** if the italicized word is used **correctly**. Write **I** if the word is used **incorrectly**.

_____14. The thing that prisoners *possess* most is freedom.

_____15. In some companies, workers can *extend* their workday by two hours and then enjoy three-day weekends.

_____16. The day was hot and sunny; *nevertheless*, almost no one showed up to use the city swimming pool.

_____17. It is a shame how spending time with the wrong people has *reformed* Nathan. He used to be a nice guy, but now he's rude and not exactly honest.

_____18. Most department stores have a few computer games for sale, but you have to go to a computer store for a really *vast* selection of games.

_____19. When Thomas tried to explain how the accident happened, he was so excited and confused that he only *clarified* the story.

_____20. Mr. Lee feels that serving high-quality food at reasonable prices is the most *senseless* way of gaining loyal customers.

_____21. Although I had the *preconception* that Mrs. Arnold would be a difficult person to work for, I soon came to like her very much.

_____22. I painted a line from the left edge of the wall all the way over to the right edge, and then I covered that *vertical* line with a colorful border design.

_____23. The police arrested a man who wrote a *commitment* describing how he had robbed the video store.

_____24. I *resent* what my brother did. After I told him what I was going to buy for our mother's birthday, he rushed out and bought it first, so I had to come up with a new idea.

_____25. Judging from the way Tina and Frank keep smiling and winking at one another, there seems to be a good deal of *spite* between them.

Score   (Number correct) _____ × 4 = _____ %

Enter your score above and in the vocabulary performance chart on the inside back cover of the book.

UNIT FIVE: Test 3

PART A: Synonyms
In the space provided, write the letter of the choice that is most nearly the **same** in meaning as the **boldfaced** word.

_____ 1. **assert**   A) state as true   B) put limits on   C) give one's time
D) make more difficult

_____ 2. **commitment**   A) location   B) promise   C) opinion   D) difficulty

_____ 3. **convince**   A) persuade   B) differ   C) listen carefully   D) own

_____ 4. **decay**   A) own   B) look for   C) break down   D) replace

_____ 5. **evade**   A) stand for   B) struggle   C) make clear   D) avoid

_____ 6. **fragment**   A) unfriendly feeling   B) a snack   C) piece of a whole
D) true statement

_____ 7. **fundamental**   A) careless   B) bored   C) stiff   D) basic

_____ 8. **illustrate**   A) replace   B) stand for   C) show through example   D) get

_____ 9. **impression**   A) argument   B) piece   C) effort   D) belief

_____ 10. **nevertheless**   A) even so   B) afterward   C) because   D) even better

_____ 11. **overwhelm**   A) receive   B) overpower   C) understand   D) come before

_____ 12. **possess**   A) lie about   B) own   C) differ   D) show

_____ 13. **precaution**   A) something done to prevent a problem   B) something done to fix a
problem   C) a problem   D) a result

_____ 14. **preconception** A) truth   B) decision   C) opinion formed before knowing
about something   D) area nearby

_____ 15. **procedure**   A) part of a whole   B) way of doing something   C) reason   D) goal

_____ 16. **reform**   A) make better   B) replace   C) learn about   D) prevent

_____ 17. **renew**   A) mention again   B) start up again   C) ignore   D) make clear

_____ 18. **resemble**   A) be ahead   B) be similar to   C) worry about   D) improve

_____ 19. **resent**   A) replace   B) rot   C) feel angry at   D) differ

_____ 20. **resources**   A) something missing   B) period of time   C) enough
D) wealth of a country

_____ 21. **solemn**   A) serious   B) noticeable   C) complete   D) careless

_____ 22. **symbolize**   A) show   B) make use of   C) get larger   D) stand for

_____ 23. **tendency**   A) anger   B) habit   C) tension   D) belief

_____ 24. **unanimous**   A) in full agreement   B) quarreling   C) carefully done   D) basic

_____ 25. **vicinity**   A) neighborhood   B) wealth   C) promise   D) opinion

(Continues on next page)

PART B: Antonyms
In the space provided, write the letter of the choice that is most nearly **opposite** in meaning to the **boldfaced** word.

____26. **abolish**   A) differ   B) create   C) give away   D) ignore

____27. **acquire**   A) make worse   B) escape   C) lose   D) see

____28. **anxious**   A) dishonest   B) tired   C) careless   D) relaxed

____29. **clarify**   A) include   B) correct   C) confuse   D) grow strong

____30. **comprehend**   A) enjoy   B) give away   C) misunderstand
D) remain the same

____31. **conflict**   A) anger   B) loss   C) profit   D) agreement

____32. **convert**   A) keep the same   B) make more expensive   C) hide from sight
D) reduce in size

____33. **corrupt**   A) useful   B) honest   C) loose   D) careless

____34. **dramatic**   A) not noticeable   B) brightly colored   C) careful   D) careless

____35. **expand**   A) agree   B) confuse   C) begin   D) become smaller

____36. **extend**   A) begin   B) give away   C) shorten   D) make worse

____37. **formal**   A) attractive   B) not sincere   C) casual   D) troubled

____38. **frank**   A) careless   B) dishonest   C) loose   D) not enough

____39. **inferior**   A) recent   B) better   C) far away   D) serious

____40. **precede**   A) get smaller   B) grow   C) happen again   D) come after

____41. **precise**   A) not serious   B) not complete   C) not exact   D) not common

____42. **promote**   A) remember   B) anger   C) increase   D) discourage

____43. **rigid**   A) dull   B) rude   C) bending   D) correct

____44. **senseless**   A) depressing   B) dirty   C) active   D) reasonable

____45. **spite**   A) reaction   B) action   C) growth   D) friendly feeling

____46. **stress**   A) relaxation   B) argument   C) question   D) idea

____47. **thorough**   A) not proper   B) harmful   C) boring   D) not complete

____48. **vary**   A) confuse   B) stay the same   C) disappear   D) make worse

____49. **vast**   A) small   B) changing   C) unpleasant   D) better

____50. **vertical**   A) small   B) better   C) not interested   D) horizontal

---

| *Score*   (Number correct) _____ × 2 = _____ % |

Enter your score above and in the vocabulary performance chart on the inside back cover of the book.

Unit Six

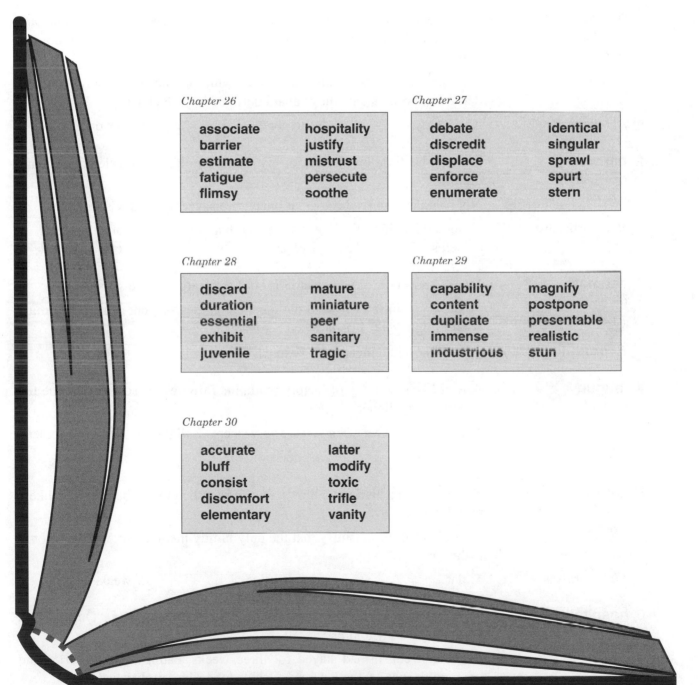

Chapter 26

associate	hospitality
barrier	justify
estimate	mistrust
fatigue	persecute
flimsy	soothe

Chapter 27

debate	identical
discredit	singular
displace	sprawl
enforce	spurt
enumerate	stern

Chapter 28

discard	mature
duration	miniature
essential	peer
exhibit	sanitary
juvenile	tragic

Chapter 29

capability	magnify
content	postpone
duplicate	presentable
immense	realistic
industrious	stun

Chapter 30

accurate	latter
bluff	modify
consist	toxic
discomfort	trifle
elementary	vanity

CHAPTER

26

associate	hospitality
barrier	justify
estimate	mistrust
fatigue	persecute
flimsy	soothe

Ten Words in Context

In the space provided, write the letter of the meaning closest to that of each **boldfaced** word. Use the context of the sentences to help you figure out each word's meaning.

1 associate
(ə-sō′shē-āt′)
– *verb*

- My sister's house is always full of African American, Asian, Hispanic, and white kids. "I want my kids to **associate** with all kinds of children, not just children who look like them," she says.

- The people next door don't **associate** with anyone in the neighborhood. They don't even attend the annual Fourth of July block party.

___ *Associate* means   A. to study.   B. to get together.   C. to work.

2 barrier
(băr′ē-ər)
– *noun*

- To keep his little brother out of his room, Tim built a **barrier** of toys and clothing.

- Not being able to read is a great **barrier** to success in today's world.

___ *Barrier* means   A. something that helps.   B. something that explains.   C. something that gets in the way.

3 estimate
(ĕs′tə-māt′)
– *verb*

- I don't know how old my doctor is, but I **estimate** that she's about 60.

- "I know you haven't figured out our final grades yet, but can you **estimate** what I might get?" Frieda asked her teacher.

___ *Estimate* means   A. to make a judgment.   B. to have hope.   C. to fear.

4 fatigue
(fə-tēg′)
– *noun*

- After Mike's first day of factory work, his **fatigue** was so great that he fell asleep during dinner.

- You shouldn't drive when you are very sleepy. **Fatigue** can cause an accident.

___ *Fatigue* means   A. tiredness.   B. mood.   C. energy.

5 flimsy
(flĭm′zē)
– *adjective*

- The next time a hard wind blows, that **flimsy** shed in our back yard is likely to fall down.

- That old chair is so **flimsy** that the only family member allowed to sit on it is the cat.

___ *Flimsy* means   A. dark.   B. expensive.   C. weak.

6 hospitality
(hŏs′pĭ-tăl′ĭ-tē)
– *noun*

- The family we visited in Mexico showed us true **hospitality**. "Our house is your house," they told us.

- After their cousin had stayed for three weeks, eating their groceries and tying up the phone, the Petersons decided their **hospitality** had to end.

___ *Hospitality* means   A. curing the sick.   B. traveling.   C. welcoming visitors.

7 justify
(jŭs′tə-fī′)
– *verb*

- Nothing can **justify** the cruel way that our neighbor speaks to her children.
- Josie tried to **justify** eating her little sister's cookie by saying, "I was afraid she might choke on it."

___ *Justify* means   A. to bother.   B. to excuse.   C. to repeat.

8 mistrust
(mĭs-trŭst′)
– *verb*

- The way Donna's new boyfriend won't give a straight answer to any question makes me **mistrust** him.
- You should **mistrust** any e-mail that says you've won some wonderful prize. Chances are it isn't true.

___ *Mistrust* means   A. to doubt.   B. to believe.   C. to harm.

9 persecute
(pûr′sĭ-kyo͞ot)
– *verb*

- A fifth-grade bully **persecuted** smaller classmates by teasing, pushing, and tripping them.
- White classmates of the African American playwright August Wilson **persecuted** him daily with written threats.

___ *Persecute* means   A. to support.   B. to treat badly.   C. to try to avoid.

10 soothe
(so͞o*th*)
– *verb*

- Sometimes the sound of a vacuum cleaner will **soothe** fussy babies and help them go to sleep.
- What **soothes** you when you're feeling tired and cranky? For me, a cup of hot tea and a warm bath usually help.

___ *Soothe* means   A. to comfort.   B. to excite.   C. to annoy.

Matching Words with Definitions

Following are definitions of the ten words. **Print** each word next to its definition. If you look closely at each word in context, you will be able to figure out its meaning.

1. _____   To give a good reason for; show to be right

2. _____   To have no trust in; doubt

3. _____   To make a guess at the size, amount, value, etc. of something

4. _____   Light, thin, and lacking strength

5. _____   Generous, friendly treatment of guests

6. _____   Something that blocks the way

7. _____   To calm or comfort someone or something

8. _____   The state of being very tired

9. _____   To spend time; join

10. _____   To harm again and again; treat cruelly, especially because of dislike of a person's ideas, race, religion, etc.

CAUTION: Do not go any further until you are sure the above answers are correct. Then you can use the definitions to help you in the following practices. Your goal is eventually to know the words well enough so that you don't need to check the definitions at all.

➤ *Check 1*

Using the answer line, complete each item below with the correct word from the box.

A. **associate**	B. **barrier**	C. **estimate**	D. **fatigue**	E. **flimsy**
F. **hospitality**	G. **justify**	H. **mistrust**	I. **persecute**	J. **soothe**

_____ 1. "If you lie down with dogs, you'll get up with fleas." This old saying means that if you ___ with bad people, you'll become more like them.

_____ 2. The saleswoman who sold the dress to me ___d that it needed to be shortened by two inches or so.

_____ 3. I'd like to go to that fancy new beauty salon in town, but I can't ___ paying so much for a haircut.

_____ 4. The little girl shivered. Her ___ dress did not protect her from the cold.

_____ 5. Esperanza wants to learn English quickly. She knows that her poor English is a ___ to getting a good job.

_____ 6. Lee says that his boss ___s him because he has long hair, but I don't think he's right. I think his boss is always yelling at him because he's lazy.

_____ 7. I think I'm getting sick. I haven't worked hard, but I still feel great ___.

_____ 8. To ___ his crying daughter, Roberto hugged her gently and sang to her.

_____ 9. It's not fair to ___ Mr. Anderson just because he looks like your dishonest Uncle Sal. His coworkers trust him completely.

_____ 10. The Thompsons are well-known for their ___. They often have guests staying with them, and people are constantly dropping in for meals.

NOTE: Now check your answers to these questions by turning to page 240. Going over the answers carefully will help you prepare for the remaining practices, for which answers are not given.

➤ *Check 2*

Using the answer lines, complete each item below with **two** words from the box.

_____
_____ 1–2. Bernie had to walk for several miles in the snowstorm, wearing only a ___ jacket. By the time he got home, he felt sick with cold and ___.

_____
_____ 3–4. Sonia arrived at her aunt's house feeling angry and tired after a bad day at work. But her aunt's warm ___ helped to ___ her, and soon she was feeling much better.

_____
_____ 5–6. Lonnie tries to ___ his ___ of people by saying, "I have no faith in people. They're all just waiting for a chance to stab you in the back."

_____
_____ 7–8. Because the bridge is unsafe to drive on, the mayor has ordered workers to put up ___s at both ends of it. He ___s that the bridge will be closed for about six weeks.

_____
_____ 9–10. How can you ___ with people who preach "white power"? Doesn't it bother you that they ___ people of other races?

➤ *Word Work*

A. Write each word next to the examples that best match it.

A. **barrier**	B. **estimate**	C. **flimsy**
D. **justify**	E. **persecute**	

_____ 1. Selling African Americans as slaves
Forcing Jews into Nazi concentration camps
Chasing Gypsies out of European towns

_____ 2. "The reason property taxes must be raised is that the money is needed for important school repairs."
"My alarm clock didn't go off, so I was late to work."
"I didn't return your call yesterday because I didn't get home until midnight."

_____ 3. I think our houses are about a mile apart.
The little girl looks about six years old.
It should take an hour or so to finish the job.

_____ 4. The cheap tennis shoes fell apart quickly.
That lightweight blanket won't keep you warm.
The walls between our apartments are so thin that we hear every word our neighbors say.

_____ 5. A two-foot pile of snow at the end of the driveway
A fence surrounding an open manhole
No high-school diploma

B. In the space provided, write the letter of the choice that best completes each item.

_____ 6. You are most likely to **mistrust** someone who
A. has lied to you before.
B. offers to lend you money.
C. has a good sense of humor.

_____ 7. Parents generally want their children to **associate** with other kids who
A. cheat and steal.　　B. do poorly in school.　　C. are helpful and polite.

_____ 8. People who are well-known for their **hospitality** probably
A. are fearful of guests.　　B. enjoy having guests.　　C. are wealthy.

_____ 9. Some people avoid **fatigue** by
A. wearing warmer clothing.　　B. taking a brief nap.　　C. being kind to everyone.

_____ 10. In order to **soothe** her crying daughter, Sonia
A. spanked the child.　　B. laughed at her.　　C. read her a story.

➤ *Word Parts*

A. The prefix *mis-* means "bad," " badly," "wrong," "incorrectly," or "lack of."

Examples: misfortune — bad luck
  mistrust — lack of trust

On each answer line, write the word from the box that means the same as the *italicized* words.

A. **misbehave**	B. **misinterpret°**	C. **misplace**
D. **misspell**	E. **misunderstanding**	

_____ 1. Those children often *behave badly*. Yesterday, they finger-painted on the walls with peanut butter and put chewing gum in the cat's fur.

_____ 2. I always *put* my glasses *in the wrong place*. I'm going to get a chain and hang them around my neck. Then I'll always know where they are.

_____ 3. Because of a *lack of understanding* about the class schedule, we thought our final exam was on May 21 instead of May 25.

_____ 4. "Don't *interpret incorrectly* what I said," the coach told the player. "I'm not trying to get rid of you; I'm simply trying to get you to play better."

_____ 5. The teacher handed out a list of words that people often *spell incorrectly*, such as "weird," "separate," "friend," and "embarrass."

B. The suffix *-fy* means "cause to become," "cause to have," or "make."

Examples: pure — clean   solid — firm
  purify — cause to become clean   solidify — make firm

On each answer line, write the word from the box that best completes the item.

F. **beautify**	G. **clarify°**	H. **falsify**
I. **satisfy**	J. **terrify**	

_____ 6. Some people enjoy Stephen King's horror stories, but they ___ me so badly I can't sleep.

_____ 7. The bank employee used his computer to ___ company records and hide the extra checks he wrote to himself.

_____ 8. If people eat only enough to ___ their hunger, they are unlikely to become overweight.

_____ 9. "I'm not sure I understand the directions for the project," one student said to the teacher. "Could you ___ them, please?"

_____ 10. People try all kinds of things in order to ___ themselves, from dyeing their hair and using makeup to having cosmetic surgery.

➤ *Final Check*

Read the passages carefully. Then fill in each blank with the word that best fits the context.

A. My Parents' Problem

A. **associate**	B. **hospitality**	C. **justify**	D. **mistrust**	E. **persecute**

Sometimes I feel sorry for parents. It must be hard to know what to do when your child is old enough to make his own choices, and you see him making improper° ones. For instance, last year my brother Jason started hanging around with a kid named Allan. When Allan first came to our house, my parents welcomed him with their usual (1)_____. But Allan was rude, as if he resented° them. Worse yet, Jason began to act that way too. There were other things that made me (2)_____ Allan. I knew some of the people he (3)_____d with. Most of them had been in trouble at school and even with the police. My parents finally said that Allan could not come to our house, and if they answered the phone when he called, they were cold to him. When they tried to talk to Jason about his new friend, Jason got angry. He said they (4)_____d Allan for no good reason—just out of spite°. It was an agonizing° time for my family. Finally, though, Jason started pulling away from Allan. And soon after, Allan was arrested for breaking into a drugstore. For Jason, that was enough to (5)_____ our parents' concern. He actually apologized for not listening to them earlier.

B. The Hike That Hurt

F. **barrier**	G. **estimate**	H. **fatigue**	I. **flimsy**	J. **soothe**

"Want to go for a hike on Saturday?" Bert's words were music to my ears. I'd been hoping for the longest time that Bert would ask me out.

City girl that I am, I thought of a "hike" as being a stroll around the park. I couldn't have been more wrong. To begin with, we started with an hour-long drive into what looked to me like the jungle. The hike, which I had (6)_____d would take about forty-five minutes, lasted six weeks. Well, not really. But it must have dragged on for at least four hours. I was tired at the end of an hour. After another two hours, I wondered if anyone had ever actually died of (7)_____. And then there were my feet. My tennis shoes were very cute, but they were also cheap and (8)_____, and soon I had blisters the size of Montana. But we kept on going . . . and going . . . and going. We climbed over large (9)_____s, including a huge tree that had fallen across the trail. "Isn't this great?" Bert kept saying, in his usual energetic° way. I just smiled weakly.

Later, as I (10)_____d my aching feet in hot water, Bert called. "Today was so much fun," he said. "Let's go for a *really* long hike next weekend!"

"I have another idea," I said. "Let's do something even *more* fun—like scrub the kitchen floor with a toothbrush."

Scores   Check 2 _____%   Word Work _____%   Word Parts _____%   Final Check _____%

Enter your scores above and in the vocabulary performance chart on the inside back cover of the book.

debate	identical
discredit	singular
displace	sprawl
enforce	spurt
enumerate	stern

Ten Words in Context

In the space provided, write the letter of the meaning closest to that of each **boldfaced** word. Use the context of the sentences to help you figure out each word's meaning.

1 debate
(dĭ-bāt′)
– *verb*

- Over dessert, we were **debating** which was best—chocolate ice cream or vanilla ice cream.
- Brad will **debate** anything. If you say it's a nice day, he'll say, "I don't know about that. Wasn't it a little too warm this morning?"

____*Debate* means   A. to agree.   B. to pay no attention to.   C. to argue.

2 discredit
(dĭs-krĕd′ĭt)
– *verb*

- When his son was arrested, Mr. Kaufman sadly said, "You've **discredited** our family name."
- The writer had stolen someone else's work and claimed it was his. When this was proved, it **discredited** him forever.

____*Discredit* means   A. to shame.   B. to honor.   C. to know.

3 displace
(dĭs-plās′)
– *verb*

- Why did the bathtub overflow when you sat down in it? The reason is that your body **displaced** the water.
- The constant warring in Afghanistan **displaced** thousands of families, who were forced to seek safety away from their homes.

____*Displace* means   A. to help.   B. to stop.   C. to move out.

4 enforce
(ĕn-fôrs′)
– *verb*

- You're not really supposed to take dogs in the park, but nobody **enforces** the rule.
- The rule in our house is "one hour of TV a day," and our parents **enforce** it. If we're caught breaking the rule, we can't watch TV for a week.

____*Enforce* means   A. to insist on.   B. to break.   C. to build.

5 enumerate
(ĭ-nōō′mə-rāt′)
– *verb*

- On her list for Santa Claus, Emily **enumerated** all the books and toys she wanted.
- As we argued, Jill began to **enumerate** all my faults. "All right, that's enough!" I finally said.

____*Enumerate* means   A. to forget.   B. to list.   C. to get rid of.

6 identical
(ī-dĕn′tĭ-kəl)
– *adjective*

- A famous story called "The Necklace" is about a diamond necklace and a necklace made of fake jewels that appear to be **identical**.
- To me, all stars look **identical**. How can anyone tell them apart?

____*Identical* means   A. the same.   B. beautiful.   C. very different.

7 **singular**
(sĭng′gyə-lər)
– *adjective*

- The word "sheep" can be **singular**, referring to just one animal, or plural, referring to a whole flock.
- Why do we say a "pair" of jeans? It's just a **singular** piece of clothing.

___ *Singular* means   A. large.   B. only one.   C. difficult.

8 **sprawl**
(sprôl)
– *verb*

- Hot and panting from his long run, the dog **sprawled** on the cool kitchen floor.
- When I was a little girl, I thought my brother's high-school friends looked like giants as they **sprawled** all over our living-room chairs and sofa.

___ *Sprawl* means   A. to stretch out.   B. to fall.   C. to sit up straight.

9 **spurt**
(spûrt)
– *verb*

- Amy's brother made her laugh so hard at breakfast that orange juice **spurted** out of her mouth and into his face.
- When I turned on the drinking fountain, the water **spurted** out higher and stronger than I expected and splashed me in the face.

___ *Spurt* means   A. to leak slowly.   B. to shoot out.   C. to hold in.

10 **stern**
(stûrn)
adjective

- On the job our principal seems like a **stern** man, but at home he's quite relaxed and friendly.
- "John, come here this minute!" As soon as I heard my father's **stern** voice, I knew I was in trouble.

___ *Stern* means   A. not dangerous.   B. warm and friendly.   C. firm and demanding.

Matching Words with Definitions

Following are definitions of the ten words. **Print** each word next to its definition. If you look closely at each word in context, you will be able to figure out its meaning.

1. _____   To name one by one; list

2. _____   To damage a good name or reputation

3. _____   To flow out suddenly and with force

4. _____   To make sure that a rule or law is obeyed

5. _____   Serious and strict

6. _____   Exactly alike

7. _____   To discuss a question by looking at different points of view; argue

8. _____   Being only one; not plural

9. _____   To sit or lie with the arms and legs thrown outward

10. _____   To move from the usual or proper place; shift the location of

CAUTION: Do not go any further until you are sure the above answers are correct. Then you can use the definitions to help you in the following practices. Your goal is eventually to know the words well enough so that you don't need to check the definitions at all.

➢ *Check 1*

Using the answer line, complete each item below with the correct word from the box.

A. **debate**	B. **discredit**	C. **displace**	D. **enforce**	E. **enumerate**
F. **identical**	G. **singular**	H. **sprawl**	I. **spurt**	J. **stern**

_____ 1. "This afternoon," Ms. Reynolds announced, "we will ___ this question: Should classes be pass/fail, or should they have letter grades?"

_____ 2. My new friend's cruel teasing of her brother ___ed her in my eyes.

_____ 3. I got soaked when I began to disconnect the pipe under our sink, and water ___ed out at me. I had forgotten to turn off the main water line.

_____ 4. The babysitter ___d the twins' 8:30 bedtime. "We don't have to go to bed that early!" they said. "Tonight you do," she answered.

_____ 5. Dad was ___ when we whined about having to walk the dog. "You promised you would take care of him. Now stop complaining," he said.

_____ 6. Patti and Renee laughed when they showed up at the party wearing ___ dresses. "I guess it just shows we both have good taste," Patti said.

_____ 7. Mr. Nelson said, "My wife's good qualities are too many to ___ here."

_____ 8. Some human organs, like the heart and the liver, are ___. Others, such as the kidneys and lungs, come in pairs.

_____ 9. Mario's mother told him, "Don't ___ on the floor like that when you're studying. You're more likely to fall asleep than to learn something."

_____ 10. The tornado destroyed many homes and ___d nearly one hundred people.

NOTE: Now check your answers to these questions by turning to page 241. Going over the answers carefully will help you prepare for the remaining practices, for which answers are not given.

➢ *Check 2*

Using the answer lines, complete each item below with **two** words from the box.

_____
_____ 1–2. "Parents should ___ their rules," said the counselor. " If they don't, they may ___ themselves in their kids' eyes. Kids respect parents who aren't afraid to be tough sometimes."

_____
_____ 3–4. Let's ___ the question of whether the English language makes sense. For example, we say "goose" for a ___ bird and "geese" for more than one. So if it's "moose" for one animal, why isn't it "meese" for two?

_____
_____ 5–6. As the man tripped and fell in the supermarket, he ___ed a stack of boxes of cereal; then he ___ed on the aisle floor.

_____
_____ 7–8. When George hit Cliff so hard that blood ___ed from Cliff's nose, our usually playful gym teacher suddenly became very ___.

_____
_____ 9–10. Libby and Sibby look ___ to me, but my sister knows the twins so well that she can ___ several differences between them.

➤ *Word Work*

A. In the space provided, write the letter of the choice that best completes each item.

_____ 1. People often **discredit** themselves by

    A. changing to a better job.
    B. mailing a letter.
    C. doing something dishonest.

_____ 2. I can **enumerate** the dwarfs in Disney's *Snow White and the Seven Dwarfs.*

    A. They are Bashful, Doc, Dopey, Grumpy, Happy, Sleepy, and Sneezy.
    B. However, I can't list them.
    C. I think the shy one is named Bashful.

_____ 3. The **singular** form of that insect's name is

    A. butterfly.   B. butterflies.

_____ 4. A person is likely to **sprawl** in a chair when

    A. chatting on the phone with a friend.
    B. speaking to a large group.
    C. trying to make a good impression at a job interview.

_____ 5. The water **spurted**

    A. gently down a window pane.
    B. when the fire fighter turned on his hose.
    C. so still I could see the reflection of the clouds in the puddle.

B. In the space provided, write the letter of the word that most closely relates to the situation in each item.

_____ 6. In class, we argued about whether there should be stricter handgun laws.

    A. displace   B. debate   C. discredit

_____ 7. When our cousins moved in with us, my brother and I had to give up our bedroom and start sleeping in the living room.

    A. enumerate   B. spurt   C. displace

_____ 8. During the test, several teachers stood watching us, to make sure that no one cheated.

    A. enforce   B. enumerate   C. debate

_____ 9. All the apartments on this side of the building are exactly alike.

    A. singular   B. stern   C. identical

_____ 10. My father glared at me and said, "Sit down. It's time we had a serious talk."

    A. singular   B. stern   C. enumerate

➤ *Synonyms and Antonyms*

A. Synonyms. Write the letter of the word or phrase that most nearly means the **same** as each boldfaced word.

____ 1. **debate**

    A. undo   B. return

    C. argue   D. agree

____ 2. **enumerate**

    A. pronounce   B. name each one

    C. explain   D. expand

____ 3. **spurt**

    A. burst   B. divide

    C. drip   D. enlarge

____ 4. **enforce**

    A. pressure   B. push out

    C. create   D. insist on

____ 5. **sprawl**

    A. spread out   B. gather in

    C. reach   D. shelter

B. Antonyms. Write the letter of the word or phrase that most nearly means the **opposite** of each boldfaced word.

____ 6. **discredit**

    A. damage   B. praise

    C. pay back   D. help

____ 7. **identical**

    A. nasty   B. alike

    C. personal   D. different

____ 8. **displace**

    A. keep in place   B. fill

    C. remove   D. borrow

____ 9. **singular**

    A. unusual   B. old

    C. many   D. outstanding

____10. **stern**

    A. strict   B. difficult

    C. young   D. easygoing

➤ *Final Check*

Read the passages carefully. Then fill in each blank with the word that best fits the context.

A. A Teacher's Lesson

A. **discredit**	B. **enforce**	C. **enumerate**	D. **singular**	E. **stern**

When Gino got his first paper back from the new English teacher, there seemed to be red ink everywhere. At the end of the paper, Ms. Robbins had (1)_____d some of his mistakes. Below the list, she wrote, "See me after class."

As he walked up to her desk, Gino felt angry and embarrassed. Why did this teacher have to (2)_____ the stupid rules of grammar and spelling?

But the meeting wasn't as bad as Gino expected. Instead of being (3)_____, Ms. Robbins was friendly and helpful. She began showing him how to correct his mistakes. She said, "You wrote 'A pile of bodys was lying in the middle of the football field.' But when the (4)_____ form of a word ends in *y*, you must change the *y* to *ies* when writing about more than one 'Bodys' should have been 'bodies.'"

"What's the difference?" Gino asked. "People can still figure out what I mean."

"Sometimes they can, and sometimes they can't," the teacher said. "But working without care (5)_____s you as a writer. Readers take your ideas less seriously if they aren't written well, and poor spelling can be a barrier° to achieving your goals."

Years later, in college, Gino wrote about Ms. Robbins, calling her the most important teacher he ever had. "She made me work hard," he wrote, "but I realize now that she didn't just teach me to write clearly. She taught me to think clearly, too."

B. My Sports Heroes

F. **debate**	G. **displace**	H. **identical**	I. **sprawl**	J. **spurt**

It all happened so fast, it's hard to for me to describe. But I'll try. While having a snack in the kitchen, my brothers Todd and Roger began to (6)_____ whether football or baseball was the more difficult sport to play well. As they argued, each trying to justify° his theory°, they jumped around and waved their arms. Then Todd's hand smashed against a table. The action (7)_____d a can of soda that was sitting there. Crash! The soda hit the floor, and foam (8)_____ed at least three feet into the air. As Todd jumped away from the foam, he stumbled and (9)_____ed on the kitchen floor. He yelped in pain, and Roger ran toward him, hoping to soothe° his pain. Unfortunately Roger slipped in the puddle of soda and fell on top of Todd. Todd yelled, "I think my wrist is broken." Roger added, "I think mine is, too." They were both right. Now the boys have (10)_____ casts on their left wrists. They proved that arguing can be a difficult sport, too.

Scores Check 2 _____%	Word Work _____%	Synonyms and Antonyms _____%	Final Check _____%

Enter your scores above and in the vocabulary performance chart on the inside back cover of the book.

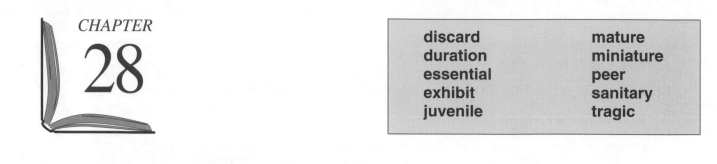

Ten Words in Context

In the space provided, write the letter of the meaning closest to that of each **boldfaced** word. Use the context of the sentences to help you figure out each word's meaning.

1 **discard**
(dĭ-skärd′)
– *verb*

- "Please don't **discard** your paper towel tubes," said the art teacher. "Save them and then bring them in for our projects."
- My uncle wishes he had the comic books he **discarded** when he was a boy. They would be worth quite a lot of money now.

___ *Discard* means   A. to show.   B. to get rid of.   C. to keep.

2 **duration**
(dŏo-rā′shən)
– *noun*

- My little sister held her hands over her eyes for the **duration** of the horror movie.
- School was closed for the **duration** of the snowstorm.

___ *Duration* means   A. a time period.   B. a place.   C. a memory.

3 **essential**
(ĭ-sĕn′shəl)
– *adjective*

- For the overnight trip, Tom packed only a few **essential** supplies, including his toothbrush, toothpaste, and a T-shirt to sleep in.
- On her desk, Holly kept **essential** study items: highlighting pens, index cards, and a dictionary.

___ *Essential* means   A. expensive.   B. needed.   C. large.

4 **exhibit**
(ĭg-zĭb′ĭt)
– *verb*

- The science teacher **exhibited** her bug-eating plants at this year's flower show.
- Many parents **exhibit** their children's artwork on the refrigerator door.

___ *Exhibit* means   A. to lose.   B. to hide.   C. to show.

5 **juvenile**
(jōo′və-nīl′)
– *adjective*

- Puppies, like most **juvenile** animals, are extremely cute. But be sure you know what that cute little puppy will grow into before you take it home.
- Some TV cartoon shows are not meant for **juvenile** audiences and are shown at night, when most children are in bed.

___ *Juvenile* means   A. young.   B. difficult.   C. older.

6 **mature**
(mə-tyŏor′)
– *adjective*

- The largest living animal is the blue whale. A **mature** blue whale, when fully grown, can be over 100 feet long and weigh 300,000 pounds!
- Although Tim is old enough to get his driver's license, his parents don't think he is **mature** enough to be a safe driver.

___ *Mature* means   A. busy.   B. brave.   C. adult.

7 miniature
(mĭn′ē-ə-choŏr′)
– *adjective*

- It can take hours to play a regular game of golf, but **miniature** golf takes much less time because the course is so little.
- Grandma gave my little sister a **miniature** tea set, made up of a tiny teapot and four little cups.

____ *Miniature* means   A. expensive.   B. small-scale.   C. ordinary.

8 peer
(pîr)
– *noun*

- In day care or nursery school, little children learn to share and play with their **peers**.
- Our history teacher is going to an education conference next week. "It's fun to meet and exchange ideas with my **peers** from other schools," she said.

____ *Peer* means   A. an equal.   B. an instructor.   C. a lesson.

9 sanitary
(săn′ĭ-tĕr′ē)
– *adjective*

- "Don't let the puppy lick the baby's face!" said my sister, snatching her child away. "A dog's tongue isn't **sanitary**! The baby might get sick."
- To protect their patients, doctors and nurses don't wear ordinary street clothes in an operating room. They wear special **sanitary** clothing.

____ *Sanitary* means   A. dry.   B. new.   C. clean.

10 tragic
(trăj′ĭk)
– *adjective*

- The **tragic** attacks on the World Trade Center and the Pentagon on September 11, 2001, resulted in the deaths of more than 3,000 people.
- The play *Romeo and Juliet* tells of the **tragic** deaths of two young lovers whose families were enemies.

____ *Tragic* means   A. honest.   B. terrible.   C. failed.

Matching Words with Definitions

Following are definitions of the ten words. **Print** each word next to its definition. If you look closely at each word in context, you will be able to figure out its meaning.

1. _____   To present for others to see; display

2. _____   The time during which something exists or happens; the time remaining for something

3. _____   Made on a small scale

4. _____   To throw away

5. _____   Young; not fully grown; like a child

6. _____   Very sad; involving death, grief, or destruction

7. _____   Necessary

8. _____   A person who is on an equal level with another person, as in age or occupation; a member of the same group as others

9. _____   Free from dirt or germs

10. _____   Adult; fully developed; like an adult

CAUTION: Do not go any further until you are sure the above answers are correct. Then you can use the definitions to help you in the following practices. Your goal is eventually to know the words well enough so that you don't need to check the definitions at all.

➤ *Check 1*

Using the answer line, complete each item below with the correct word from the box.

A. **discard**	B. **duration**	C. **essential**	D. **exhibit**	E. **juvenile**
F. **mature**	G. **miniature**	H. **peer**	I. **sanitary**	J. **tragic**

_____ 1. Last year Maddie liked her dress with Winnie-the-Pooh on it, but now she thinks it makes her look too ___.

_____ 2. Before you put a bandage on that cut, wash it with soap and water to make the area as ___ as possible.

_____ 3. At the bottom of our goldfish bowl lies a ___ pirate's ship.

_____ 4. Lewis likes to restore° old furniture, so he checks what his neighbors put outside in the trash. "You'd be surprised what people ___!" he says.

_____ 5. Mrs. Walker scolded her son for calling their elderly neighbor by her first name. "She's not a ___ of yours. Treat her with more respect."

_____ 6. For me, popcorn is an ___ part of the movie experience. I just don't enjoy a film without it.

_____ 7. "Why do you look so sad?" my father said. "You only failed a test. That's not so ___. It's not as though someone died."

_____ 8. On Hobby Night, Joy ___ed her collection of coins from other countries.

_____ 9. Two rude women whispered throughout the ___ of my father's speech.

_____ 10. Lions live together in groups, with the ___ animals watching out for the younger ones.

NOTE: Now check your answers to these questions by turning to page 241. Going over the answers carefully will help you prepare for the remaining practices, for which answers are not given.

➤ *Check 2*

Using the answer lines, complete each item below with **two** words from the box.

_____
_____ 1–2. When our family has a New Year's Eve party, the little kids have to go to bed at ten o'clock. But the more ___ ones can stay up for the ___ of the party.

_____
_____ 3–4. The movie star ___ed her first husband's love letters. Later, a reporter found them in her trash and ___ed them on TV.

_____
_____ 5–6. "Before you begin cooking," said the TV chef, "it is ___ to make sure your work area is well scrubbed and ___."

_____
_____ 7–8. Recently, a ___ Siberian tiger died at the zoo. The loss of the baby tiger was ___ because there are only a few hundred Siberian tigers left in the world.

_____
_____ 9–10. Making ___ furniture for dollhouses is a popular activity with my third-grade niece and her ___s.

➤ *Word Work*

A. Write each word next to the examples that best match it.

A. **duration**	B. **essential**	C. **exhibit**
D. **juvenile**	E. **sanitary**	

_____ 1. Maria scrubbed the bathroom sink.
  Before giving Randy an injection, the nurse wiped his arm with alcohol.
  Jim washed the apple before he ate it.

_____ 2. A newly hatched bird
  Three little kittens
  A kindergarten student

_____ 3. A ball for playing soccer
  Eggs to make an omelet
  Wheels for a skateboard

_____ 4. The movie lasted an hour and a half.
  A week contains seven days.
  The couple had been married for forty-seven years.

_____ 5. Tack students' stories on the bulletin board.
  Hang a painting on the living-room wall.
  Place a statue of a queen in a museum.

B. In the space provided, write the letter of the choice that most closely relates to the situation in each item.

_____ 6. Workers' **peers** include their

  A. children.   B. coworkers.   C. sports heroes.

_____ 7. People **discard** items that they

  A. are very fond of.   B. know are valuable.   C. do not want anymore.

_____ 8. Many people feel it would be **tragic** if the world's tigers

  A. died out.   B. had no stripes.   C. hunted for food.

_____ 9. The nine-year-old is **mature** for his age. He

  A. reads as well as most twelve-year-olds.
  B. still sucks his thumb.
  C. enjoys computer games.

_____ 10. Jack keeps his **miniature** cars in a

  A. garage.   B. shoebox.   C. parking lot.

➤ *Word Parts*

A. The prefix *dis-* means "not," " lack of," "the opposite of," or "remove."

> *Examples:* *disorder* — lack of order; confusion
> *discard* — to remove from a group of items; throw away

On each answer line, write the word from the box that means the same as the *italicized* words.

A. **disagree**	B. **discourteous**	C. **dishonest**
D. **disloyal**	E. **displace°**	

_____ 1. My bookcase is so full that if I buy a new book, I'll have to *remove from its place* one of the books I already have.

_____ 2. I consider myself a true friend of Molly, but she thinks I was *not loyal* because I went to Disneyland with my family instead of to her birthday party.

_____ 3. Brian paid for his purchase with a $20 bill, but the *not honest* cashier gave him change for $10 and kept the difference.

_____ 4. When the restaurant manager heard a server being *the opposite of courteous* to a customer, she fired him on the spot.

_____ 5. My twin cousins love to argue. Sometimes I think they *do not agree* just for the fun of it.

B. The suffix *-ary* means "of," "connected with," or "relating to."

> *Examples:* *imaginary* — of the imagination
> *sanitary* — relating to health

On each answer line, write the word from the box that best completes the item.

F. **complimentary**	G. **customary°**	H. **dietary**
I. **honorary**	J. **solitary°**	

_____ 6. Common ___ problems are skipping breakfast and getting too much sugar in beverages and foods.

_____ 7. Even if you don't like someone's outfit, you can still make an honest ___ remark such as, "Your shirt is a pretty color."

_____ 8. Although having a birthday cake is ___ in the United States, that's not the tradition in some other parts of the world.

_____ 9. Ms. Lopez never attended classes at the college, but it gave her an ____ degree to recognize her good work in building the children's hospital.

_____ 10. Dogs love the company of other dogs, but cats tend to be ___ animals, keeping pretty much to themselves.

➤ *Final Check*

Read the passages carefully. Then fill in each blank with the word that best fits the context.

A. A Childish Collection

A. **discard**	B. **exhibit**	C. **juvenile**	D. **mature**	E. **miniature**

Have you ever had a collection? When I was younger, I collected (1)_____

horses. They were so tiny that a dozen of them could sit on one bedroom shelf. No two of them

were identical°; each one was different. I loved to (2)_____ them there, where

my friends could admire the spectacle°. But when I was about 13, I decided to displace° them,

thinking that my little horses were too (3)_____ for a teenager's bedroom. I

couldn't bring myself to (4)_____ them entirely, though, so I wrapped them up

carefully and put them away. Recently I found them again, and I felt sorry that I had hidden them

away in a dark drawer. I decided that at my age, I should be (5)_____ enough not to

care if anyone else thinks my horses are childish. I brought them out and arranged them once

again on my bedroom shelf. And guess what? My very "grown-up" friends like to play with them.

B. Clara Barton

F. **duration**	G. **essential**	H. **peer**	I. **sanitary**	J. **tragic**

Clara Barton was born on Christmas Day, 1821. As a young girl, she was too shy to go to a

regular school. So Clara was educated at home. Along with her lessons, her mother taught her to

keep a house (6)_____ so that germs didn't spread there. Perhaps that is why

Clara became a nurse. When the Civil War began, in 1861, Clara learned that doctors on the

battlefield did not have enough (7)_____ medical supplies, such as bandages.

Clara thought it was (8)_____ that soldiers were dying unnecessarily. She

talked people into donating supplies. Then she went to the battlefield herself to nurse wounded

soldiers. She worked there for the (9)_____ of the entire war. After the war,

she helped many families locate missing soldiers. On a visit to Europe, Clara associated° with

other nurses who had helped during wars. She learned that on the battlefield, her European

(10)_____s wore red crosses to identify them. Clara took the idea back home.

In 1882, the once-shy girl founded the American Red Cross.

Scores	Check 2 _____%	Word Work _____%	Word Parts _____%	Final Check _____%

Enter your scores above and in the vocabulary performance chart on the inside back cover of the book.

capability	magnify
content	postpone
duplicate	presentable
immense	realistic
industrious	stun

Ten Words in Context

In the space provided, write the letter of the meaning closest to that of each **boldfaced** word. Use the context of the sentences to help you figure out each word's meaning.

1 capability
(kā-pə-bĭl′ĭ-tē)
– *noun*

- Ellen has a great **capability** for science. She started taking college science courses when she was just 15.
- Some people don't have much **capability** for foreign languages. My father studied German for five years but can barely speak it.

____ *Capability* means   A. fear.   B. talent.   C. place.

2 content
(kən-tĕnt′)
– *adjective*

- How **content** that cat looks, curled up and purring in the sunny window!
- The children's story "The Fisherman's Wife" tells of a women who was never **content**, no matter what wonderful things she had

____ *Content* means   A. busy.   B. pleased.   C. worried.

3 duplicate
(dōō′plĭ-kāt′)
– *verb*

- Chuck does a great imitation of Elvis Presley. He **duplicates** Elvis's voice and movements perfectly.
- The vacuum-cleaner salesman said, "Many people have tried to **duplicate** our product, but they all failed! Only *this* vacuum cleaner is the real thing."

____ *Duplicate* means   A. to copy.   B. to believe.   C. to enjoy.

4 immense
(ĭ-mĕns′)
– *adjective*

- An adult grizzly bear really is **immense**. It can be eight feet tall and weigh 850 pounds.
- We felt an **immense** sense of relief when the neighbor's missing child was found safe.

____ *Immense* means   A. smart.   B. awful.   C. huge.

5 industrious
(ĭn-dŭs′trē-əs)
– *adjective*

- The phrase "busy as a beaver" comes from the fact that beavers are **industrious** builders.
- Feeling **industrious** last Saturday, I cleaned the house, did the laundry, and baked four loaves of bread.

____ *Industrious* means   A. lonely.   B. ready to work.   C. playful.

6 magnify
(măg′nə-fī′)
– *verb*

- A microscope can **magnify** a blood cell hundreds of times, making it large enough for us to see.
- Somehow, the water **magnified** the fish at the end of my fishing line. Once I pulled the fish in, I was surprised how small it really was.

____ *Magnify* means   A. to see.   B. to fool.   C. to make larger-looking.

7 postpone
(pōst-pōn′)
– *verb*

- Because of a snowstorm, our school's winter concert had to be **postponed** for a week.
- Can we **postpone** this conversation for just five minutes? First I need to finish what I'm working on.

___ *Postpone* means   A. to put off.   B. to begin.   C. to record.

8 presentable
(prĭ-zĕn′tə-bəl)
– *adjective*

- "We're leaving for Grandma's house in ten minutes, and I want you looking **presentable** by then!" the children's mother told them.
- In order to make the kitchen **presentable** in a hurry, I hid the dirty dishes under the sink.

___ *Presentable* means   A. colorful.   B. comfortable.   C. fit to be seen.

9 realistic
(rē′ə-lĭs′tĭk)
– *adjective*

- To be **realistic**, I must admit that my weekend job at the grocery store will not ever allow me to buy a Cadillac.
- Doug says it takes a half-hour to get to his house, but forty-five minutes is more **realistic**.

___ *Realistic* means   A. hopeful.   B. true-to-life.   C. different.

10 stun
(stŭn)
– *verb*

- The news that I had won a million dollars would probably **stun** me. I don't think I'd be able to speak at first.
- After a lifetime spent in the Midwest, my grandfather was **stunned** the first time he saw the ocean. "It's just unbelievable," he kept saying.

___ *Stun* means   A. to teach.   B. to amaze.   C. to ruin.

Matching Words with Definitions

Following are definitions of the ten words. **Print** each word next to its definition. If you look closely at each word in context, you will be able to figure out its meaning.

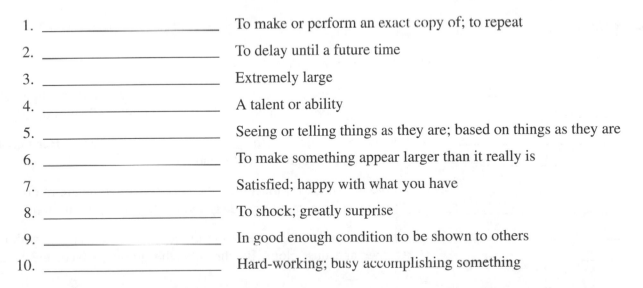

1. _____ To make or perform an exact copy of; to repeat

2. _____ To delay until a future time

3. _____ Extremely large

4. _____ A talent or ability

5. _____ Seeing or telling things as they are; based on things as they are

6. _____ To make something appear larger than it really is

7. _____ Satisfied; happy with what you have

8. _____ To shock; greatly surprise

9. _____ In good enough condition to be shown to others

10. _____ Hard-working; busy accomplishing something

CAUTION: Do not go any further until you are sure the above answers are correct. Then you can use the definitions to help you in the following practices. Your goal is eventually to know the words well enough so that you don't need to check the definitions at all.

➢ *Check 1*

Using the answer line, complete each item below with the correct word from the box.

A. **capability**	B. **content**	C. **duplicate**	D. **immense**	E. **industrious**
F. **magnify**	G. **postpone**	H. **presentable**	I. **realistic**	J. **stun**

_____ 1. When the guest of honor said that he'd be out of town that night, the surprise party had to be ___d until next week.

_____ 2. Every day, you have the ___ to make someone else happy. Try using it!

_____ 3. Telescopes ___ objects that look small because they are far away.

_____ 4. This year, the team will try to ___ its victory at last year's Super Bowl.

_____ 5. I offered to give Sue the comfortable chair I was sitting in, but she said, "No thanks, I'm ___ where I am."

_____ 6. Before she went to her job interview, Alice asked her sister if she could borrow some ___ shoes.

_____ 7. The principal stopped in to visit our busy classroom. "I'm glad to see your students looking so ___," she told the teacher.

_____ 8. For Grandma's ninetieth birthday party, we ordered an ___ cake. It was seven layers high and served sixty people.

_____ 9. It would ___ Mom if my brother cleaned his room without being asked.

_____ 10. A long-term goal may not seem ___ at first, but you may reach it by taking one small step at a time.

NOTE: Now check your answers to these questions by turning to page 241. Going over the answers carefully will help you prepare for the remaining practices, for which answers are not given.

➢ *Check 2*

Using the answer lines, complete each item below with **two** words from the box.

_____
_____ 1–2. I knew that seeing Mount Everest, the world's highest mountain, would ___ Rick. "I had no idea how ___ it really is," he said.

_____
_____ 3–4. My aunt no longer has the ___ to read without glasses. Her glasses ___ the print enough for her to read it easily.

_____
_____ 5–6. People who feel they must have the best of everything are rarely ___. It's better to have more ___ ideas about what is important in life.

_____
_____ 7–8. When Dad yelled, "Company's coming!" we were very ___ with the sweeper and dust cloth. By the time the guests arrived, the house looked ___.

_____
_____ 9–10. To celebrate their anniversary, the couple wanted to ___ their first date. But they had to ___ the celebration because the restaurant where they'd eaten was closed for two weeks.

➤ *Word Work*

A. In the space provided, write the letter of the choice that best completes each item.

_____ 1. I prefer **realistic** movies, such as
A. *Santa Claus versus the Martians.*
B. *The Basketball Incident.*
C. *The Little Mermaid.*

_____ 2. Thomas looked quite **presentable** after he
A. showered, shaved, and put on a nice outfit.
B. came in from playing football on a muddy field.
C. had been sick for several days.

_____ 3. In school, the students learned to **magnify** items using a

A. ruler.   B. calculator.   C. microscope.

_____ 4. The rat was so **immense** that it
A. looked more like a cat than a rat.
B. hardly ate anything at all.
C. could hide in tiny spaces.

_____ 5. The baseball player pitched a no-hitter, then **duplicated** his performance in the next game by
A. pitching poorly.
B. pitching another no-hitter.
C. being replaced.

B. In the space provided, write the letter of the word that most closely relates to the situation in each item.

_____ 6. Tom dropped into his favorite chair, smiled happily, and said, "What a great day this has been."

A. immense   B. realistic   C. content

_____ 7. After school, the kids raked the leaves from the yard, took out the garbage, did the dishes, and tidied up the house.

A. realistic   B. industrious   C. capability

_____ 8. We delayed our family reunion by two weeks so that more people could attend.

A. magnify   B. postpone   C. duplicate

_____ 9. When he met the twin brother he'd never known he had, Rick was speechless with shock.

A. stun   B. magnify   C. presentable

_____10. Although he's never had a music lesson, Justin plays the piano very well.

A. duplicate   B. capability   C. presentable

➤ *Synonyms and Antonyms*

A. Synonyms. Write the letter of the word or phrase that most nearly means the **same** as each boldfaced word.

_____ 1. **duplicate**

    A. fool
             B. repeat
    C. grow
            D. draw

_____ 2. **realistic**

    A. lazy
             B. quick
    C. strong
          D. true-to-life

_____ 3. **postpone**

    A. delay
             B. mail
    C. encourage
       D. rush

_____ 4. **stun**

    A. annoy
            B. surprise
    C. dare
            D. burn

_____ 5. **capability**

    A. weakness
        B. guilt
    C. power
           D. pride

B. Antonyms. Write the letter of the word or phrase that most nearly means the **opposite** of each boldfaced word.

_____ 6. **content**

    A. happy
            B. unhappy
    C. cozy
            D. rude

_____ 7. **immense**

    A. large
           B. sensible
    C. soothing
       D. tiny

_____ 8. **industrious**

    A. simple
           B. frightened
    C. lazy
           D. hard-working

_____ 9. **magnify**

    A. look up
         B. make smaller
    C. show off
       D. make larger

_____ 10. **presentable**

    A. clean
           B. messy
    C. generous
       D. returnable

➤ *Final Check*

Read the passages carefully. Then fill in each blank with the word that best fits the context.

A. From Poor Girl to College President

| A. **capability** | B. **content** | C. **industrious** | D. **presentable** | E. **realistic** |

Ruth Simmons grew up as a poor child living in a shack in Texas. The idea that she would become a college president couldn't have seemed (1)_____. Nevertheless°, in the year 2000, Dr. Simmons was named president of Brown University. She became the first African American to lead an Ivy League school.

Ruth's father was a farmer, and her mother was a maid. The family was so poor that for Christmas, each of the twelve children received an apple, an orange, and ten nuts. Ruth always wore hand-me-down clothing. When she won a scholarship to attend college, her high-school teachers bought her a coat so she would look (2)_____ on campus. But Ruth always had a great (3)_____ for learning. She says that when she first started school, "it was like waking up."

Today, Dr. Simmons is not (4)_____ to enjoy her own success. She wants to see other poor young people succeed as well. She tells them to be proud of being (5)_____. According to Dr. Simmons, "Any work done out of love for one's family and out of duty is noble work."

B. Snowflakes

| F. **duplicate** | G. **immense** | H. **magnify** | I. **postpone** | J. **stun** |

You've probably heard the statement "No two snowflakes are alike." But can this be true? When you think of the (6)_____ amount of snow that falls each year, is it possible that nature never (7)_____s a snowflake? No, it probably isn't true. What is true is that no one has ever found two snowflakes that are identical°. A snowflake is made up of up to 100 million tiny pieces. These pieces can be arranged in so many ways that it seems that no two snowflakes are alike.

Probably no one has ever cared more about snowflakes than a Vermont farmer named Wilson A. Bentley. In 1885, Mr. Bentley discovered that he could (8)_____ a snowflake, to see it better, and then photograph it. After he saw the photo, he was amazed by the snowflake's beauty. He wrote, "It seemed a shame that this beauty should not be seen and appreciated by others. . . . When a snowflake melted, that design was forever lost." Bentley could not (9)_____ the melting of snowflakes, but he did manage to keep and exhibit° a record of their beauty. He collected photographs of 2,400 snowflakes and published them in a book that would (10)_____ readers with the incredible° beauty and variety° of snowflakes. By the time he died in 1931, he was known across the country as "Snowflake" Bentley.

Scores   Check 2 _____%   Word Work _____%   Synonyms and Antonyms _____%   Final Check _____%

Enter your scores above and in the vocabulary performance chart on the inside back cover of the book.

accurate	latter
bluff	modify
consist	toxic
discomfort	trifle
elementary	vanity

Ten Words in Context

In the space provided, write the letter of the meaning closest to that of each **boldfaced** word. Use the context of the sentences to help you figure out each word's meaning.

1 accurate
(ăk′yər-ĭt)
– *adjective*

• When you're measuring medicine, it's important to be **accurate**. Too much or too little could actually harm the patient.

• The spell checker program on my computer helps me make sure that my spelling is **accurate**.

___*Accurate* means   A. generous.   B. healthy.   C. exactly right.

2 bluff
(blŭf)
– *verb*

• During her job interview, Yolanda didn't try to **bluff**. Instead of trying to suggest that she knew a lot about accounting, she simply said, "I will work hard to learn."

• A good card player knows how to **bluff**. If he or she has a bad hand, none of the other players knows it.

___*Bluff* means   A. to pretend.   B. to tell the truth.   C. to leave.

3 consist
(kən-sĭst′)
– *verb*

• Middle schools usually **consist** of grades five through eight.

• "Egg creams" **consist** of milk, soda water, and syrup—but no egg and no cream.

___*Consist of* means   A. to leave out.   B. to be like.   C. to include.

4 discomfort
(dĭs-kŭm′fərt)
– *noun*

• My nephews always suffer **discomfort** the day after Halloween. They eat far too much of the candy they collect.

• Jen felt such **discomfort** when she lied to her friend that she promised herself she'd never tell a lie again.

___*Discomfort* means   A. physical or mental upset.   B. peace.   C. great danger.

5 elementary
(ĕl′ə-mĕn′tə-rē)
– *adjective*

• An **elementary** rule of science is this: What goes up must come down.

• In her first computer class, Wanda learned some **elementary** skills, such as how to start up the computer.

___*Elementary* means   A. difficult.   B. false.   C. basic.

6 latter
(lăt′ər)
– *noun*

• When I was offered pumpkin pie or cherry pie, I chose the **latter**. Cherry pie has always been my favorite.

• When two things are mentioned, the first one is often called "the former" and the second is called "the **latter**."

___*Latter* means   A. first one.   B. second one.   C. least.

7 modify
(mŏd′ə-fī′)
– *verb*

- A mechanic can **modify** a car so it can be driven by someone who can't use his or her legs.
- The dress Krystal made is like one she saw in a magazine, but she **modified** it by giving it long sleeves.

___ *Modify* means   A. to buy.   B. to make different.   C. to harm.

8 toxic
(tŏk′sĭk)
– *adjective*

- After they learned that a company had dumped **toxic** waste nearby, Mr. and Mrs. Miller no longer wanted to buy the house they'd looked at.
- It's very dangerous to mix bleach with other household cleaners. The mixture can create **toxic** gas.

___ *Toxic* means   A. a small amount of.   B. heavy.   C. unhealthy.

9 trifle
(trī′fəl)
– *verb*

- Gina broke up with Ed because he **trifled** with her feelings. He would insult her in public and then say, "Why get upset? I was just kidding around."
- "Never **trifle** with the truth," my dad used to say. "Nobody respects a liar."

___ *Trifle with* means   A. to play with.   B. to treat seriously.   C. to question.

10 vanity
(văn′ĭ-tē)
– *noun*

- The wicked queen in "Snow White" was famous for her **vanity**. Every day, she asked a magic mirror who the most beautiful woman in the country was, and it said, "You are." One day, the mirror answered, "Snow White is more beautiful than you." That day, the queen decided Snow White had to die.
- Because of Mark's **vanity** about his expert piano playing, he refuses to play anything for others, even for fun, unless he's learned it perfectly.

___ *Vanity* means   A. kindness.   B. too much pride.   C. concern for health.

Matching Words with Definitions

Following are definitions of the ten words. **Print** each word next to its definition. If you look closely at each word in context, you will be able to figure out its meaning.

1. _____   To be made up

2. _____   To treat as if it has little value

3. _____   The second of two things or persons mentioned

4. _____   To change somewhat

5. _____   A feeling of pain or uneasiness; lack of comfort

6. _____   Poisonous; very bad for one's health

7. _____   A feeling of too much pride in one's appearance, ability, etc.

8. _____   Correct; without errors; precise°

9. _____   To pretend to know more or feel more confident than one really does

10. _____   Basic; simple

CAUTION: Do not go any further until you are sure the above answers are correct. Then you can use the definitions to help you in the following practices. Your goal is eventually to know the words well enough so that you don't need to check the definitions at all.

➤ *Check 1*

Using the answer line, complete each item below with the correct word from the box.

A. **accurate**	B. **bluff**	C. **consist**	D. **discomfort**	E. **elementary**
F. **latter**	G. **modify**	H. **toxic**	I. **trifle**	J. **vanity**

_____ 1. "Why aren't you wearing your glasses?" I asked Eileen when I saw her at the dance. "___," she answered. "I look better without them."

_____ 2. Your addition here is not ___; 28 plus 73 is not 104.

_____ 3. My sister's new apartment ___s of just two rooms.

_____ 4. "Don't ___ with me," the movie detective told the suspect. "Tell me what you know, and tell it to me quickly."

_____ 5. Here's an ___ fashion tip: Don't wear plaid pants with a striped shirt.

_____ 6. When the beggar asked for money, you could see ___ in people's faces.

_____ 7. January has thirty-one days, and February has only twenty-eight. But of the two months, the ___ always seems longer to me.

_____ 8. Dan ordered a tuna sandwich, but then he called the waitress back so he could ___ his order: "May I have that on rye instead of white bread?"

_____ 9. A sign on the truck warned that it was carrying ___ materials.

_____ 10. As I took my friend over to meet my neighbor, I realized I'd forgotten the neighbor's name. I tried to ___ by saying, "Why don't you two introduce yourselves to each other?"

NOTE: Now check your answers to these questions by turning to page 241. Going over the answers carefully will help you prepare for the remaining practices, for which answers are not given.

➤ *Check 2*

Using the answer lines, complete each item below with **two** words from the box.

_____
_____ 1–2. ___ has led people to do dangerous things. For instance, women used to put drops of a ___ liquid in their eyes to make them brighter.

_____
_____ 3–4. Before you visit a foreign country, it's good to learn some ___ phrases, such as "Please" and "Thank you." Beyond that, don't try to ___. Just say, "I'm sorry; I don't speak the language."

_____
_____ 5–6. When my father had stomach ___, his doctor ordered a test. "This test gives ___ results, so we'll know exactly what's the matter," the doctor said.

_____
_____ 7–8. When my uncles Mike and Leonard came to this country, one of them decided to ___ his last name. The former kept the name Mike Barrenski, but the ___ is now known as Leonard Barr.

_____
_____ 9–10. Because my brother has ___d with so many girls' feelings, his female friends now ___ of only my mom and my sister.

➤ *Word Work*

A. In the space provided, write the letter of the choice that best completes each item.

_____ 1. The **discomfort** Ellen was feeling was due to

    A. the happy news she had just received.

    B. her new shoes, which pinched her feet.

    C. her fluffy, warm bathrobe.

_____ 2. Dennis and Mitchell were talking when the **latter** suddenly became angry and pushed

    A. Dennis.   B. Mitchell.   C. both Dennis and Mitchell.

_____ 3. A person who **trifles** with your feelings

    A. cares deeply for you.

    B. feels bad about what he or she is doing.

    C. is not concerned about your feelings.

_____ 4. If the Weather Bureau's prediction of two feet of snow turns out to be **accurate**, our area will receive

    A. no snow at all.   B. two feet of snow.   C. less than a foot of snow.

_____ 5. You might **modify** a recipe in order to

    A. share it with a friend.

    B. know where to find it easily the next time.

    C. make it lower in fat.

B. In the space provided, write the letter of the word that most closely relates to the situation in each item.

_____ 6. "Of course I know how to multiply fractions! But it's pretty complicated, and it would take me too long to explain it or show it to you."

    A. latter   B. vanity   C. bluff

_____ 7. That spider's bite is so poisonous that most victims die within four hours.

    A. latter   B. toxic   C. elementary

_____ 8. New York City is made up of five boroughs: Manhattan, the Bronx, Queens, Brooklyn, and Staten Island.

    A. modify   B. vanity   C. consist

_____ 9. Two plus two equals four. *Cat* is spelled C-A-T.

    A. elementary   B. latter   C. modify

_____ 10. Many celebrities have face-lifts to make themselves look younger than they are.

    A. trifle   B. consist   C. vanity

➤ *Analogies*

Each item below starts with a pair of words in CAPITAL LETTERS. For each item, figure out the relationship between these two words. Then decide which of the choices (A, B, C, or D) expresses a similar relationship. Write the letter of your choice on the answer line. (All the repeated words in these items are from this unit.)

_____ 1. ACCURATE : WRONG ::

    A. magnify° : telescope   B. factual : story

    C. essential° : unimportant   D. identical° : same

_____ 2. BLUFF : PRETEND ::

    A. duplicate° : copy   B. play : poker

    C. lie : truth   D. sprawl° : gather

_____ 3. CONSIST OF : CONTAIN ::

    A. cook : recipe   B. throw out : discard°

    C. create : destroy   D. postpone° : date

_____ 4. DISCOMFORT : PLEASURE ::

    A. poverty : wealth   B. happy : joy

    C. flood : water   D. exhibit° : paintings

_____ 5. TOXIC : POISON ::

    A. realistic° : imagination   B. sweet : sugar

    C. tragic° : funny   D. magic : magician

_____ 6. ELEMENTARY : ALPHABET ::

    A. large : immense°   B. school : classroom

    C. childish : mature°   D. green : grass

_____ 7. LATTER : SECOND ::

    A. numbers : enumerate°   B. before : after

    C. last : final   D. stern° : teacher

_____ 8. VANITY : MODESTY ::

    A. mirror : reflection   B. plane : pilot

    C. enforce° : law   D. strength: weakness

_____ 9. TRIFLE WITH : TAKE SERIOUSLY ::

    A. emotion : anger   B. tell : secret

    C. mistrust° : believe   D. work : industrious°

_____ 10. MODIFY : HAIRDO ::

    A. debate° : argue   B. repair : fix

    C. truck : highway   D. rewrite : paragraph

➤ *Final Check*

Read the passages carefully. Then fill in each blank with the word that best fits the context.

A. Three Little Words

A. **bluff**	B. **elementary**	C. **consist**	D. **discomfort**	E. **vanity**

Three little words can make the world a better place. No, they're not "I love you." They are simply these: "I don't know." Although the words seem (1)_____, many people find them difficult to say. They will do almost anything to evade° admitting they don't know something. For instance, a teacher might ask a student, "What were some of the causes of the Civil War?" Instead of saying, "I don't know," the student will try to (2)_____ his way out of the situation by saying, "Well, there were a lot of them, but they're pretty hard to enumerate°." Or at a news conference, a reporter might ask a politician a difficult question. The politician's (3)_____ about being an expert won't allow her to say the simple truth: "I don't know." So she spends ten minutes giving an answer that (4)_____s of nothing but hot air. The truth is that people respect someone who is honest enough to say, "I don't know." So the next time you're asked a question you can't answer, admit it — *say* you can't. The brief (5)_____ you may feel is less than the immense° trouble you'll avoid.

B. A Child-Safe Home

F. **accurate**	G. **latter**	H. **modify**	I. **toxic**	J. **trifle**

When Elena was expecting her first child, she wanted to do everything right. She saw her doctor regularly during the duration° of her pregnancy. She took special vitamins. She kept (6)_____ records of her weight gains from week to week. She exercised and ate a balanced diet. She wouldn't think of smoking or drinking.

But Elena hadn't thought of everything. A few weeks before the baby was due, Elena's mother, Anna, came over for a visit. Elena and Anna sat and talked for a little while, and then the (7)_____ looked around the apartment. "You know, this isn't a child-safe home," Anna said. "Look at all the dangers there are for a baby or a toddler."

Elena was stunned°. She knew that her mother was right and that if they postponed° doing something about the problem, there could be tragic° results. The two spent the rest of the afternoon doing a thorough° job of making the apartment safe for a baby. They took (8)_____ household cleaners, such as bleach and ammonia, and locked them away on high shelves. They had to (9)_____ the doors on the cabinets so that little fingers could not open them. They fitted child-proof plugs into electrical outlets and put a baby gate across the top of the stairs. When they were finished, Elena breathed a sigh of relief. "I'll take every precaution° I can to keep my baby safe," she said. "A child's health is much too important to (10)_____ with."

Scores Check 2 _____% Word Work _____% Analogies _____% Final Check _____%

UNIT SIX: *Review*

The box at the right lists twenty-five words from Unit Six. Using the clues at the bottom of the page, fill in these words to complete the puzzle that follows.

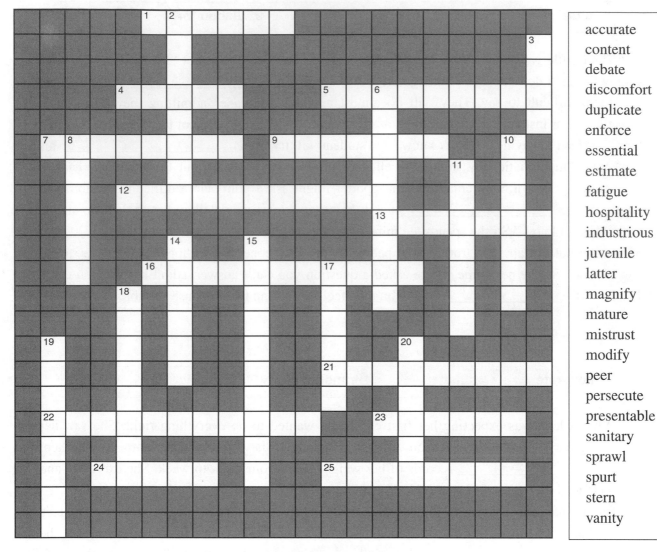

accurate
content
debate
discomfort
duplicate
enforce
essential
estimate
fatigue
hospitality
industrious
juvenile
latter
magnify
mature
mistrust
modify
peer
persecute
presentable
sanitary
sprawl
spurt
stern
vanity

ACROSS

1. Too much pride in one's appearance or ability
4. To flow out suddenly and with force
5. To make or perform an exact copy of; repeat
7. To make a guess at something's size, amount, or value
9. To make sure that a rule or law is obeyed
12. In good enough condition to be shown
13. Satisfied; happy with what you have
16. Generous, friendly treatment of guests
21. Necessary
22. Hard-working; busy accomplishing something
23. Adult; fully developed
24. Serious and strict
25. Young; not fully grown

DOWN

2. Correct; precise
3. A person who is on an equal level with another person
6. To harm again and again; treat cruelly
8. To sit or lie with arms and legs thrown outward
10. To make something appear larger than it really is
11. The state of being very tired
14. To change somewhat
15. A feeling of pain or uneasiness
17. The second of two things or persons mentioned
18. To have no trust in; to doubt
19. Free from dirt or germs
20. To discuss a question by looking at different points of view

230

UNIT SIX: Test 1

PART A
Choose the word that best completes each item and write it in the space provided.

_____ 1. Communities ___ their laws by using fines and jail time.

    A. estimate   B. enforce   C. magnify   D. mistrust

_____ 2. Instead of washing cloth diapers, most people now use diapers that they can ___.

    A. discard   B. enumerate   C. justify   D. exhibit

_____ 3. When they arrived at the party, Henry said something that made Irina angry. For the ___ of the party, Irina didn't speak to him.

    A. essential   B. fatigue   C. duration   D. toxic

_____ 4. Tomorrow's test will ___ of short essay and multiple-choice questions.

    A. postpone   B. consist   C. modify   D. persecute

_____ 5. I ___ that the drive from here to Florida will take about twenty hours.

    A. trifle   B. displace   C. enumerate   D. estimate

_____ 6. ___, cough, and fever are often signs that you have the flu.

    A. Fatigue   B. Hospitality   C. Peer   D. Vanity

_____ 7. Cheap clothing rarely lasts a long time; it's too ___.

    A. elementary   B. industrious   C. miniature   D. flimsy

_____ 8. To me, all chicken eggs look ___. Can a mother hen tell which are hers?

    A. content   B. essential   C. identical   D. stern

_____ 9. ___ redwood trees line the "Avenue of the Giants" in northern California. Some are more than 360 feet high.

    A. Singular   B. Flimsy   C. Immense   D. Presentable

_____ 10. The shoplifter tried to ___ his stealing by saying, "The store's owner makes so much money, he'll never miss what I take."

    A. associates   B. enforce   C. persecute   D. justify

_____ 11. We'd been lost for half an hour, but Dad's ___ wouldn't allow him to ask for directions. "I know exactly where we are!" he kept insisting.

    A. fatigue   B. hospitality   C. peer   D. vanity

(Continues on next page)

_____ 12. Aisha had planned on serving roast chicken with baked potatoes and salad for dinner. When she realized she had no potatoes, she had to quickly ___ her menu.

      A. modify   B. magnify   C. debate   D. enumerate

_____ 13. On top of the wedding cake stood a ___ bride and groom, only about five inches tall.

      A. sanitary   B. miniature   C. mature   D. singular

PART B

Write **C** if the italicized word is used **correctly**. Write **I** if the word is used **incorrectly**.

_____14. Since Marva wanted her checkbook to be *accurate*, she used a calculator to do the addition and subtraction.

_____15. The kindergarten teacher's sweet smile and *stern* voice made even the shyest child feel relaxed.

_____16. In the Spanish course for beginners, we learned to ask and answer a few *elementary* questions.

_____17. Barry's favorite books are *realistic* ones about creatures from other planets that travel through time.

_____18. You can sense our neighbor's *hospitality* as soon as you see the signs in his yard saying, "Beware of Dog," "No Trespassing," and "Go Away."

_____19. Adding sweet-smelling, *toxic* oils to the water makes bathing a delightful treat.

_____20. Sharing a toothbrush is not a very *sanitary* thing to do.

_____21. Samuel *soothed* the frightened puppy by patting it and talking to it gently.

_____22. "It's *essential* that Mrs. Peterson have her medicine every four hours," the doctor said. "Otherwise, she could become very ill."

_____23. The high-school seniors were asked to read to their *peers* in kindergarten.

_____24. "You won't believe what just happened!" Roberta cried. From the joyful look on her face, I could tell she had *tragic* news.

_____25. *Mature* female animals have been known to take care of motherless babies in addition to their own.

Score (Number correct) _____ × 4 = _____ %

Enter your score above and in the vocabulary performance chart on the inside back cover of the book.

UNIT SIX: Test 2

PART A
On the answer line, write the word from the box that completes each item below. Use each word once.

A. **associate**	B. **debate**	C. **discomfort**	D. **discredit**	E. **displace**
F. **industrious**	G. **juvenile**	H. **latter**	I. **mistrust**	J. **persecute**
K. **presentable**	L. **sprawl**	M. **trifle**		

_____ 1. I didn't like the woman who interviewed me. I asked her seriously when I might hear about the job, but she just ___d with me, laughing and saying, "Sooner or later."

_____ 2. Trying to ___ one of his coworkers, Gino told the boss that the man had been caught stealing.

_____ 3. The thoughtless man ___ed across the seat on the bus, taking up as much room as three other people.

_____ 4. "Can you wait for me to shower and shave?" Randall said. "I want to look ___ when we go out."

_____ 5. Cruel people on the block ___d the new family because of their race, sending them hateful letters.

_____ 6. "Your money or your life!" the robber said. I preferred to save the ___, so I handed over the money.

_____ 7. The shopkeeper ___s everyone. "Anyone will cheat you if you're not careful," she claims.

_____ 8. Although a grown-up Dalmatian dog is white with black spots, a ___ Dalmatian is pure white.

_____ 9. The boss fired the lazy worker. "I need to find someone more ___," he said.

_____ 10. "I can't find anything," Juan complained. "When Hal cleaned up the apartment, he ___d everything."

_____ 11. Since her family moved across town, Sandy doesn't ___ with her old friends anymore.

_____ 12. The two candidates for mayor are going to ___ about whether to raise taxes or not.

_____ 13. I don't know if Sharon was embarrassed, angry, or sad at the meeting, but it was clear she was feeling some sort of ___.

(Continues on next page)

PART B

Write **C** if the italicized word is used **correctly**. Write **I** if the word is used **incorrectly**.

_____14. At her interview, Janice *enumerated* all the reasons she should be given the job.

_____15. Being able to speak three languages is a wonderful *barrier* to Francesca at her office, where she meets many people from other countries.

_____16. After the rainstorm, puddles of water *spurted* quietly on the sidewalk.

_____17. A fortuneteller claims to have the *capability* to see into the future.

_____18. Some words that are well-known in the *singular*—such as "cactus"—are less well-known in the plural. More than one cactus would be "cacti."

_____19. Pastor Stevenson never gives the same sermon twice. He *duplicates* a new talk for every situation.

_____20. The couple upstairs are clearly *content* with each other. Their fights wake us up almost every night.

_____21. Because he was ashamed of his poor report card, my brother *exhibited* it in the back of his desk drawer.

_____22. Because he doesn't want to admit he is unemployed, Scott *bluffs* when he is asked what he does for a living. He says things like, "I'm doing a little bit of this and that right now."

_____23. "I will introduce the graduates one by one," said the principal. "To save time, please *postpone* your applause until all the names have been called."

_____24. At the street fair, an artist offered to write our names in an unusual way. She said she would *magnify* the letters so that the whole name could fit on a single grain of rice.

_____25. When I came to the kitchen for breakfast, I was *stunned*—my father said, "Good morning," as usual.

Score   (Number correct) _____ × 4 = _____%

UNIT SIX: Test 3

PART A: Synonyms
In the space provided, write the letter of the choice that is most nearly the **same** in meaning as the **boldfaced** word.

_____ 1. **barrier**   A) something that helps   B) something that is similar
                              C) something that gets in the way   D) something that is different

_____ 2. **bluff**   A) pretend   B) reject   C) realize   D) limit

_____ 3. **capability**   A) action   B) excuse   C) talent   D) victim

_____ 4. **consist of**   A) be made up of   B) be sure of   C) be missing   D) be worth

_____ 5. **discomfort**   A) dishonesty   B) pleasure   C) ability   D) pain

_____ 6. **displace**   A) name   B) move away   C) throw away   D) show

_____ 7 **duplicate**   A) copy   B) erase   C) purchase   D) envy

_____ 8. **duration**   A) amount something weighs   B) time something lasts
                              C) value something is worth   D) material something is made of

_____ 9. **elementary**   A) basic   B) difficult   C) recent   D) complete

_____ 10. **enforce**   A) ignore   B) suggest   C) release   D) carry out

_____ 11. **enumerate**   A) give away   B) reduce   C) choose   D) list

_____ 12. **estimate**   A) measure   B) guess   C) separate   D) confuse

_____ 13. **industrious**   A) hard-working   B) badly made   C) tired   D) not honest

_____ 14. **justify**   A) throw away   B) permit   C) give a reason for   D) listen

_____ 15. **juvenile**   A) strange   B) large   C) happy   D) young

_____ 16. **magnify**   A) make appear larger   B) make ready   C) shrink   D) hide

_____ 17. **mistrust**   A) doubt   B) believe   C) know   D) blame

_____ 18. **modify**   A) keep   B) change   C) scare   D) hurry

_____ 19. **peer**   A) equal   B) enemy   C) boss   D) servant

_____ 20. **persecute**   A) praise   B) harm   C) love   D) expect

_____ 21. **realistic**   A) exciting   B) true to life   C) very large   D) accidental

_____ 22. **sprawl**   A) spread out   B) repeat   C) regret   D) encourage

_____ 23. **spurt**   A) loosen   B) flow suddenly   C) drip   D) fasten tightly

_____ 24. **stun**   A) respect   B) surprise   C) forget   D) refuse

_____ 25. **trifle**   A) put away   B) treat lightly   C) hide from   D) set up

(Continues on next page)

PART B: Antonyms
In the space provided, write the letter of the choice that is most nearly **opposite** in meaning to the **boldfaced** word.

_____26. **accurate**   A) timid   B) full of mistakes   C) active   D) honest

_____27. **associate**   A) stay away from   B) accept   C) copy   D) make fun of

_____28. **content**   A) not wealthy   B) not fair   C) not satisfied   D) not honest

_____29. **debate**   A) repeat   B) allow   C) agree   D) bore

_____30. **discard**   A) keep   B) enter   C) notice   D) let

_____31. **discredit**   A) agree   B) honor   C) cause pain   D) pretend

_____32. **essential**   A) possible   B) expensive   C) not needed   D) borrowed

_____33. **exhibit**   A) hide   B) chase   C) purchase   D) need

_____34. **fatigue**   A) worry   B) peppiness   C) humor   D) sadness

_____35. **flimsy**   A) funny   B) untrue   C) strong   D) colorful

_____36. **hospitality**   A) blame   B) generosity   C) action   D) unfriendliness

_____37. **identical**   A) common   B) famous   C) cheap   D) different

_____38. **immense**   A) tiny   B) clever   C) pretty   D) noisy

_____39. **latter**   A) best   B) easiest   C) lowest   D) first

_____40. **mature**   A) stupid   B) young   C) smooth   D) active

_____41. **miniature**   A) recent   B) lost   C) comical   D) large

_____42. **postpone**   A) do earlier   B) do better   C) do again   D) do badly

_____43. **presentable**   A) messy   B) careful   C) same   D) best

_____44. **sanitary**   A) modern   B) cold   C) dirty   D) shiny

_____45. **singular**   A) many   B) bright   C) careless   D) boring

_____46. **soothe**   A) disturb   B) trust   C) hide   D) forget

_____47. **stern**   A) friendly   B) worried   C) interested   D) strong

_____48. **toxic**   A) sweet   B) dusty   C) harmless   D) simple

_____49. **tragic**   A) unusual   B) long-lasting   C) happy   D) foolish

_____50. **vanity**   A) modesty   B) honesty   C) confusion   D) agreement

Score (Number correct) _____ × 2 = _____%

Enter your score above and in the vocabulary performance chart on the inside back cover of the book.

Appendixes

A. Limited Answer Key

Important Note: This answer key contains the answers for the "Check 1" activity that is on the third page of each chapter. You should not look at these answers until you have tried your best to pick the word that belongs in each sentence of this activity.

If you use the answer key correctly, it will help you learn and remember the words in the chapter. It will also help you prepare for the other activities and tests, for which the answers are not given. To make this key easier to use, the titles of each chapter's readings are written after the chapter number.

Chapter 1 (Johnny Appleseed; The Lovable Leech?)

1. transform
2. fertile
3. preference
4. surplus
5. peculiar
6. solitary
7. principal
8. challenge
9. suitable
10. dependent

Chapter 2 (Finding Fault—And What to Do About It; What Do Your Hobbies Reveal About You?)

1. frustration
2. deliberate
3. Excessive
4. indicate
5. attitude
6. fragile
7. category
8. analyze
9. critical
10. contrast

Chapter 3 (Fixing Up Furniture; Barbara's Date with Her Cousin)

1. desperate
2. evident
3. accompany
4. improper
5. dispose of
6. rejection
7. preserve
8. determine
9. pursue
10. restore

Chapter 4 (The Vacuum-Cleaner Salesman; Peace at Last)

1. reduction
2. betray
3. exaggerate
4. abundant
5. neutral
6. comparison
7. demonstrate
8. distinct
9. inhabit
10. dispute

Chapter 5 (Study Skills to the Rescue!; Training a Puppy)

1. unstable
2. utilize
3. aggravate
4. considerable
5. obnoxious
6. intentional
7. coincide
8. interference
9. humane
10. cease

Chapter 6 (Toasters; A Mean Man)

1. reliable
2. advise
3. minimum
4. penalize
5. originate
6. current
7. deprive
8. hesitate
9. objection
10. maintain

Chapter 7 (A Special Memory; Watch Your Manners!)

1. endure
2. classify
3. recollect
4. astonish
5. exclaim
6. abrupt
7. eager
8. complex
9. horizontal
10. consent

Chapter 8 (Big Brothers and Sisters; Kevin's First Date)

1. potential
2. vanish
3. variety
4. appeal
5. wholesome
6. adequate
7. establish
8. customary
9. respond
10. awkward

Chapter 9 (Differences in a Gym Program; Through a Child's Eyes)

1. discipline
2. ultimate
3. resort
4. vague
5. interpret
6. propose
7. eliminate
8. furthermore
9. emphasis
10. brutal

Chapter 10 (Knowing How to Argue; A Change of School, A Change of Heart)

1. linger
2. anticipate
3. occur
4. reluctant
5. version
6. particular
7. miserable
8. accustomed
9. misinterpret
10. revise

Chapter 11 (Coming Out of a Coma; The Office Doughnut Contest)

1. internal
2. external
3. maximum
4. remedy
5. incredible
6. conscious
7. spectacle
8. protest
9. assume
10. verdict

Chapter 12 (The People's Choice; The Christmas Wars)

1. triumph
2. artificial
3. counsel
4. frequency
5. complicate
6. conscience
7. temporary
8. represent
9. transparent
10. detect

Chapter 13 (What's Your Type?; What a Circus!)

1. withdraw
2. energetic
3. strive
4. trait
5. foresight
6. tolerance
7. agonizing
8. interval
9. substance
10. prosper

Chapter 14 (Practicing Kindness; The Stinking Rose)

1. consistent
2. significant
3. evaluate
4. plea
5. random
6. cope
7. phrase
8. sole
9. practical
10. approximately

Chapter 15 (A Modern Fairy Tale; Wolf Children)

1. shallow
2. authentic
3. harsh
4. concept
5. disrupt
6. thrive
7. remote
8. confront
9. eligible
10. characteristic

Chapter 16 (A Mismatched Couple; A Campaign to Become Class President)

1. transfer
2. burden
3. influence
4. extravagant
5. sympathize
6. apparent
7. fulfill
8. security
9. economical
10. automatic

Chapter 17 (The Famous Detective; Why So Quiet?)

1. outspoken
2. deceive
3. communicate
4. bewilder
5. theory
6. investigate
7. legible
8. earnest
9. fiction
10. emotion

Chapter 18 (Fear of Speaking; Do You Believe in Magic?)

1. humiliate
2. divert
3. assure
4. revive
5. impulse
6. crucial
7. perceive
8. hostile
9. frantic
10. extraordinary

Chapter 19 (The Miracle Runner; One of Those Days)

1. alert
2. primary
3. idle
4. theme
5. overcome
6. abandon
7. devote
8. circumstances
9. function
10. dominate

Chapter 20 (The All-Too-Common Cold; A Criminal with a Tail)

1. misleading
2. prey
3. exclude
4. hinder
5. severe
6. monotonous
7. obtain
8. excerpt
9. seize
10. disregard

Chapter 21 (Traveling with Children; Saving Earth's Natural Supplies)

1. resources
2. unanimous
3. conflict
4. vicinity
5. possess
6. vary
7. procedure
8. convert
9. renew
10. stress

Chapter 22 (More Fat, Anyone?; Is Prison Effective?)

1. precise
2. nevertheless
3. decay
4. expand
5. promote
6. vast
7. corrupt
8. reform
9. tendency
10. abolish

Chapter 23 (She Changed My Mind; So Sue Me)

1. clarify
2. assert
3. rigid
4. evade
5. extend
6. preconception
7. resemble
8. senseless
9. precaution
10. vertical

Chapter 24 (Fear of Public Speaking; Mrs. Thornton's Condition)

1. comprehend
2. inferior
3. impression
4. overwhelm
5. thorough
6. anxious
7. dramatic
8. frank
9. convince
10. illustrate

Chapter 25 (Wacky Weddings; The Cost of Hatred)

1. fragment
2. commitment
3. formal
4. acquire
5. spite
6. resent
7. precede
8. solemn
9. fundamental
10. symbolize

Chapter 26 (My Parents' Problem; The Hike That Hurt)

1. associate
2. estimate
3. justify
4. flimsy
5. barrier
6. persecute
7. fatigue
8. soothe
9. mistrust
10. hospitality

Chapter 27 (A Teacher's Lesson; My Sports Heroes)

1. debate
2. discredit
3. spurt
4. enforce
5. stern
6. identical
7. enumerate
8. singular
9. sprawl
10. displace

Chapter 28 (A Childish Collection; Clara Barton)

1. juvenile
2. sanitary
3. miniature
4. discard
5. peer
6. essential
7. tragic
8. exhibit
9. duration
10. mature

Chapter 29 (From Poor Girl to College President; Snowflakes)

1. postpone
2. capability
3. magnify
4. duplicate
5. content
6. presentable
7. industrious
8. immense
9. stun
10. realistic

Chapter 30 (Three Little Words; A Child-Safe Home)

1. vanity
2. accurate
3. consist
4. trifle
5. elementary
6. discomfort
7. latter
8. modify
9. toxic
10. bluff

B. Dictionary Use

It isn't always possible to figure out the meaning of a word from its context. That's where a dictionary comes in. Following is some basic information to help you use a dictionary.

HOW TO FIND A WORD

A dictionary contains so many words that it can take a while to find the one you're looking for. But if you know how to use guide words, you can find a word rather quickly. *Guide words* are the two words at the top of each dictionary page. The first guide word tells what the first word is on the page. The second guide word tells what the last word is on that page. The other words on a page fall alphabetically between the two guide words. So when you look up a word, find the two guide words that come before and after the word you're looking for.

- Which of the following pair of guide words would be on a page with the word *litigate*?

    liquid / litter   **lodger / longhand**   **light / lily**

The answer to this question and the questions that follow are given on the next page.

HOW TO USE A DICTIONARY LISTING

A dictionary listing includes many pieces of information. Here is a typical listing. Note that it includes much more than just a definition.

> **thun•der** (thŭn′dər) *n.* **1.** The explosive sound following an electrical charge of lightning. **2.** Any loud, resounding noise. — *v.* **3.** To give forth thunder. **4.** To make a loud, resounding noise like thunder. **5.** To utter loudly or threateningly.

Key parts of a dictionary entry are listed and explained below.

Syllables. Dots separate entry words into syllables. Note that *thunder* has one dot, which breaks the word into two syllables.

- To practice seeing the syllable breakdown in a dictionary entry, write the number of syllables in each word below.

    out•pa•tient _____   **Mis•sis•sip•pi** _____   **re•frig•er•a•tor** _____

Pronunciation guide. The information within parentheses after the entry word shows how to pronounce the entry word. There are two types of symbols: pronunciation symbols and accent marks.

Pronunciation symbols represent the consonant sounds and vowel sounds in a word. The consonant sounds are probably very familiar to you, but you may find it helpful to review some of the sounds of the vowels—*a, e, i, o,* and *u*. Every dictionary has a key explaining the sounds of its pronunciation symbols, including the long and short sounds of vowels.

   Long vowels have the sound of their own names. For example, the *a* in *pay* and the *o* in *no* both have long vowel sounds. Long vowel sounds are shown by a straight line above the vowel: ā, ō.

   In many dictionaries, the *short vowels* are shown by a curved line above the vowel. Thus the *u* in the first syllable of *thunder* is a short *u* (ŭ). The pronunciation chart on the inside front cover of this book shows that the short *u* has the sound of *u* in *up*. It also shows that the short *a* (ă) has the sound of *a* in *hat*, that the short *e* (ĕ) has the sound of *e* in *ten*, and so on.

- Which of the words below have a short vowel sound? Which has a long vowel sound?

    camp (kămp) _____   **pie** (pī) _____   **silk** (sĭlk) _____

Another pronunciation symbol is the *schwa* (ə), which looks like an upside-down *e*. It stands for certain rapidly spoken, unaccented vowel sounds, such as the *a* in *above*, the *e* in *item*, the *i* in *easily*, the *o* in *gallop*, and the *u* in *circus*. Most of the time, it has an "uh" sound, like the "uh" a speaker says when hesitating. Here are three more words that include the schwa sound:

a•like (ə-līk′)   **an•swer** (ăn′sər)   **pro•nounce** (prə-nouns′)

• Which syllable in *thunder* contains the schwa sound, the first or the second? _____

Accent marks are small black marks that tell you which syllable to emphasize, or stress, as you say a word. An accent mark follows *thun* in the pronunciation guide for *thunder*. This mark tells you to stress the first syllable of *thunder*. Syllables with no accent mark are not stressed. Some syllables are in between, and they are marked with a lighter accent mark.

• Which syllable has the stronger accent in *automatic*? _____

au•to•mat•ic (ô′tə-măt′ĭk)

Parts of speech.   After the pronunciation key and before each set of definitions, the entry word's parts of speech are given. The parts of speech are abbreviated as follows:

noun—*n.*   pronoun—*pron.*   adjective—*adj.*   adverb—*adv.*   verb—*v.*

• The listing for *thunder* shows that it can be two parts of speech. Write them below:

_____   _____

Definitions.   Words often have more than one meaning. When they do, each meaning is usually numbered in the dictionary. You can tell which definition of a word fits a given sentence by looking at the context—the rest of the sentence. For example, the word *copy* has several definitions, including these two: **1.** To make a copy of. **2.** To imitate.

• Show with a check which definition (1 or 2) applies in each sentence below:

The boy learned to swear by *copying* his father.   1 ___   2 ___

The students *copied* the homework assignment into their notebooks.   1 ___   2 ___

Other information.   After the definitions in a listing in a hardcover dictionary, you may find information about the *origin* of a word. This information, usually given in brackets ([ ]), explains which languages contain earlier forms of the word. And you may sometimes see one or more synonyms or antonyms for the entry word. *Synonyms* are words that are similar in meaning to the entry word; *antonyms* are words that are opposite in meaning.

WHICH DICTIONARIES TO OWN

You will find it useful to own two recent dictionaries: a small paperback dictionary to carry to class and a hardcover dictionary, which contains more information than a small paperback version, to keep at home. Here are several good dictionaries that are published in both paperback and hardcover editions:

The American Heritage Dictionary
The Random House College Dictionary
Webster's New World Dictionary

ANSWERS TO THE DICTIONARY QUESTIONS

Guide words: *liquid / litter*   Accent: stronger accent on third syllable *(mat)*
Number of syllables: 3, 4, 5   Parts of speech: noun and verb
Vowels: *camp, silk* (short); *pie* (long)   Definitions: 2; 1
Schwa: second syllable of *thunder*

C. Topics for Discussion and Writing

Note: The first five items for each chapter are intended for discussion; the last two, for writing. Feel free, however, to either talk or write about any of the items.

Chapter 1 (Johnny Appleseed; The Lovable Leech?)

1. Everyone has some personal habits that might seem odd to others. For instance, one person might put all her books in alphabetical order, while another might constantly jingle the **surplus** change in his pocket. Describe something that you do, or that someone you know does, which might seem **peculiar** to other people.

2. If you could **transform** one room in your home, which one would it be and how would you change it?

3. Think of a friend of yours and decide, from what you know of that person, what a **suitable** job would be for him or her. To do so, first think about the person's talents, likes, and dislikes.

4. Who is a person you feel is **dependent** upon you in some way? Describe the ways in which that person relies on you.

5. Some people feel strongly that they should have their dogs and cats "fixed" so that they are no longer **fertile**. Others think they should let their pets have babies at least once, or even many times. What is your opinion about letting pets reproduce?

6. Write about a **challenge** that you have faced and dealt with successfully. What was the **principal** reason that this challenge was difficult for you? How did you go about dealing with it?

7. When you are feeling blue or depressed, which is your **preference**: to cheer yourself up by being with people, or to be **solitary**? At such a time, would you need to be with other people, or to have quiet time alone? Tell about a time that makes your preference clear.

Chapter 2 (Finding Fault—And What to Do About It; What Do Your Hobbies Reveal About You?)

1. What do your favorite leisure activities reveal about you? Tell about one or more of your principal° interests and what they **indicate** about your personality.

2. Many people feel that a positive, hopeful **attitude** is more likely to lead to success than a negative one. Do you agree? Explain your answer.

3. What are you most **critical** about in other people? What are you most critical about in yourself? Is your answer the same in both cases? Or is there a **contrast** between the faults you focus on in someone else and those you see in yourself?

4. What is your favorite **category** of reading material? If you don't like to read, what type of reading do you least dislike?

5. We are likely to think that if someone hurts us **deliberately**, it is worse than doing the same harm by accident. But why? Aren't we hurt just as much either way?

6. Write about something in your life that causes you **excessive frustration**. It might be a personal relationship, a chore you hate, or a problem that keeps coming up. Explain why it makes you feel so discouraged.

7. In a paper, **analyze** what makes learning easy or hard for you. Give examples to show what you mean.

Chapter 3 (Fixing Up Furniture; Barbara's Date with Her Cousin)

1. Do you own something special that you hope to **preserve** throughout your life? What is it, and how could you keep it in good condition?

2. What kind of items do you frequently use that other people **dispose** of, and what do you use them for? What would you have to do if such items were no longer available?

3. If a visitor went shopping with you, what would become **evident** to him or her about your taste in clothes?

4. What career do you plan on **pursuing**? How did you **determine** your career choice? What ways can you pursue it in addition to going to school?

5. Who is the actor or actress you would most like to **accompany** to the Academy Awards ceremony? Why?

6. What is one goal in life that is important for you to **pursue**? When did it become **evident** to you that this was a meaningful goal for you? Write about that goal and its meaning in your life.

7. Write about a time when you experienced a feeling of **rejection**. How did you feel? What did you do afterward to **restore** your feeling of self-confidence?

Chapter 4 (The Vacuum-Cleaner Salesman; Peace at Last)

1. If you found out that someone you love very much had committed a crime, would you **betray** him or her and tell the police?

2. Imagine that you are working at a company that needs to save money. It gives you and your coworkers this choice: Everyone takes a **reduction** in pay, or half of the workers will lose their jobs. You don't know, of course, who will be fired and who won't. Would you take the cut in pay? Why or why not?

3. When something bad happens, do you tend to **exaggerate** it ("This is the end of the world!") or do you tend to play it down ("It's no big deal")? Discuss the **contrast** between each of these attitudes° toward trouble.

4. Describe a **dispute** in which you felt strongly about one side, and a debate in which you felt **neutral**. Why did you have strong feelings about the first issue, but not about the second one?

5. Do you think human beings will ever **inhabit** another planet? Why or why not?

6. If you could make one thing on Earth more **abundant**, what would it be, and why? Write about your choice.

7. Write about how you would **demonstrate** to others something you know how to do very well, such as baking a cake or riding a bike. How would you give your audience a **distinct** idea of the process?

Chapter 5 (Study Skills to the Rescue!; Training a Puppy)

1. Think of several things that upset you, disturb you, or make you angry or annoyed. These things may happen in the world, in your community, or in your family. Now suppose that you can make one of them—but only one—**cease**. Which one would you stop, and why?

2. Have you ever experienced an interesting **coincidence**—two things that happened at the same time, as if they had been planned? For example, someone may have called you on the phone just as you were beginning to think of that person. Tell about an interesting coincidence in your life.

3. Have you ever been in a situation where telling a lie seemed more **humane** than telling the truth? Why was the lie kinder? In such a situation, is it all right to lie? Why or why not?

4. What do you think makes the difference between a solid, lasting relationship—in a marriage, for example—and an **unstable**, troubled one? Do you think one single thing is most important, or is it a combination of many things?

5. Recycling is an issue of **considerable** importance to many people today. Do you or your family members save and **utilize** anything out of the ordinary, something that other people might not have thought to put to use? If so, what is it, and how do you use it?

6. People sometimes **aggravate** an already bad situation by well-meant but harmful **interference**. Write about a time in your own experience when someone (perhaps even you!) made things worse, even though the harm wasn't **intentional**.

7. Everyone has faults, of course, but have you ever known someone whose fault or faults were especially **obnoxious**? Write about what it was like to know this person, and how you reacted to his or her unpleasant qualities.

Chapter 6 (Toasters; A Mean Man)

1. Does someone you know have a nickname? How did that nickname **originate**?

2. Who do you think is a **reliable** person in your life? Who is *not* reliable? Would you **maintain** a friendship with someone who is not reliable? Explain your answers.

3. Name one **current** song, movie, or TV show that you enjoy. Then explain why you like it.

4. What do you think should be the **minimum** legal age for people to drive? To buy alcohol? To vote? To serve in the military? Explain.

5. Is there a time when it was clear to you that a friend was making a mistake? Did you try to **advise** the friend to do things differently, or did you **hesitate** to interfere? Tell about what your friend was doing and what you did, if anything.

6. Write a paper about what you think are some proper ways to **penalize** children when they misbehave. For example, do you think it is ever right to punish a child by spanking? Or do you think a better punishment is to **deprive** children of something they want?

7. What is a movie you've seen that you have strongly disliked? Explain your **objection** to the film. End your paper by telling what you would **advise** the filmmakers to do in order to improve the movie.

Chapter 7 (A Special Memory; Watch Your Manners!)

1. Scientists think there may once have been some kind of life on Mars—not little green men, but simple life forms. If this turns out to be true, would it **astonish** you? Why or why not?

2. Which do you find harder to **endure**: a heat wave in the summer, or bitter cold in the winter? How do you try to make yourself more comfortable?

3. Can you think of an **abrupt** event you have experienced—something that happened suddenly and without warning? It might have been something important, like the end of a relationship, or something minor, like a sudden rainstorm. Tell what it was like.

4. What things in your life would you **classify** as too **complex**? How could you make these things simpler for you?

5. Did you ever **exclaim** something without meaning to—in class, for instance, or on a bus, or at a movie? Can you **recollect** how it happened? Can you remember how you felt and what happened afterwards?

6. Write about a time when, as a young child or later, you were **eager** to do something, but your parents wouldn't **consent** to it. Try to explain both points of view, yours and theirs. How do you feel now about what happened?

7. **Classifying** items helps to show the similarities and differences among them. Write a paper in which you classify something into two or three categories°. Explain the features of each group and how each member of the group fits in. For instance, you might divide your courses into those in which the teacher teaches the whole class for the entire period and those in which students work in small groups.

Chapter 8 (Big Brothers and Sisters; Kevin's First Date)

1. Have you and your parents ever disagreed about whether or not a person was a **wholesome** influence in your life? How did you see that person, and how did that differ from the way your parents saw him or her?

2. What holiday is celebrated in a big way in your family? What are some of the **customary** ways you have **established** to celebrate that holiday each year?

3. If a genie offered you just one wish before **vanishing** in a puff of smoke, how would you **respond**?

4. Think of someone you know who has the **potential** to develop a talent. Who is the person, and what is his or her special ability? How do you think he or she can develop that ability?

5. Do people on the street ever **appeal** to you for money? Does this make you feel **awkward**? What do you do when that happens?

6. Write about a time when you thought that you were doing an **adequate** job at home or in school, but someone else—perhaps a parent or a teacher—thought you weren't working up to your **potential**. How did you **respond** to the person who encouraged you to do better?

7. What are some **wholesome** activities that you enjoy? How do you feel that they improve your mind, body, or character? Write about a **variety** of such activities and how they affect you.

Chapter 9 (Differences in a Gym Program; Through a Child's Eyes)

1. Have you ever watched someone acting in a **brutal** fashion—on TV, in a movie, or in real life? What did the person do? How did you feel about what was happening?

2. Think about some of the major problems of our society, such as drug abuse, unemployment, poverty, hunger, and crime. Which problem do you think it is most important to **eliminate**? Why did you choose the one you did?

3. Why might parents sometimes **resort** to spanking their children? **Furthermore**, do you think that spanking is a good way to **discipline** children? Why or why not?

4. What are some of your earliest, most **vague** memories? Why do you think you still remember these events?

5. What, for you, would be the **ultimate** vacation? Where would you go, and what would you do?

6. Write a paper describing a change you would like to **propose** in how your school, workplace, or household is run. Describe in detail—not **vaguely**—how your suggestion would work.

7. TV, movies, and magazines are constantly giving us messages about fashion, body image, and other things having to do with outward appearance. How do you think people **interpret** these messages? Write a paper about whether or not there is too much **emphasis** today on "looking good."

Chapter 10 (Knowing How to Argue; A Change of School, A Change of Heart)

1. Describe something that **occurs** regularly—perhaps every day, or every week, or every year—that you **anticipate** with pleasure. What makes you look forward to it?

2. Has a friend ever asked you for a favor that you were **reluctant** to do? Describe what he or she asked for and why you did not want to say yes. Did you end up doing what your friend asked you to do?

3. Have you ever read something and then seen a television or movie **version** of the same story? Which did you prefer? Why?

4. Tell about a time when someone **misinterpreted** something you did or said. What did you mean? What did the person *think* you meant?

5. What are some reasons why a student might **linger** after school instead of going straight home?

6. Write about something that **occurred** that made you feel **miserable**. What happened? Why did you feel so bad about it? Did you ever become **accustomed** to what happened, or does it still bother you?

7. Write a paper about the best or worst job (or class or teacher) you ever had. Provide plenty of details that make very clear to the reader just why that **particular** job (or class or teacher) was a good one or a bad one. **Revise** the paper at least once, adding even more details when you do so.

Chapter 11 (Coming Out of a Coma; The Office Doughnut Contest)

1. Describe a time when something **incredible** but true happened to you. Or tell of a time when something hard to believe happened to someone you know.

2. What is an interesting **spectacle** you recently witnessed? Describe what made it noticeable.

3. What do you think should be the **maximum** number of students in a sixth-grade class? A high-school writing class? A college lecture class?

4. Most families have a few of their own **remedies** for minor illnesses or injuries. Tell about some ways your family deals with bruises, sickness, or maybe even hurt feelings. Are these remedies applied **internally** or **externally**? How do they work?

5. When have you **assumed** that something was true and then became **conscious** that you were mistaken? For example, you might have assumed that two people were related and later found out they weren't. Or you may have believed that someone agreed with you on some point and then found out he or she did not. Explain your reaction.

6. Think of a disagreement that two of your friends have had. If they asked you to decide who was right, what would be your **verdict**? Why?

7. Write about a time when you **protested** against something you thought was wrong or unfair. Did you protest quietly, or did you do something to make a **spectacle** of yourself?

Chapter 12 (The People's Choice; The Christmas Wars)

1. Why do fans have a sense of **triumph** when their team wins? After all, the fans didn't do any of the playing; they only watched and cheered. What might their team's victory **represent** to them?

2. How would you **counsel** a teenager who wanted to drop out of school? Can you think of anything special to say about this—something that doesn't just repeat the advice that kids usually hear?

3. People tend to think that something that is "**artificial**" is worse than something that is "natural." Can you think of an opposite example—a human-made product that is better than the natural thing?

4. When someone is lying to you, do you think you can usually **detect** it? If so, how? If not, why not?

5. **Transparent** objects have various advantages. One obvious benefit of a window, for example, is letting more light into a room. What are some other ways in which something transparent can be useful?

6. Henry David Thoreau wrote that our lives are too cluttered by detail, and he urged us to "Simplify, simplify." Write about some ways you might make your own life simpler by getting rid of activities that **complicate** it, or at least by reducing their **frequency**.

7. Write about a time you had to do something difficult because your **conscience** demanded that you do it. For instance, you may have had to say no to a friend in order to avoid doing something you felt was wrong. Explain the situation and the choices you faced. Then tell what you finally decided to do and why.

Chapter 13 (What's Your Type?; What a Circus!)

1. Do you know someone in your community who has **prospered** more than most of the people around him or her? How did this person manage to succeed? Do you think this success was a matter of luck, ability, **energetic** effort, or all three?

2. Think of a time in your past when you had to **strive** to achieve something difficult. What were you trying to do, and why did you succeed or fail?

3. Describe a time in your life when you demonstrated **tolerance** for another person's opinions or behavior. How were that person's thoughts or actions different from what you were accustomed° to? How did you show your acceptance?

4 Think of a close friend or family member, and describe several of that person's **traits**. Which of those qualities have influenced you the most?

5. Some people like waiting for something nice to happen. They are able to enjoy the **interval** between deciding to do something—for instance, buying some new clothes—and actually doing it. Others hate to wait. As soon as they decide to buy something new, they want to be at the store, buying it. Which kind of person are you? Can you patiently look ahead to a nice event? Or does waiting spoil your enjoyment of the experience?

6. What's the most **agonizing** physical pain you have experienced? Did a person, an event, or a **substance** cause this pain? Explain what caused it and what it was like.

7. Think of a situation in your life in which you wish you had shown more **foresight**. Describe what happened. Then explain how things might have turned out differently if you had planned ahead better. Or, instead, tell about a time when you were very glad that you did have foresight.

Chapter 14 (Practicing Kindness; The Stinking Rose)

1. How do you **cope** with tension? Are you someone who deals with pressure well, without becoming overly upset? Or do you "fall apart" and become helpless? Describe a tense situation in your life, and **evaluate** how you have coped (or are coping) with it.

2. Do you know someone who is very **practical**? Do you know someone who is not so practical and often does not consider things realistically? Describe those two people, giving examples of how one is sensible and the other is not so sensible.

3. What is a **phrase** that you associate with a particular person in your life? Did a parent, a grandparent, or a friend have a saying that he or she repeated often? What was that phrase, and when was the person likely to say it?

4. **Approximately** how much free time do you have in a week? Do you have a **significant** amount of free time in your life, or only a small amount of free time? What are some of the things you prefer to do in your free time?

5. While your life may change from day to day, there are some parts of your life that are **consistent**, that you can depend on routinely. For example, you may wake up every day to the sound of your alarm clock, or you may have a relationship that you can always count on. What are some of the consistent things in your life that you like best?

6. What is one behavior that you'd really like to see someone change? Perhaps you wish that a parent would stop smoking, or that a friend would quit asking to borrow money from you. Write a **plea** to that person, asking him or her to change this particular° behavior and explaining why.

7. Some people believe that everyone has only one "perfect match"—that there is a **sole** romantic partner for each of us. Others think that people get together at **random** and that there are a number of people out there who would make a good life partner. Write about whether you believe in "just one true love" or in "lots of possibilities."

Chapter 15 (A Modern Fairy Tale; Wolf Children)

1. Some words can be used to describe people as well as things. For example, a **shallow** person does not think deeply about things. People who are **authentic** say what they really mean and actually do what they say they will do. Describe someone you know who is **shallow** and someone else you know who is **authentic**.

2. Tell about a time you **confronted** another person about something he or she had done. What were you upset about? How did you express your feelings to that person?

3. Name a **remote** place, a spot hardly anyone else knows about, where you go to relax or study. Tell about that place, including what you like about it.

4. What are some common ways that students **disrupt** classroom activities? What are some of the more unusual classroom disruptions you have seen?

5. Tell about a time that you spoke to someone in a **harsh** way, then wished you had not. Why do you think you spoke so unpleasantly?

6. What qualities do you think are **characteristic** of a good friendship? Write a paper explaining your **concept** of friendship.

7. Imagine that you could design your own school—one in which you could truly **thrive**. How would it meet your mental, emotional, and physical needs? What subjects would be taught? How would they be taught? Would the teaching be done in classrooms, or in some other setting? Could just anyone attend your school, or would only certain people be **eligible**? Write a description of your ideal school.

Chapter 16 (A Mismatched Couple; A Campaign to Become Class President)

1. What gives you a sense of **security** at home or at school? What makes you feel insecure? If you had to **transfer** to a different school, would you feel less secure? If so, what could you do to feel more comfortable?

2. Once people had to do their laundry by hand. Now there are **automatic** washers to do it for them. What automatic machine do you wish someone would invent to help you with some other task?

3. Think of one person who has had a big **influence** on your life. Describe how he or she has affected you.

4. Have you ever made a promise that was difficult to **fulfill**, yet you kept it? What was it?

5. Describe one way that your family tries to be **economical**.

6. Write about a time when it was **apparent** that something was bothering a friend. What made it apparent to you that something was bothering him or her? How did you help your friend deal with that **burden**? Did you just express your **sympathy**, or did you assist in some more active way?

7. If you had one day in which you could be as **extravagant** as you liked, what would you do? What dreams would you **fulfill** during that day?

Chapter 17 (The Famous Detective; Why So Quiet?)

1. Which member of your family is most **outspoken**? Give an example of a time that person has boldly stated his or her opinion.

2. Think of a friend who has moved away, but with whom you have stayed in touch. In what ways do the two of you **communicate**?

3. Tell about a time when a person seemed to you to be **earnest**, but then did something that showed he or she was not sincere at all. How did that person **deceive** you, and how did you discover the truth?

4. Describe a work of **fiction** that you have read and enjoyed. What about it maintained° your interest?

5. Lots of television shows are based on police officers, private detectives, or even scientists who **investigate** crimes or unusual events. What is one such show that you've watched? How do the people in the show go about their work?

6. Have you ever been involved in a mystery that was never solved? It might be the disappearance of something that belonged to you or a change in a friend that you never understood. What happened to **bewilder** you? Do you have any **theory** about what might have really happened?

7. Select a particular **emotion**, such as sadness, embarrassment, joy, fear, or another feeling. Write about a time when you experienced that emotion strongly. Tell what happened, how you felt, and why you felt that way.

Chapter 18 (Fear of Speaking; Do You Believe in Magic?)

1. Of all the friendships you've had, which one seems the most **crucial** to you? Why has that one friendship been so important to you?

2. Describe a person you know who often seems **hostile**. Is this person unfriendly to everyone or only to certain people? How does the person express his or her hostility?

3. When have you seen one person try to **humiliate** another? What did he or she do in order to embarrass the other person? Describe what the first person did and how the other person reacted.

4. Tell a story about a time when you spoke or acted because of an **impulse**. Did you feel OK later about what you had said or done? Or did you wish you had thought it through more carefully first?

5. When you were a child, what kind of situation made you feel **frantic**? Losing a favorite plaything? Getting lost? How did you act when you were feeling so anxious? (If you can't remember, think of a young child you know, and describe what might make this child feel frantic and how he or she would act.)

6. Write about how and where you like to study. Where do you prefer to sit? What do you like to have around you? Do you like to have music playing and people around, or do those things **divert** your attention? When you get sleepy or bored as you study, what do you do to **revive** yourself?

7. Write about the trip that you take to reach school. What route do you follow? Do you walk, or do you travel in a car or bus? Describe some of the sights, smells, and sounds that you usually **perceive** in the course of your trip. What **extraordinary** things have you ever seen or experienced along the way?

Chapter 19 (The Miracle Runner; One of Those Days)

1. Have you ever wished you could **abandon** your responsibilities—school, family, work— and just take off somewhere? Explain what **circumstances** made you feel that way.

2. When you have free time, do you **devote** yourself to some activity, or do you prefer to be **idle**? Why?

3. Prisons are the topic of many arguments these days. What do you think the **function** of a prison should be? To help criminals become better citizens? To punish them? Or just to keep them where they can't do any more harm? Explain.

4. Has anyone ever tried to **dominate** you or someone you know by threats or bullying? What are some things a person could do to **overcome** this kind of abuse?

5. Have you ever been to a **theme** park? If so, what was the theme, and how was it carried out?

6. When you are bored or sleepy, what do you do to make yourself more **alert**? Do you drink tea, cola, or coffee? Go for a fast walk? Take a shower? Describe something that wakes you up when you need a lift.

7. Write about your **primary** goal in getting an education. Is it to prepare for a good job? To please your family? To gain self-respect? To learn more about things that interest you?

Chapter 20 (The All-Too-Common Cold; A Criminal with a Tail)

1. When have you **disregarded** the advice someone gave you, and later wished you had paid attention to it? Tell about what happened.

2. How do you feel about the previews that are shown in theaters before the feature? Do you think that the **excerpts** give a good idea of what those movies will be like?

3. Tell about a time when you were trying to leave the house to get to work or school, but something **hindered** you. What was it that got in the way of your leaving?

4. Do you ever see advertisements for products or hear claims that you think are **misleading**? Describe one such ad or claim. In what way do you believe it might lead people to a mistaken conclusion?

5. What was the most **severe** weather you have ever experienced? How bad was it, and how did you deal with it?

6. What is the most **monotonous** thing that you have ever had to do? Did you make it more exciting by playing music? By watching TV? Describe the task and what was so boring about it. Then tell how you made it more fun for yourself.

7. How do you feel about hunting? Would you enjoy following your **prey**—perhaps a deer— and then shooting it? Do you think that hunting is an acceptable way to **obtain** food? Or are you bothered by the idea of hunting wild animals? Write about your attitude° toward hunting.

Chapter 21 (Traveling with Children; Saving Earth's Natural Supplies)

1. After you woke up this morning, what **procedure** did you go through to get ready for your day? Do you ever **vary** your routine? If so, when—and why?

2. How do you **renew** the food supplies in your cupboard and refrigerator? Are you very organized, writing lists for once-a-week shopping trips? Or do you shop a little bit every day?

3. Name a few of your favorite places in the **vicinity** of your home. Why are these your favorites?

4. Do you think juries should always have to reach a **unanimous** verdict° to convict someone of a crime? Why or why not?

5. The United States has abundant° natural **resources**. Should they be **converted** to practical° uses (for example, drilling for oil or cutting down trees for paper and building materials)? Or should some be preserved as natural parklands and forests? Explain your answers.

6. Write about a time that you were in **conflict** with one or more other people. What was the argument about? Did you experience a lot of **stress** as a result of the conflict? How was the conflict finally settled?

7. Write about a close friend. What traits° does your friend **possess** that make you like him or her so much?

Chapter 22 (More Fat, Anyone?; Is Prison Effective?)

1. Tell about a home or building that has started to **decay**. What were the causes of the problem, and what could have been done to avoid it? What do you think will become of that home or building?

2. If you could **expand** one room in your home, which would it be? How would you use the increased space?

3. Some people say that commercials for candy, fast food, and salty snacks should not be broadcast during Saturday morning cartoons, because they **promote** bad eating habits among kids. Do you agree? Or should television stations be allowed to schedule these ads whenever they choose?

4. Think of a process in which it is important to be **precise**. Why is it important to do this in an exact way? What would happen if you were *not* precise?

5. Do you believe that prison actually **reforms** criminals? Why or why not? Can you think of a better way to deal with people who have broken the law?

6. If you had unlimited power, what is one thing that you would **abolish** from the world? Write in a serious or humorous style about something you would get rid of if you had **vast** power.

7. Why do you think that some people grow up to be honest, while others become **corrupt**? Are there reasons why certain people have a **tendency** to commit dishonest acts? Write about why a person growing up may become an honest or a dishonest adult.

Chapter 23 (She Changed My Mind; So Sue Me)

1. What is one responsibility you have in your life—around the house, at school, or at work—that you would like to **evade**? What are some ways you could try to escape that responsibility?

2. In your opinion, do dreams have any meaning? Or are they just **senseless** collections of pictures and sounds? Explain why you feel as you do.

3. What are some **precautions** that you take to keep from becoming a victim of crime? Explain how the things you do help keep you safe.

4. Describe a time when you formed a **preconception** of something—perhaps a particular job, course, or activity—that turned out to be incorrect. Where did you get the ideas that led to your first opinion? After you actually experienced this situation, did you **rigidly** hold on to your earlier belief, or did you change your opinion—either for the better or for the worse? Explain.

5. Who are the two people in your family (or a family you know) who **resemble** each other the most? In what ways are they alike? Are they similar only in looks, or also in the way that they act?

6. Most people are lucky if they can go away for one or two weeks of vacation in a year. Imagine that somehow you have been able to **extend** your vacation to last an entire year—and that you have plenty of money to spend on it. Write a description of how you would spend your year.

7. Pretend that you are a scientist from Mars who has been sent to study the planet Earth. Your assignment today is to look out one window and describe all the **vertical** objects that you see. Since your Martian boss has never visited Earth, you will have to **clarify** what each object is and what it does, so be sure to include plenty of details about each object.

Chapter 24 (Fear of Public Speaking; Mrs. Thornton's Condition)

1. Did you ever try to **convince** a friend to give up a bad habit? What was the habit, and what did you do to convince your friend to give it up?

2. Tell about a time when your first **impression** of a person turned out to be mistaken. What happened to make you **comprehend** what the person was really like?

3. Do you know people who seem to like to make other people feel **inferior** to them? How do they do it?

4. Talk about a time when work or other responsibilities **overwhelmed** you. How were you overwhelmed, and how did you react?

5. How might someone go about doing a very **thorough** job of studying the words in this chapter? Name specific steps that the person could take.

6. Write about a time when you were **frank** about your feelings, even though you knew that someone else might not like what you said. How did you feel about speaking out honestly? Did the experience make you feel **anxious**? How did other people respond°?

7. Write about a particular° quality of someone you know. First, give a brief definition of this quality. Then go on to use an example to **illustrate** what you mean. For instance, you might first say what stubbornness is. Then you could describe one particular event that showed a person's stubbornness in a **dramatic** way.

Chapter 25 (Wacky Weddings; The Cost of Hatred)

1. Of all the things that you have **acquired** in your life, which one is the most meaningful? Where and how did you get it? Is it something that is valuable in terms of money, or does it have another kind of value to you? Is it **fundamental** to your sense of who you are?

2. Think of one **commitment** you have made. It could have been to study harder, to break a bad habit, or to get more exercise. What led you to make that promise? Were you able to live up to it?

3. Describe a **formal** ceremony that you have seen. During that ceremony, were people more excited, more relaxed, or more **solemn** than usual? Give examples.

4. Think of a time when you **resented** another person's words or behavior. What did he or she do that angered you? How did you respond°?

5. The world is full of things that **symbolize** other things or ideas. For example, a diamond ring on a woman's left hand may symbolize her engagement. What are some other common things that stand for something else?

6. Pretend that you are an archeologist a thousand years from now. You are digging up the area that used to be your bedroom and finding **fragments** of things you once owned. Write about what you find there. What would a scientist learn or guess about life today by studying your room?

7. Write about an experience that left you feeling full of **spite** toward someone. What happened to stir up that angry feeling? In the time that **preceded** the experience, had you liked or disliked the other person? Afterward, did you express your anger openly, or did you keep it to yourself?

Chapter 26 (My Parents' Problem; The Hike That Hurt)

1. If someone you know thought you had insulted him or her, what could you do to **soothe** that person's hurt feelings?

2. Have you ever met anyone whom you instantly **mistrusted**? What was it about that person that made you mistrustful? Do you think you were right to feel the way you did?

3. Are there people in your school who **persecute** others because of their race, religion, or other reasons? If so, give an example of the type of behavior you're thinking of. Why do you think that these people act this way?

4. Identify a goal that you have for your own life. What do you think might be the biggest **barrier** to your achieving that goal? Can you think of at least one way to overcome that barrier?

5. Tell about a time when you were shown great **hospitality**. Who treated you that way? Just what was done that made you feel so welcome?

6. How long would you **estimate** you have known your oldest friend? Why do you like to **associate** with that person? Answer these questions in a paper about this friend.

7. Write about a time you made a decision that made other people unhappy. What happened? How did you **justify** the decision? Do you feel now that you made the right choice?

Chapter 27 (A Teacher's Lesson; My Sports Heroes)

1. Would you enjoy having an **identical** twin? Why or why not?

2. What is a rule that you think should be put into effect at your school or workplace? How would you **enforce** that rule?

3. What is one topic that you hear people **debate** about? What is your opinion on that topic?

4. Have you ever admired someone—maybe a public figure—and then learned something that **discredited** that person in your eyes? If so, explain what you learned that changed your mind about the person.

5. Do you know of anyone who was **displaced** by losing a home to fire or as a result of family problems? Tell how that person dealt with the loss.

6. Write a paper in which you **enumerate** and explain three things that you like about one of these things: your school, your job, or a close friend.

7. Think about a time that someone had a **stern** talk with you, a talk that you've never forgotten. Describe what the talk was about and how you felt about it afterward.

Chapter 28 (A Childish Collection; Clara Barton)

1. Think about the things that you own. What is one possession that you plan never to **discard**? Why is that item so special to you?

2. If you were going to adopt a cat or dog, would you prefer to get a **juvenile** or an adult animal? What would be the advantages of either choice?

3. What do you **exhibit** in your bedroom (or another room)? A particular poster? A collection of, say, **miniature** animals or cars? Photographs? Explain what you've chosen to display and why.

4. We usually think of "**peer** pressure" as the pressure a person feels from his or her friends to do bad or unhealthy things. But can peer pressure be positive? If so, give some examples.

5. Imagine that you're going to live on a desert island for six months. Food, water, and shelter will be provided for you. You may bring along only one item. What would that item be, and why is it so **essential** to you?

6. Have you ever known someone who had to go through a **tragic** experience? In addition to causing pain, did the experience make that individual become more **mature** in some way? Write about what the person experienced, and how he or she responded.

7. Pretend you have an entire month—and all the money you need—to do anything you want. Write a paper describing what you would do for the **duration** of that month. Would you stay in one place and do one thing, or would you travel and do a variety of things?

Chapter 29 (From Poor Girl to College President; Snowflakes)

1. Think of someone you know who is **industrious**. Give examples that show why you chose that person.

2. If you could suddenly have the **capability** to do one thing extremely well, what would it be? Would you play a musical instrument, excel at a sport, speak a foreign language, or do something else? Why?

3. If you learned that very important guests were coming to visit in half an hour, what would you do in that time to make your home (or room) more **presentable**?

4. Think of a day in your life that was so enjoyable you'd like to **duplicate** it. What was so special about that day?

5. What qualities or possessions do people really need in their lives in order to be **content**? Why are these qualities or possessions so important?

6. Write about a time that an event or a piece of news **stunned** you. What was it about the event or news that caused you to feel such **immense** surprise?

7. In a paper, explain one goal you'd like to achieve during the next year—a **realistic** goal, not an unlikely one. Describe one or more steps you might take to reach your goal. Is there anything that might cause you to **postpone** taking these steps?

Chapter 30 (Three Little Words; A Child-Safe Home)

1. What do you feel is the most **elementary** rule about being a good friend? Why is this rule so basic to a good friendship?

2. What does your favorite meal **consist** of? Why do you like these foods so much?

3. Have you ever been bothered by the way a stranger was acting? Describe what was going on, and why you felt the **discomfort** you did.

4. Which would you rather be—rich, or talented? If you prefer the first choice, explain why. If you chose the **latter**, tell why it appeals to you more.

5. If you could **modify** just one thing about your home, what would it be, and why would you want to change it?

6. Do a thorough search of your bathroom, kitchen, or garage, and make an **accurate** list of all the **toxic** materials that you find there. What is the purpose of each one? Also, what can you do to use, store, and dispose° of them safely? Write a brief report on what you found.

7. **Vanity** sometimes causes us to try to **bluff** our way out of situations. In other words, our pride makes us pretend to know more than we really do. Write about a time you (or someone else) tried to bluff about something. Did you (or the other person) get away with it?

D. Word List

abandon, 142
abolish, 168
abrupt, 54
abundant, 28
accompany, 22
accurate, 224
accustomed, 72
acquire, 186
adequate, 60
advise, 48
aggravate, 34
agonizing, 98
alert, 142
analyze, 16
anticipate, 72
anxious, 180
apparent, 124
appeal, 60
approximately, 104
artificial, 92
assert, 174
associate, 200
assume, 86
assure, 136
astonish, 54
attitude, 16
authentic, 110
automatic, 124
awkward, 60
barrier, 200
betray, 28
bewilder, 130
bluff, 224
brutal, 66
burden, 124
capability, 218
category, 16
cease, 34
challenge, 10
characteristic, 110
circumstances, 142
clarify, 174
classify, 54
coincide, 34

commitment, 186
communicate, 130
comparison, 28
complex, 54
complicate, 92
comprehend, 180
concept, 110
conflict, 162
confront, 110
conscience, 92
conscious, 86
consent, 54
considerable, 34
consist, 224
consistent, 104
content, 218
contrast, 16
convert, 162
convince, 180
cope, 104
corrupt, 168
counsel, 92
critical, 16
crucial, 136
current, 48
customary, 60
debate, 206
decay, 168
deceive, 130
deliberate, 16
demonstrate, 28
dependent, 10
deprive, 48
desperate, 22
detect, 92
determine, 22
devote, 142
discard, 212
discipline, 66
discomfort, 224
discredit, 206
displace, 206
dispose, 22
dispute, 28

disregard, 148
disrupt, 110
distinct, 28
divert, 136
dominate, 142
dramatic, 180
duplicate, 218
duration, 212
eager, 54
earnest, 130
economical, 124
elementary, 224
eligible, 110
eliminate, 66
emotion, 130
emphasis, 66
endure, 55
energetic, 98
enforce, 206
enumerate, 206
essential, 212
establish, 60
estimate, 200
evade, 174
evaluate, 104
evident, 22
exaggerate, 29
excerpt, 148
excessive, 17
exclaim, 55
exclude, 148
exhibit, 212
expand, 168
extend, 174
external, 86
extraordinary, 136
extravagant, 124
fatigue, 200
fertile, 10
fiction, 130
flimsy, 200
foresight, 98
formal, 186
fragile, 17